DENNIS TUEART

MY FOOTBALL JOURNEY

I dedicate this book to my wife, Joan, and our three sons, Mark, Leigh and John. Joan has shown unwavering love, patience and support over more than 40 years. She knows how to manage me better than anyone else, and has done so through all my highs and lows. Our sons are a credit to us and have given me total encouragement since I decided to write this book, and I have welcomed their personal views and critiques.

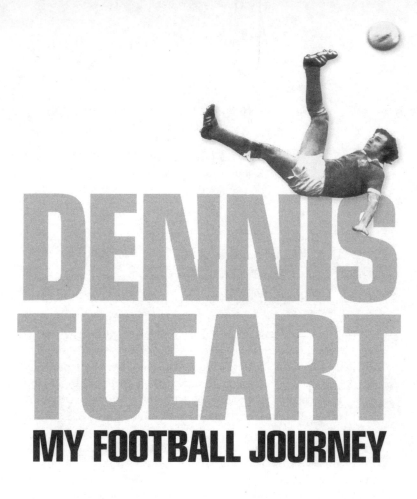

DENNIS TUEART

MY FOOTBALL JOURNEY

VSP

Published by Vision Sports Publishing in 2011

Vision Sports Publishing
19-23 High Street
Kingston upon Thames
Surrey
KT1 1LL

www.visionsp.co.uk

ISBN: 978-1-907637-23-0

Co-author: Jon Spurling
Edited by: Justyn Barnes
Copy editing: Alex Morton
Cover design: Doug Cheeseman

Typeset by Palimpsest Book Production Limited,
Falkirk, Stirlingshire

Printed and bound by CPI Group (UK) Ltd, Croydon, CR0 4YY

A CIP Catalogue record for this book
is available from the British Library

CONTENTS

"The iconic shot of Dennis scoring that overhead kick at Wembley in '76 is etched into the memory of all City fans. For 34 years it was all we had. King of all Geordies and honorary Mancunian."
Noel Gallagher

"Dennis Tueart was my hero as a kid."
Johnny Marr

"Dennis Tueart was one of my Seventies football heroes. I loved everything about him, from his amazing skill, speed and goalscoring ability to those trendy tie-ups and sweatbands he used to wear as he bombed down the wing. He was the coolest player and he played for us!"
Paul Lake

ACKNOWLEDGEMENTS

Dennis Tueart

My father, Norman, and father-in-law, Tony, both gave me many discipline and work ethic values. Schoolteacher Bob Maddison and my first real manager, Alan Brown, contributed immensely to that development.

Huge thanks to all my team-mates who played in those three exciting, winning teams at Sunderland, Manchester City and the New York Cosmos. They showed what can be achieved when the word "team" is applied professionally. To all my managers, special thanks because, as Joan knows, I am not the easiest person to manage, but all I have ever wanted to do was to be successful and win. And to those special supporters who have followed and supported me, thank you and I hope I have given you some happy memories to treasure.

Joan and my sons fully endorsed the decision to donate all of my royalties from this book to the Teenage and Young Adult Cancer Unit at The Christie in Manchester. Louise Hadley and Jenny Haskey from The Christie have worked extremely hard to ensure that maximum funds will be raised to benefit more teenagers. My brother Kevin, who after contracting the disease in his early 20s has been a credit with his positive attitude, is an excellent example for modern-day young cancer sufferers.

A great thank you to my literary agent, David Luxton, and my ghostwriter, Jon Spurling, whose patience and many hours spent with me and on trains have been invaluable. Toby, Jim and Alex from Vision Sports Publishing have shown great tolerance and support with this project. Thanks to my secretary, Marion, who must have been fed up with me coming in and making changes to the changes I had already made, but she knows I wanted the final script to be as accurate and interesting as the life I've had.

Jon Spurling
To Dennis and Joan – thanks for all the hospitality and for making me feel so welcome in their home. For all the chaps at Vision Sports Publishing – it's been a pleasure working with you again. Thanks to my agent, David Luxton, for the encouragement and the opportunities. And, finally, to Helen and Phoebe xx.

FOREWORD

By Carlos Alberto

During my career as a footballer I won the World Cup with Brazil in 1970 and played with some of the greatest players in the history of the game – like Pele, Beckenbaur and Zico – and I can honestly say that Dennis was one of the best I ever saw or had the pleasure of playing with. I can give my word on that!

He was very, very skilful at dribbling the ball and he always ran hard and fast at the defence. He was a very quick player and always played for the team. Unlike a lot of wingers and attacking players, he would always come back and help out his full-back when the opposition had the ball. He always gave more than 100 per cent.

I had heard about Dennis as a player before he joined the Cosmos, so I wasn't at all surprised at how good he was. When he arrived in New York we got on very well and have remained good friends to this day.

The time we spent together at the New York Cosmos was one of the best times of our lives, playing in front of huge crowds each week. I spent a total of six years in the States, and the time I spent there, developing football in the country, was fantastic. If you ask Franz Beckenbauer, he would say exactly the same thing – we brought a lot of happiness to a lot of people.

One of the things that people remember about the NASL in those days is the 35-yard shoot-outs which we had instead of penalties, and Dennis is always reminding me about the time I scored the winning goal in one of these. I never normally took those kicks in training or in matches, but in the conference semi-final against Minnesota the coach came up to me and asked me to take one. I was a little nervous about it, because we were at sudden death by then, and if I missed then we were out, but I said, "Okay, why not, I'll do it". So I flicked the ball up, juggled it towards the goal and lifted it high over the 'keeper. I hadn't planned to flick the ball up and juggle it towards the goal – it was just a spur-of-the-moment thing.

That shoot-out is still talked about today as one of the greatest in history, and the 60,199 fans in the stadium went crazy when I scored. Every time I go back to New York now, the people there are emotional when they talk about those days with the Cosmos, and the great players who played there, like Pele, Beckenbauer and Dennis Tueart.

I also go to England several times a year and always make sure that I phone Dennis to arrange to meet up with him. He is the kind of person you want to spend time with. Dennis is one of the greatest, both as a player and as a person.

I am honoured that he has asked me to write the foreword to his autobiography and I am sure you will enjoy what is a fascinating read.

Carlos Alberto
Rio de Janeiro
October 2011

INTRODUCTION

When my almost ten years as a director of Manchester City Football Club came to an end, it wasn't wholly unexpected. There had been rumblings about a takeover for months; the grey suits jockeying for position in the new order. It hadn't escaped my notice that I was being increasingly marginalised and excluded from issues which I had been employed to deal with. Issues I still felt I was best qualified to find solutions to. I'd seen the signs. And yet, when it came, the manner of my dismissal seemed unimaginably heartless and unprofessional.

On June 20, 2007, after nine and a half years serving as non-executive director of Manchester City, I received my resignation letter via email. None of my fellow board members had spoken to me face-to-face, or even telephoned, to warn me of their decision beforehand. No discussion, no dignity, no thanks. Just goodbye. My time was up. A day later, the controversial £81.6 million purchase of the club by Thaksin Shinawatra, former Prime Minister of Thailand, was completed.

Why did it hurt so much? Of course, there was the sense of feeling abandoned by colleagues. The complete absence of warmth or any appreciation for the work I'd put in as a director during some of the toughest times in the club's 127-year history stung too. Serving on the Manchester City board may have been ostensibly a part-time role, but it was a full-time passion which had affected every other aspect of my life, a passion with deep roots.

Born and raised in football-mad Newcastle in an era when the city's team, inspired by the great Jackie Milburn, were winning FA Cups almost as a matter of routine, the game grabbed me from the cradle. Competitive by nature and with a work ethic ingrained in me by my father, I was determined to become a professional footballer. Never mind that I was small for my age, growing up I would fight against the odds, with a single-minded focus to achieve my goal. Nothing would stop me, not even rejection by my hometown club, unable to see beyond my lack of height. Instead, I journeyed across the North East divide, to Wearside where United's rivals Sunderland gave me my chance.

At Sunderland, I played under Alan Brown, whose innovative methods have influenced generations of managers up to the likes of Jose Mourinho, and Bob Stokoe, who led the club to its greatest triumph. Urged on by the "Roker Roar", Second Division Sunderland won the 1973 FA Cup and, amid the spiralling unemployment and strikes of that time, I witnessed the power of football in raising the spirits of an entire city and bringing people together.

On the road to Wembley that year, we played Manchester City, English football giants of the late Sixties and early Seventies, and I got a glimpse of what it must be like to play for one of England's greatest clubs. Their manager, Malcolm Allison, described us as "little Sunderland", a jibe which fired us up to beat them. And in the wake of the FA Cup triumph, I felt that, with Sunderland's fanbase, they had the potential to be much more than a little club. When it was clear that the club's ambitions did not match my own, though, I had to move on.

Fate took me back to Maine Road in 1974, to Manchester City, and from the moment I pulled on that sky-blue shirt it felt right. It was the start of a love affair that continues to this day. As a City player, among the highs, such as scoring the winning goal in the 1976 League Cup final with an overhead kick, there were disappointments and missed opportunities. City would never be the most reliable of mistresses, and we've had our fall-outs along the way, one of which led to an exciting interlude for me in America, replacing the legendary Pele at the New York Cosmos. But I always came back.

Years after my playing career had ended, in 1997, it was that magnetic attraction which distracted me from running three thriving businesses to join City's board of directors. The following years would see numerous battles behind the scenes and City plunge into football's third tier for the first time in its history. We hit many bumps along the way, but I was proud to assist in the rebuilding process. I always tried to apply the same honest endeavour to the task that I had in my playing days, drawing on all my experiences at Sunderland, the Cosmos and City and, subsequently, in business. The organisations that are most successful are the ones who maintain stability, unity and team spirit. By pulling together within the club, connecting with the community and tapping into the club's huge fanbase, I believed Manchester City could fulfil its massive potential.

Sadly, the power of the grey suits and their mindset had taken over. Football is all about passion, emotion and creativity; business is about brand, growth and profitability. I'm not sure how well they mix.

CHAPTER ONE

BEGINNING

May 8, 1955. Here I am, a five-year-old boy hoisted high on my dad's shoulders, with my black-and-white Newcastle rosette and my zebra scarf. I wriggle around, straining my eyes to see if the lads are getting closer. "When are they gonna be here, Dad? When are they gonna be here?" I pester him. There is a sea of expectant faces inside St James' Park, and we are hemmed in on the heaving Gallowgate End, waiting, waiting. They have poured in from everywhere. From Blyth, where the gigantic power stations tower over the town, and from the mining towns of Blaydon and Ashington, where terraced houses are dwarfed by huge chimneys belching out black filth, and where groups of women have written to their local MPs complaining about the constant smog and smoke in the air, which makes their children cough and leaves their washing looking permanently grey. Hordes have made the short trip from Gateshead across the Tyne Bridge, and then there are those, like my family, the Tuearts, who hail from Walker in the East End of Newcastle, where the giant cranes in the Swan Hunter shipyard loom above everything else like giant tripods. You see them wherever you go, high on the murky skyline.

Tens of thousands are also lining the streets outside St James' to welcome home the lads after their FA Cup win at Wembley. This is the third FA Cup triumph in five years. It's a doddle, this Wembley lark, the North East press are saying. All the lads and lasses, jammed together like sardines, are clad in dark hats and dark coats over dark suits on a chilly North East afternoon. All around me, they're taking gulps from brown ale bottles, and drags from cigarettes. A wave of excitement hits us as we're told that the team bus has somehow nudged its way through the masses to the stadium.

Twenty four hours earlier, Bobby 'The Dazzler' Mitchell, George Hannah and local hero Jackie Milburn put Manchester City to the sword down in London. The lads won 3–1, and have brought the pot back to the North East. Stories circulated before the match about City forward Don Revie's "masterplan". Playing as a deep-lying centre-forward, the idea was that he would wreak havoc and go for our occasionally pedestrian defence's jugular.

Some of the writers in the North East had got wind of City's perceived "Flash Harry" approach before the match: City's tactical masterplan, City's new-fangled sky-blue tracksuits – "Geordies v Gaudies", some journalists had dubbed it. But Newcastle won anyway. We don't go for Flash Harrys where I come from. It makes us rise to the challenge all the more. I'm straining my eyes to try to see the team. "Any minute now son, any minute now," my dad reassures me. He works on the lathes as a fitter and a turner in the Swan Hunter yards, which over the last 50 years have constructed the RMS *Mauritania* and the *Carpathia*, the first vessel to rescue the survivors of the *Titanic* disaster. He must be good, too, because at a time when heavy industry is slipping into decline, and unemployment has become a grim reality for many workers across the North East, Dad always has regular work and a regular wage. He works hard. Very hard. Mum works as a cleaner in a local office, and they both provide me and my younger brother, Kevin, with a secure and happy childhood. There isn't the money for luxuries. The odd family holiday away consists of a bus trip to a wooden chalet up the coast to Newbiggin, or days out at Tynemouth long beach, where we wolf down egg-and-tomato sandwiches, prepared by Mum. The need for regular work dominates people's lives. That, and the fortunes of the Toon.

Finally, amidst the din of roars, cheers and rattles, the team appear in the directors' box with the cup. Somewhere over there is Bobby Mitchell, with his dark hair swept back and grinning broadly, showing off his tombstone teeth, and George Hannah, a modest forward who plays in the most unfussy way, and who is looking a bit bemused by the whole thing. And there's 'Wor Jackie', who until a couple of years earlier had been working part-time as a fitter at Hazelrigg Colliery, holding the FA Cup aloft in one hand and smoking a cigarette with the other. Next to Milburn stands the team's cheerleader, known as 'Mr Newcastle'. He's wearing a zebra hat, zebra pyjamas, and a giant zebra rosette. He's encouraging the crowds to start singing. And so it starts, the Newcastle United anthem:

> Oh me lads, yeh shud hev seen us gannin,
> Pass'd the foalks alang the road, just as they wor stanin,
> Al the lads an' lasses there, all wi' smilin' faces,
> Gannin along the Scotswood Road, to see the Blaydon Races.

The song is unrelenting, and all the players join in. All of us. Singing it like our lives depend on it. The players salute the crowd, milking the applause for all it's worth, and then, finally, as if acting on some invisible signal, they're gone, out of sight. Next day in the press, the manager, Stan Seymour, talks about how this will be a springboard to greater success for the team, but over the next decade the majority of the headlines will revolve around tales of behind-the-scenes bust-ups, arguments over the club's meanness with money, and storm-outs over dirty team baths and unfit club houses for players. A classic tale of lost hope in a one-club city. Apart from a solitary Fairs Cup win back in 1969, there hasn't been another day quite like that FA Cup homecoming since. Newcastle United – the talk of the Toon.

Fifty-five years or so later, I look back on that afternoon and am still struck by the symbolism of the whole thing. Of course I was blissfully unaware at the time, but the clubs involved in that FA Cup final – Manchester City and Newcastle – would loom large throughout my life. I, too, would be on the Wembley pitch on cup final day when Bob Stokoe, Newcastle's craggy central defender, a Tyneside boy who ended up on Wearside like me, and Don Revie would once again cross swords 18 years later on a famous May afternoon in 1973, an unforgettable occasion which still flashes back to me pretty much every day. That afternoon at St James' in 1955 is my earliest football memory, and the enduring feeling that has stayed with me ever since is the raw, magnetic power that the game yields. I could feel it then, and I felt it throughout my football career. It's almost a force of nature. Around 200,000 Geordies turned out, maybe more, to toast Newcastle's success, and the cup was won by a team whose core was drawn from the local area, a side with which the locals could identify. The victory was talked about in the city for years afterwards. That's what football can do to people's lives. It can bond people, it can give them hope and a new lease of life. During my time as a player and as a director, I never forgot that fans are the lifeblood and the beating heart of any football club. Lose them, and the game is meaningless.

As a kid, home for me was a two-bedroom flat on the second floor of a three-floor council block in Lancefield Avenue, Walker. Eric Burdon, lead singer of The Animals, is a famous son of Walker. I shared a bedroom, and a three-quarter-sized bed, with my brother Kevin, who is six years younger than me. There was a middle brother, Paul, who was born roughly three and a half years after me. Before we moved to Lancefield Avenue, Mum, Dad, myself and Paul lived in a prefab in Walker. One night, I was woken up by screaming and shouting in the house, and I wandered out of my room to see my dad cradling 18-month-old Paul in his arms, trying to get him warm next to an electric fire. It was too late, though. Paul had suffered a cot death. I was too young to comprehend what had happened and, although I'm sure my parents suffered terrible emotional trauma at the time, it was never discussed afterwards, even when I was an adult. I think that was how things were dealt with back then. Whatever happens to you in the North East, no matter how terrible and unpleasant, you dust yourself down and move on with your life. It's a philosophy which I have always believed in, partly because it was instilled in me from a very young age.

Because of the age gap between Kevin and myself, socially I didn't have much to do with my brother until he was older, but I do recall that whenever he was able, we'd play diving headers with a tennis ball at one end of our bedroom. Luckily, we were at the end of the block, so there were no neighbours to complain about the endless banging of the ball against the wall. The walls in our bedroom were plastered with cut-outs of footballers from *Charles*

Buchan's Football Monthly, or any other pictures of players that I could get hold of from magazines or newspapers. The pictures weren't just of Newcastle players, but any big stars from any clubs who captured my imagination, like Stan Matthews or Nat Lofthouse. Like many boys in Newcastle, I became obsessed with football from an early age, and I grew up dreaming that one day I might be lucky enough to pull on the famous black-and-white stripes. I've still got a photograph of myself wearing a black-and-white striped cotton shirt, aged about three, although I've no idea where Dad got hold of it from, as replica shirts were quite rare in those days.

On Saturday nights, after Dad had been out to the working men's club, he would come home late after his regular skinful. In our lounge, we had a piano which dominated the room, and Dad, who was an excellent pianist, would start tinkling away on the ivories and singing. I can't imagine that the neighbours underneath were too happy, but I can't recall anyone ever complaining about the noise levels. Then the next day we would go to get some fresh air and watch my dad's working men's club's Sunday League side with my dad's brother, Lawrence (everyone called him 'Uncle Lol'), and my mum's brother, Uncle Tommy, who helped run the team. I loved the feel of the whole thing; the competitiveness, the shouting, the cajoling and the energy.

I was always reasonably happy at school. I wasn't the best scholar in the world, but my mum and dad always encouraged me to work hard and do my best. Dad was keen that I should also play football, but he would always remind me, "Concentrate on your schoolwork, son." In every way, Dad was always a hard taskmaster. If I'd done well in something at school, he'd always be interested and encouraging, but he'd often say, "Work harder." I knew I was doing alright when he simply said nothing. As I made my way in football, I realised that many men of his generation were taciturn by nature. The less they said to you, the better. If they spoke to you, it often meant that there was an issue of some sort. A problem. In football coaching and management, the "say nothing" philosophy is no good at all for the development of players, yet thousands of players have played the game receiving precious little positive, one-on-one input from their coaches, especially those of my generation.

Virtually every boy in Newcastle at that time started kicking a ball as soon as they could walk, and I was no exception. Contrary to the clichéd images people may have of "jumpers for goalposts" in that era, ball games were not encouraged in the streets surrounding our flats in the early 1960s, but we played anyway, on a big, square green in the middle of our four council blocks. Actually, there wasn't too much that was green about it, because the space was so worn that only a few tufts of grass survived. The space was really, really tight. On such a rough surface, your control had to be good, and you had to adjust quickly to the bounce and movement of the ball to keep it glued to your foot. It sharpened me up mentally and physically, and taught me how to react when other players were virtually on top of me, trying to boot me out of the way. You could have anything from five-a-side to 15-a-side in those games outside our flat, and as the games got bigger I'd have to fight and scrap for time on the ball and space.

It was hugely important to me, that steep learning curve on the big, square green, because I learnt how to get stuck in and make my presence felt, something which was always a major part of my game as a professional. I was always small for my age, a good inch or two shorter than the other boys in my peer group, so I felt that I had a great deal to prove, and that I had to stand out from the crowd. That feeling never changed from when I was a young kid scrapping it out in Walker, to playing for Sunderland, Manchester City or the New York Cosmos. Even as a seven- or eight-year-old, I was aware that others around me were less skilful than me, but more physical, so what I lacked in size, I was going to have to make up for in effort and aggression.

Before Mum and Dad got me a pair of boots, I'd had to be creative about what I wore on my feet, because like lots of boys in my area I had a pair of shoes for school and a pair for best. There was no way Mum and Dad could stretch to buying me another pair of shoes for football. So when Dad finished with his work shoes, I would cut out soles from a piece of linoleum and fix them to the bottom. They were actually a bit too big, but it did help me sharpen up my control. When I finally did get my first pair of boots with screw-in studs, I remember walking around the house, showing them off to my mum. My parents would have to have saved hard for those boots, and getting them was one of those unforgettable moments in life. From that point on I was always particular about the state of my boots. Throughout my career they had to be spotless because I saw them as my tools. They were part of who I was. The following day, I trip-trapped across the playground at school, making as much noise as possible, making sure everyone knew I had those boots, feeling about ten feet tall (which, unfortunately, I wasn't).

As well as playing football outside my flat, I also played at school and for a local boys' club, Welbeck Juniors. I would play for the school on a Saturday morning and then the boys' club in the afternoon. The afternoon kick-off was usually 2pm, and if we were playing away on the west side of Newcastle we would rush down to St James' Park after our game and get in free as the stadium gates would be open for supporters leaving early, and catch the last 15 minutes. It was quite easy to meet the Newcastle team in the early and mid-Sixties. During school holidays, I'd often shoot over to Hunters' Moor, where the players trained, to take a peek at what they were up to. In those days, the team would walk to and from the training ground from St James' Park, along with a couple of dozen other autograph hunters and those other supporters who just loved swaggering along the road like a professional footballer. I'd be there, walking with the players, trying to make small talk with them, grabbing their signatures. "How are you son?" they'd ask me, ruffling my hair as I strutted alongside them. There was Dave Hollins, the goalkeeper (brother of John, the future Chelsea, QPR and Arsenal player), striker Barrie Thomas, and the midfielder Jim Iley. Small-town heroes all of them, even though they couldn't hold a candle to Stan Seymour's team of the early and mid-Fifties. Opposite St James' Park was the brewery, and all year round you could smell the sweet, often overpowering, smell of the hops any time you went near the ground. To me as a kid, it was just the "football smell", and it never occurred to me until I started making my way in the game that other grounds have their own unique character and aromas.

Making my presence felt in schools' football was a long and hard process. It still is for any youngster who has dreams of making it in the game – it's a dog-eat-dog world, with desperate young players clamouring to attract the attention of the club scouts who float around games. In the late Fifties and early Sixties, it was often a case of separating the (big) men from the (small) boys. Conventional wisdom at the time held that if you were tall, physically strong, and could boot the ball a long way on pitches which were often waterlogged, frozen and full of holes and bumps, you had half a chance of making it in the game. I had a good level of natural ability, and good hand-to-eye coordination. In time, I would captain all my school teams at football and cricket, and I was an excellent cross country runner as well. I graduated to play for Newcastle Schoolboys and played as a centre-forward. The problem was, although I could score goals, I was not your big, bustling front-man type. I was tiny, and tiny lads who played as a centre-forward back then, as I did, were not exactly seen as having a long and rosy future in the game. I was competing with literally thousands of kids. It was survival of the fittest. Nevertheless, I thought I was good enough to become a footballer, even though I knew there were tonnes of other kids dreaming of pulling on Newcastle's black-and-white stripes. And despite my size I was doing okay.

Being captain of all my football teams gave me a massive sense of pride, a feeling of responsibility, and an inner confidence. I was also the eldest grandchild of 24 on both sides of the family, and I did feel a sense of responsibility within the family because of that. I wouldn't say that Mum and Dad constantly reminded me of the fact that I was the eldest cousin, and that I should therefore set an example to the others, but I was certainly aware of it. That, together with being a sports captain, helped me carry myself more confi-dently than other boys in my year group. I knew I was a good footballer, and I was determined to give it my best shot.

I also adhered to certain rules which I stick to even now. Part of being captain of a team is looking the part, and I've always believed in dressing smartly on the right occasion, as it shows you in a positive light when you meet others. Very unusually for a young boy – and especially for a footballer – I always liked to plan ahead. As I was juggling school, football, cricket and running, I needed to be organised. So at the start of any season, I wanted to have the fixture list, and if we were travelling away I wanted to have an itinerary. Some of my team-mates used to laugh at me about my fussiness, but I'm no different now. If I'm going away on holiday, or planning a business conference, I like everything sorted well in advance, and hate being late for anything. Occasionally it drives my family mad, and I suppose it makes me something of a control freak, but I'd like to think I'm a contingency man and it's had a positive effect on me down the years, serving me well in both my football and business career.

As any footballer knows, making it in the game often comes down to lucky breaks. Being seen at the right time by the right scout. Staying injury-free. Meeting a coach with whom you can work effectively. One of the unique innovations of Newcastle Schools at that time was that they offered gifted young players an opportunity to sit a soccer exam when they approached the age of 11. It was effectively an 11-plus in football. There were about six criteria, revolving around your ability to pass the ball, trap it, shield it, dribble it and strike it. It was predominantly all about ball work, which may sound blindingly obvious, but so much coaching at that time revolved around a player's ability to run all day that this was quite revolutionary. I passed the exam.

The real key to my progress at that time was a man called Bob Maddison, the sports teacher at my secondary school, Manor Park Technical Grammar. A hard little basket was Bob, but he was one of the few coaches I met who I can genuinely say shaped my career. He was everything that a budding 12-year-old footballer needed at that time of life: a disciplinarian, an organiser, a cajoler, sometimes a joker and, most importantly for me, an innovator. He genuinely cared about all his footballers. Clad in his tracksuit and with a whistle around his neck, he would shout instructions ("Dennis, make the run!" "Dennis, track back!" "Beat your man, Dennis!") – constructive criticism, and encouragement. He also had a great sense of humour. After Sunderland were promoted in 1963 under Alan Brown, I went to see him in his office. As I walked in through the open door, he put his hand up and shut the door in my face. There on the outside, was a picture of the promoted Sunderland team, and Bob knew that as a Newcastle fan it would annoy me. It did!

No one dared to mess Bob around. I remember once when he laid on an optional evening coaching session in the gym at Wharrior Street School near to my home. There was snow on the ground and, as young kids do, at the end of the evening we started lobbing snowballs at each other. I was a dead-eye shot, and smashed one of the gas lamps outside the school. The school complained to Bob, and he hauled me up the next day and threatened to ban me from playing again. He tore me to pieces and really made me suffer for a while before he let me back into the team. I was in tears, because I knew that not only had I let him down, but I also needed his support in school to keep progressing in the football teams.

Bob was excellent at working on tactical moves. One of his little ploys was to get the goalkeeper to collect the ball, who would then throw it to the full-back who'd broken out wide. Then the full-back would feed the ball into the channel into the path of the forward. This is a common tactic in modern-day football, where the full-back breaks out wide and links up with the forwards, but it was very rare in the early Sixties when full-backs rarely crossed the halfway line. Another of his methods was to give A4 forms to the team captains of the 12–16 age group teams, and get us to write a report on how our games had gone and how we judged individual performances. He then asked us to feedback and present to our PE teachers on a Monday morning. It encouraged us to take responsibility for our teams and gain a greater understanding of the game. I certainly think that Bob's influence encouraged me, even at that age, to think about the mechanics of a game, and what contributes to teams winning or losing.

If you look at the players who came through under Bob, it speaks volumes for his ability to nurture talent. We had about four or five years of solid representation in the Newcastle Boys team. The first to come through with Bob was John Barnwell, who went to Middle Street School before Manor Park opened, and who went on to play for Nottingham Forest and Arsenal, managed several clubs and then went on to become a top administrator in the League Managers' Association. There was Jimmy Husband, who played for Everton, Geoff Allen, who turned out for Newcastle, and Dave Young, who was the Sunderland substitute in the 1973 FA Cup Final. And then Derek Foster, from Walker like me, who holds the record for being the youngest-ever goalkeeper in the top flight when he made his debut for Sunderland aged just 15 years and 185 days. Then I broke through into the Newcastle Schoolboys team as well. All of us worshipped Bob, and it was a golden era for him in terms of his school teams, and his city boys' sides.

I was still fighting against the odds, though, because of my height. I knew I was pretty good, and I was already developing a skill which served me well throughout my professional career; the art of volleying the ball. One time my Aunty Doreen bet me ten bob that I couldn't score eight goals in a game. I won the bet, and I felt a massive thrill when one of my scissor kicks screamed past the opposition goalkeeper. It's a difficult skill to be able to pick up the line of the ball very early in flight, but luckily I had a natural gift for being able to spot it. I'd been playing for Newcastle Schoolboys since I was 12, and I was scoring plenty of goals, but all the time the general consensus was that my height would prevent me from having a crack at becoming a professional player. Decision time arrived when I reached 15. This was the age at which clubs would decide whether or not to give young players a two-year apprenticeship. Newcastle decided against taking up that option. Hull City watched me too. They said, "Thanks, but no thanks. Too small." And there was still the unresolved issue of what exactly my best position was on the park, because with my speed I was also capable of pulling out onto the wings.

In the year below me at Rutherford Grammar School, Paddy Lowrey, a centre-forward who at 15 years old was signed by Newcastle, but then went on to play for Sunderland, was making waves, and the scouts swarmed around him like bees around a honey pot. He seemed set to become the Sixties equivalent of Wayne Rooney. Good for Paddy – but it didn't look like good news for me. Added to that, the Newcastle Schoolboys team already had a right winger, so because of my goalscoring ability they shoved me out on the left wing.

I wasn't very happy about that, but eventually it turned out to be a blessing in disguise, because in those days the concept of a right-footer cutting in from the left was a bit too unorthodox for some defences to cope with. Of course, this tactic is now used at the top level, where many clubs switch wingers such as Messi at Barcelona, Di Maria and Ronaldo at Real Madrid, Robben at Bayern Munich, Ashley Young at Manchester United and Adam Johnson at Manchester City. I had to adapt quickly. I had no other choice, and it wasn't long before I was reaping the rewards of playing there. Right full-backs were used to wingers going down their outside, and I saw the panic on their faces as I darted inside and shot away from them. To be honest, I never dreamed that it was anything other than a temporary state of affairs, and I didn't imagine that I'd stay out there on the left for as long as I played football. I stuck at it, but it didn't feel right, and then Bob Maddison left Manor Park in my third year and went to another school.

I felt like I might lose my way, and that I could easily tumble into a chasm, a black hole. For some 15-year-olds that might well have been the case, but not me. The fact that Newcastle, my home-town club, declined to take me on as an apprentice stung me badly, but I wouldn't let it destroy me. Not for a second. I'd been a scrapper ever since I kicked a ball with my mates outside our flat in Walker – always battling against the odds because I was smaller than the others. But I was seriously annoyed, and hurt. I was the eldest son, and the eldest cousin. I'd been captain of the school team. And now this. I had enough self belief to know that I was too good to be discarded and thrown on the scrap heap. There were no tears, no tantrums. I'd have got no sympathy from my family with that approach. It wasn't the Tueart way. They'd have told me to grow up and get on with it. I internalised the whole thing, and became even more steely and determined. Somehow, I knew that if I stuck to doing what I was doing, then success would come from it somewhere along the line.

Sometimes, I think about what might have been. Mum and Dad, who by then also doubted that I would ever have a crack at the big time, wanted me to get some qualifications and a stable job. For a while Mum insisted I scan the small ads in the local papers. I went for an interview as an office clerk. It would never have been my thing, running around an office, doing some filing and making the tea, so I was dead lucky they never offered me the job, because even though I had a great determination to play profes-sional football and was still playing for Newcastle Schoolboys I would have probably had little option but to take it.

Bob Maddison, whom I still kept in touch with, had suggested an alternative to a traditional office job. Why not consider becoming a PE teacher like him? After all, I could carry on playing amateur football, gain some O-Levels, and then a get a "steady" job. I still wanted to play the game professionally, but I accepted that I needed something to fall back on, so I stayed on at school and took some more exams. I'd also grown an inch or two more, and reached about five feet eight inches. In the end, it was Bob, a huge Sunderland fan, who saved me. All the scouts in the area were in regular contact with him, and Bob kept on recommending me to Charlie Ferguson, the famous Sunderland scout. Charlie wasn't the tallest either, and didn't seem to have the same hang-ups about my lack of inches as other coaches, so he offered me schoolboy terms. The fact that Sunderland had always been Newcastle's big rivals didn't deter me one bit, and my overriding feeling at the time was one of sheer relief. Finally, I'd been vindicated in my decision to stick at it, and my initial rejection by Newcastle made the feeling even sweeter. I felt like I'd earned my chance, and that somehow, after all that happened, I was more armour-plated than other boys of my age, because there's nothing worse when you are 15 than the feeling of rejection, and nothing sweeter than fighting your way back from it, either.

I signed schoolboy forms with Sunderland and trained with them on a Tuesday and a Thursday night. I would continue to play for the school team, but if they didn't have a game I could play for the Sunderland youth team. It was made clear to me that after a year, the club would decide whether or not they wanted me to sign professional terms. My position in the youth team remained the same as it had been with Newcastle Schoolboys; I was a left-winger who cut inside whenever possible.

Although I'd signed forms with "the enemy", I was still something of an outsider, commuting from Newcastle. Apart from training and playing matches there, I barely spent any time in Sunderland at all. To get to training, I had to undertake a fairly unforgiving 30-minute bus journey from my school in Longbenton to Worsick Street in the centre of Newcastle. Then I would get the bus to Sunderland, get off near the local greyhound stadium, and take a 20-minute walk down to Roker Park for training. It was two hours, door-to-door, and it was the same on the way home, in the dark, the drizzle, the fog and the cold. I wouldn't get home until 10.30 in the evening. It certainly tested my resolve, but the youth team we had there at the time, which included fantastic players like the defender Colin Todd and forwards Billy Hughes and Colin Suggett, was phenomenal, and reinforced my belief that I'd made the right choice in joining Sunderland.

Only four members of the youth team didn't make it in top-class football, so clearly Charlie Ferguson knew what he was doing, and was an excellent spotter of talent. As a youngster, being in the right place at the right time, with a coach who rates you, is absolutely crucial.

I knew that I'd have to be aggressive to make it in the game. One of my youth-team colleagues was Brian Chambers, who, in terms of natural skill, was way ahead of me. He was top boy in the area, and seemed set to be a leading light. Compared to a little scrapper like me, Brian was a real thoroughbred. One night, when we got off the bus in Newcastle after travelling back from Roker Park after training, we started talking about the attitude and desire you need to make it at the top level. I asked Brian, "If you and I were fighting for a place in the team, and there was just the one place, would you kick me to get it?"

He looked a bit uncomfortable and after a while said, "No. I probably wouldn't."

"I'd kick you," I said.

It probably sounds unpleasant and horrible, but I didn't mean it that way. Brian was and still is a great mate. It was just that I was willing to do pretty much anything to break through into top-level football.

Brian had a decent enough career at Luton, Millwall and Bournemouth. He was transferred to Arsenal just before the 1973 cup final and yet he admits he didn't achieve as much as he might have done in the game. I knew I wasn't in his league skill-wise, but it takes more than that to be a professional footballer.

It also seemed that Paddy Lowrey had the world at his feet at Sunderland, and he did go on to score a couple of goals for the first team. But Paddy enjoyed life outside football rather too much. Our then manager Alan Brown's parting words to Paddy were, "I like you Paddy, but you're a rogue." So off he went.

My concerns about my height and the fact that for a while it seemed that I might not make it in the game meant I was always acutely aware that a footballer's career could be both short and full of trials and tribulations. I knew very well that I couldn't match Brian and Paddy in terms of their skill levels, so I had to be mentally tougher than them and those around me, and do what I needed to do to fulfil my aims, regardless of what others expected of me. As my sons grew up I used to say to them, "If you want to be the best, you have to be different from the rest." I know it sounds corny, and I don't want to come across like David Brent, but that's what you have to do in order to be successful. Do what *you* need to do to make it in your field, not what others are trying to get you to do.

Being different from other players never bothered me. I never drank. I did try it. As teenagers, we'd occasionally go to pubs in Newcastle, and I'd try the brown ale, but I couldn't stand it. When we socialised as a team at Sunderland, I'd order a coke or a lemonade. Even when I bought a car, I still lived in Newcastle, so I was never part of the social scene in Sunderland anyway. When we won the FA Cup at Sunderland, I remained stone-cold sober the whole time. It certainly didn't dampen my enjoyment or elation at what we'd achieved, and I loved seeing the whole thing through clear eyes. I was the butt of jokes at first ("Come on Dennis, what's the matter with you? Have a drink."), but that faded after a while, because I never let the ribbing affect me in any way, and my team-mates knew that I'd never change my drinking habits.

It was the same with gambling. Once or twice I joined the card school on the coach, but I couldn't really understand the excitement behind it, and certainly didn't want to lose my hard-earned wages playing poker.

I liked to stay firmly in control of what I was doing, and focus on the football, the job in hand. I'd never preach to others how to live their lives, and I'm very happy with the way I've always lived mine.

My breakthrough with Sunderland came in 1967 while I was still at school, when I was picked for the FA Youth Cup quarter-final against Manchester United, whose team included Brian Kidd. I scored one, typical of my unusual wing style, when I cut in from the left and hit a right-foot shot high into the United net. I also had a hand in a second goal, in front of over 11,000 supporters at

Roker Park. "New boy Tueart is the toast of Roker," ran the local *Newcastle Journal* headline. My headmaster summoned me the next day and congratulated me. My classmates teased me, albeit in an affectionate way.

This game gave me a higher profile within the club during the rest of that season when I was a part of the squad that won the FA Youth Cup, although I didn't play in the final. Typical of how things were done at clubs at the time, no one on the coaching staff ever spoke to me about how I was progressing, or whether I might be offered professional terms at the end of the season, but I trusted my judgement, and I always believed that I would make it. I could also compare myself with other youth-team players. In my first season as a young pro, before a Youth Cup quarter-final match with Everton at Goodison Park, I got injured, and my replacement, Colin Beesley, played poorly and we lost the game. I had a real go at him afterwards, which I felt a bit guilty about, but part of the problem was that Colin was a year younger and let the occasion get to him. I knew even at that age that I wasn't going to be the kind of player who was intimidated by anything.

In May 1967 the Sunderland manager, Ian McColl, invited me and my dad to discuss an offer of a professional contract. We were sat in his office, and he made a one-year contract offer of £15 a week. My dad was questioning the offer, but I was so desperate to sign the contract I was kicking him under the table. I eventually signed my first professional contract for £16 a week. As we left McColl's office, Dad congratulated me, although he warned me to keep thinking about my education. I listened to him, and took on board his advice. But my mind was racing. I was now officially a professional footballer.

CHAPTER TWO

BOMBER & THE MESSIAH

I absolutely loved the feeling of being a professional footballer from the moment I signed those forms in Ian McColl's office. The feeling never left me for the next 17 years. I'd worked so hard to have a crack at being a professional that I wasn't going to waste a second. At first, I trained with the youth team and the reserves at Sunderland, and from the moment the sessions began at ten in the morning I loved every aspect of it – the physical encounters, the running and the ball play. Not every player enjoys training, and there were a few who would come in and whinge, but not me. I even found the air up in Sunderland bracing and invigorating – it certainly woke me up in the morning!

We got some extreme weather up there. Some days we'd train on the beach at Roker or Seaburn, and occasionally we'd have to wait around for ages until the tide went out. If it was in, we had seemingly endless sessions of running up and down the beach steps to fill the time, and build up the stamina in our leg muscles. I guess that sounds fairly Spartan, but it toughened me up, I know that. Modern-day Sunderland players, who train at Cleadon, have it slightly easier than we did. When they constructed the complex 14 years ago, they built in hillocks to block the wind that howls in off the North Sea. But the gales never did me any harm, and it would get me used to the conditions at Roker Park, when the wind would sometimes blow so hard that I had tears in my eyes and could barely catch my breath.

When I was training we had some fine players on their way up through the youth and reserve team, including Billy Hughes, a Scottish attacker with a sharp turn of pace, who would make his name like I did during the 1973 FA Cup run. I was still playing out on the left, and by 1968 I was a regular in the reserves. On occasions, I was invited to train with the first team, which I took to mean that the club was pleased with my progress. I was like a whirling dervish out on that training pitch. I once block-tackled our forward, Colin Suggett, and he wasn't too happy with me and reckoned I'd gone over the top, but I don't recall feeling particularly nervous about training alongside more experienced players, and never felt overawed at all. Under Ian McColl, the team was treading water in the First Division, and it was pretty clear to me what the problem was.

We were definitely strong in the 18–21 age group. Bobby Kerr and Colin Todd were starting to make names for themselves, and Ian Porterfield, a McColl signing from Raith Rovers and a strong, decisive midfielder, was also breaking through. But a team needs more than that, and we were definitely short of experienced players. When I started out at Sunderland, we had 'Slim' Jim Baxter at the club who was, along with Denis Law, my boyhood hero. McColl knew Jim through his time as manager of the Scotland national team, and pinned his hopes on him displaying the kind of form which had made him such a hero north of the border with Rangers. In fact, thanks to his boozing, he wasn't so slim anymore and, although his talent was phenomenal, he was inconsistent.

"Gae it to the claw," he'd yell during training, referring to his left foot, and when he received the ball you could tell that he had been a supreme talent. The problem was that he'd come into training with his eyes almost on stalks from the night before. One of our trainers told us that he'd once been chatting to Jim, who happened to be eating a meat pie for breakfast as he arrived for training. Jim opened the boot of his flashy Ford Zodiac, and inside were wads of notes from his night out at the casino the night before.

For me it was an honour to play alongside him in training. He still had unbelievable vision and would dictate the play, but thanks to his lifestyle his influence was on the wane. He wasn't the best example to youngsters of how to live your life, but I remained in awe of his talent, nonetheless. I was much younger than Jim, and wasn't really on his radar, so to speak, but I was very sad for him when his life spiralled into decline after he left the club in 1967. Jim went to Nottingham Forest and continued drinking, bloated out, and eventually needed a liver transplant.

Ian McColl was soon sacked after a run of poor results and our new manager, Alan 'Bomber' Brown, sold him. Before I'd even got to know him, he sold Baxter and told the press, "Experienced players can be both an asset and a risk to youngsters."

In my role as a player and later as a club director, I'd eventually see that Brown's statement was spot on, but when he took over as manager for the second time at the start of the 1968/69 season I was far more interested in his comment to local journalists that he intended "to give every opportunity to young Sunderland players." As an 18-year-old, it was frankly music to my ears, and over time I'd see that Brown was as good as his word.

Alan Brown was definitely the most influential coach that I ever played under. He was six feet one, an ex-policeman, and he had a steely gaze that could slice right through you. It regularly did. Brown knew only too well the frustrations of managing Sunderland, a club which embraced false dawns like no other club.

In his first spell at the club in the early 1960s, Bomber had placed Brian Clough in charge of the youth team. When I was a youngster at Sunderland, my future team-mates Jimmy Montgomery and Bobby Kerr raved about their time under about Cloughie. Bomber Brown was Cloughie's mentor. Jimmy and Bobby remembered Cloughie barking out words of encouragement here, and biting invective there. Clough was all about innovation and discipline, like Brown. They should have served the club for years, and Sunderland could have lived up to its label as a "hotbed of football." But Brown walked out, back to Sheffield Wednesday, and the board quickly decided that they could do without Clough who, they reasoned, was already getting a little too big for his boots. From that time on, Sunderland meandered along in Division One, doing precious little. Clough went to Hartlepools, a place he described as being "almost at the end of the world", but he still reckoned his new team had more ambition than the Sunderland board. The shame of it.

Two years after Brown first resigned, the board decided that some of the senior players like Baxter were taking a few too many liberties, and invited him back for his second spell in the Roker hot seat. His return wasn't universally popular with the players and, as I would see, he was certainly no public relations man, but he was certainly a one-off and, tactically, miles ahead of his time.

Knowing that the purse strings were tight at Sunderland, Brown was zealous about nurturing the talent within the youth and reserve team. The board agreed to fund the construction of a new training complex at Washington, comprising several pitches and a gym. Later, when the gym had been constructed, after training one day Browny got some of us to lay the car park with cement. He hired the cement mixer himself, mixed the sand and water, and showed us how to spread the cement around. He'd walk around, towering over us, telling us to "Hurry up" and "Spread it more evenly" in his broad Northumberland brogue, and now and then even tell us we were doing okay.

Some of the lads got lime burns from it – I didn't, thankfully – but no one said anything to Brown because of the authority he wielded. He was intimidating. But did he thank any of us? No. All he said was, "Right, you lot have got somewhere to park your cars now." I suppose that he had a point.

As a policeman, we heard that Brown had been trained in the art of hand-to-hand combat. I don't know whether that story was true. It may have been tittle-tattle that did the rounds, but he did have an air about him which meant that no one dared question his ideas. I certainly wasn't about to. Not just because I tried to only speak when spoken to, but because my future at Sunderland depended on Alan Brown being satisfied with my performances.

One time, Brown decided that the defence was weak in the air. So he lined up the defenders and one by one invited them to head away golf balls he threw into the air with all the power they could muster. The rest of us stood and watched as each defender staggered away, seeing stars, Brown stood on the side, unmoved and impassive. Anyone who refused to head the balls or dallied around got an earful. I remember him yelling at defender Dick Malone: "That's it Dick, head it away son. Strengthen those muscles in your forehead." Anyone who complained of a headache or watery eyes or whatever got yelled at. None of us watching strikers intervened, fearing that Bomber might devise some form of corporal punishment for us too. Sometimes, you have to take care of number one in football.

Brown was the original dispenser of the "hairdryer" treatment, for which Sir Alex Ferguson later became famous. It was simple. At Sunderland, you did it his way.

He was almost evangelical about his training methods. It reflected how he lived his life. By the time he had rejoined the club, he had become a member of the Moral Rearmament Group, a spiritual organisation based on honesty, purity, unselfishness and love. Brown detested swearing, and would chastise us if he heard us curse. As you can imagine, stopping a large group of footballers from swearing is no mean feat, but he succeeded.

Very occasionally he did break his own non-swearing rule, though. When I was 19, he told me there were three ways to solve a problem. You could look at others and think, "I'm not that badly off," or you could whinge and come to the conclusion that the whole world is against you, or you could get off your bloody backside and do something about it yourself. I thought that that was pretty sound advice for a teenager, and I have taken that approach throughout my life.

In the era before Sports Science was common at football clubs, Brown was way ahead of his time. "Make sure you keep a scrapbook of your achievements, son," he told me. I always did, and I still have books full of clippings and photos from my career because Browny realised, and I came to in time, that if your form took a dip at some point, then looking back at reports and photos of your goals could work wonders for your confidence. I began to read specialist sports magazines, and look into what types of foods might give me an edge. I started eating white fish with honey poured over it – a mixture of protein and sugar – something which is actively encouraged these days.

By the start of the 1968/69 season, I was training far more frequently with the first team. I was scoring regularly for the reserves from my position out on the left, and I felt I was becoming physically and mentally sharper all the time. I hoped that I was nudging my way closer to the first team but, typical of Brown wanting to keep his players on their toes, he never gave me any hint that I was in his thoughts.

The average age of the squad was falling, but Brown still knew that he needed a blend of youth and experience in the side. He brought in Joe Baker from Nottingham Forest, Calvin Palmer from Stoke and Gordon Harris from Burnley. Senior professionals who've been successful in the game have a certain swagger, a particular way in which they hold themselves, and sometimes it's hard for a manager to get them to change old habits. Joe had a great track record with Hibs, Torino and Arsenal, but he was on the wane when he came to us. Later, when I'd established myself at the club, one of Browny's rules on away trips was that players couldn't drink. Joe used to get around that rule by tipping vodka into his coke or lemonade.

Harris had won the title at Turf Moor, and one day he turned to me and said, "I've got something that you'll never have."

"Oh aye, what's that then?" I asked.

"An England cap. And with a left foot like yours, you'll never have one," he claimed.

Although Harris' comment annoyed me, I did take it on board, and I always made sure that I worked hard on developing the skills on my left foot, because so many players in this country are ridiculously right-footed that to have a good degree of skill with your left foot is massively important.

Brown had no qualms about getting rid of seasoned professionals – even those whom he'd worked with over many years during his two spells at the club. His readiness to dispense with experience and ring the changes was to my benefit late in 1968.

My Sunderland debut came about after a one-to-one training session which Brown ran with myself and George Mulhall late in 1968. George was a lovely man, and he still holds the record for the most consecutive appearances for the club, but by '68 he was in his thirties and I'd just turned 19. I was hungry and ready for a crack at the first team. It was an all-consuming desire – that wish to push on and prove myself. Brown's session involved George and I, both left-sided players, going forward and checking back, trying to create space and make darting runs. It was an exhausting session, and afterwards George vomited at the side of the pitch. He literally bent double and threw up. I looked at him, and I could see Alan Brown look at him as well. His days were numbered. We all knew it.

I was named in the first-team squad on the Friday, but that didn't overly excite me, because I'd been in the squad before and not made it into the first team. The following day, when the team sheet went up at 1.45 for the Boxing Day match against Sheffield Wednesday at Roker Park – just an hour and a quarter before the game – my name was on it and George's wasn't. I was in. I confess that I went into the boot room and had a little cry. My tears were partly due to the fact that I was replacing an iconic player, which George most certainly was, and also because the enormity of the fact that I'd nudged my way in. It just got to me at that moment.

I was 19 years and one month old. I'd only signed professional terms 18 months before, so my progress to the first team was fairly rapid. I doubt that I'd have made it so quickly were it not for Alan Brown's belief in the power of youth, so I'm eternally grateful to him.

The build-up to the match – if you can call it that – went by in a flash. I just didn't have time to be nervous. I read the match-day programme and did some stretching. This became my usual pre-match routine, particularly in the era before we warmed up on the pitch. I never had any superstitions of any kind. I just wanted to focus and to disappear into my "zone".

Shortly before we ran out onto the pitch, Alan Brown walked over, looked me in the eye, and said, "Son, good luck. Go out there, do your best and, don't forget, you can do nothing wrong."

The game was played on a typical Sixties Boxing Day pitch, Sixties style. In those days before undersoil heating, it was rock hard and unforgiving. You needed tight control, otherwise the ball would simply run away from you.

The crowd was supportive and encouraging toward me because the only bright spot on the horizon was the emergence of youth-team players like myself, Billy Hughes and Bobby Kerr. I immediately struck up a good rapport with the Clock Stand. It was known to have some fairly sharp characters on it, real working class fans who had made some wingers' lives a misery over the years. That can be the lot of a winger. Possibly with the exception of the goalkeeper, you are most at risk from getting a hard time from the crowd if things go wrong. But they serenaded me with the song, "Nice one Dennis, nice one son," and I got on with them immediately.

Marking me that day was Wednesday right-back Wilf Smith, a hard-nosed defender. Early on when I received my first pass, I tried to turn around sharply. Smith came flying in on the blind side and dumped me on the cinder track surrounding the pitch. He'd certainly let me know he was there, put it that way, and he shot me a look as if to say, "You'll remember me, won't you son?"

I got up straight away to show him I wasn't intimidated, but I'd learnt the lesson that you had to look after yourself in this game, and you had to toughen up quickly. It was a poor game and it finished goalless, and after that I was in and out of the side for the next season or so.

I felt that when I played, I was adapting well. I learnt to stand up to tough players like Chelsea's Ron Harris and relished the physical side of the game. I loved it, and never doubted that I would be able to establish myself as a professional at Sunderland.

I scored my first goal for the club in a 4–1 win against Stoke City, my third game for Sunderland. Gordon Banks, the Stoke goalkeeper, had been taken off injured after a collision with our forward, Colin Suggett. He had been replaced by their centre-forward, David Herd, the former Manchester United player. I received the ball just inside the penalty area, controlled it with my right foot and cracked it into the net with my left. I guess I should thank Gordon Harris for that one.

Alan Brown would pitch me in to the team and then take me out me so as not to put too much pressure on me. It's an approach which the likes of Sir Alex Ferguson use today, but in those days it was often a case of, "If he's good enough, he's old enough", which doesn't always do young players too many favours. The pace of young players' development has to be managed on an individual basis, and these days clubs are far more sophisticated in that area than they were in the Sixties. But Alan Brown was excellent at that kind of nurturing all those years ago.

So much of what Brown did was spot on. When I was breaking through at Roker Park, the apprentices and the first team changed in different dressing rooms, to create a culture of aspiration. Some might have considered that approach elitist or divisive, but I think it drove young players on. Both dressing rooms reeked of linament, that all-pervading olive oil smell, but the apprentices knew that, until they cracked the first team, they wouldn't get a sniff of the seniors' patch. It was always just up the corridor. Just out of reach. You could hear the hubbub emanating from there. There were journalists milling about there. It was busy and buzzing; the place to be. It was almost like a holy grail. Almost within touching distance, if you just worked that bit harder.

Whether you liked Brown's methods or not, he treated all the players as if they were his sons, with him as a stern, yet encouraging father figure. He certainly was a guru when it came to training methods. Malcolm Allison and Howard Wilkinson, as well as Cloughie, have all claimed that they later used many of his methods. Then, when you consider that as a youngster, when his father was one of Allison's assistants at Sporting Lisbon, a young Jose Mourinho cited Allison as his "hero" you begin to realise the scope of Brown's influence.

I became a first-team regular during the 1969/70 season. I was able to wade in with seven goals in 35 games and felt that my overall play and contribution to the team had improved. This was, in no small measure, down to Brown's coaching. I knew that he wasn't to everyone's taste though, and his jackboot approach often irritated me as well, and that was a large part of the reason why he wasn't as successful at Sunderland as he should have been. His blanket approach to discipline backfired.

In the summer of 1970, Brown took a backpack and a tent, and completed the Pennine Walk, from the Peak District to the Scottish Borders. He must have had a great deal of time to ponder, because when he returned he unveiled a whole raft of new training techniques at pre-season training. He invented several drills where two lines of players faced each other, passed the ball and spun off to the end of their lines to encourage passing and movement. The likes of Arsene Wenger now use this training method all the time, but Brown was the first to introduce it.

Lenny Hepple, a ballroom dancer, was brought in to help us with our balance, and I found his one-to-one advice invaluable.

Lenny pointed out that, as a right-footer, I would naturally push away with my left foot, and that in time this would put pressure on my left side. He taught me how to centralise my position of gravity, and take the strain off my body. In the dressing room prior to games, we'd all practise what we called the "diddly-dees." That meant linking our arms at shoulder height in a circle, to tone and refine our upper-body strength. I never forgot Lenny's advice, and I'm convinced that it helped me make best use of my upper body throughout my career.

Brown, on Lenny's advice, also installed two table-tennis tables at the new training centre where the players would play pre- and post-training sessions, assisting their movement and balance. Jimmy Montgomery was one of the stars at the table, and he told me that it helped him sharpen up his reflexes in goal no end. Brown also introduced the concept of "shadow play", where we would move the ball around from the back to the front from our allocated positions and roles on the pitch with no opposition. It was all about Brown giving us some shape. It got us thinking as one, and I thought it was beneficial, although I know that Billy Hughes, for instance, didn't feel it added a great deal to his game. One time, Billy cut in from the left-hand side to make a near-post run after I crossed the ball, and he poked it home. Next thing we knew, Browny came down from the back of the stand and started yelling at Billy.

"What the hell are you doing in there?" Browny yelled. "That's Dave Watson's domain. You stay over on the left."

Brown worked on your mind, and did everything in his power to get inside your head. All his young professionals were made – not asked – to take their preliminary coaching badge so that they started to think about tactics and approach play. I passed mine at the age of 21.

He'd also put you on the spot after training on a Friday. He'd ask if anyone had a question about training, or the forthcoming match, but because we became fed up with his discipline we agreed as a team not to respond. There was one time when he did his usual routine, and everyone looked at the floor in silence. I felt him tower over me. I looked up, and there he was, staring directly at me.

"I know that *you've* got a question," he said.

I hadn't actually, and knew he was just trying to intimidate me, so I stayed quiet. It certainly kept young players like me in check, but as I said, the free spirits like Billy Hughes would never respond to that kind of intimidation. On away trips with the first team, not only was alcohol barred, but non-drinkers like me had to ask Browny if it was okay to have another coke. It got a bit ridiculous at times.

Brown wouldn't let you get away with anything. He knew what you were up to, almost before you did! There was a time in the early Seventies when white boots were all the rage. Alan Ball and Alan Hinton wore them, and I thought I'd follow suit. There was no money in it, not like today, at least not for a Sunderland youngster trying to make it in the game. Being a bit fussy, I wasn't happy with how one of the apprentices was cleaning my pair, so I decided that I would take them home and do it myself from then on. One Saturday I forgot to bring them in, and I was in a huge panic because I knew that Browny would crucify me if he found out. The only other player at the club who wore white boots was a young pro by the name of Freddie McIver, so I had to borrow his. The problem was, they were a size too big, and that afternoon against Everton I was tripping around all over the place and played awfully.

Browny took me off at half-time and pulled me to one side. He never missed a trick and he'd worked out straightaway what had happened. He glared at me and said, "You know why you played like that, don't you?" I learnt a couple of valuable lessons that day. One was that you could never pull the wool over Alan Brown's eyes. The second was that you have to play pretty damned well to get away with wearing white boots.

Although my stock as a player seemed to be rising, the 1969/70 campaign turned out to be disastrous for Sunderland, and ended up with us being relegated from Division One. The problem was that the youngsters weren't developing quickly enough, and Brown couldn't get what he needed out of the senior professionals at the club, like Baker. It was difficult for all of us, and even as a 20-year-old I began to become frustrated with the situation at the club, and the fact that, even though I'd just broken into the team, my career might be in serious danger of stalling. I only had to look around me to realise that, before I knew it, my time as a professional footballer could be over. In the early Seventies, we had a young Scottish midfielder with us at Sunderland called Bobby Park whose style was compared favourably to Jim Baxter. He was a fantastic midfielder who, in March 1970, during the 100th Tyne–Wear derby, scored what I still reckon was actually my goal. On a really blustery day at Roker, in front of 50,000, I nudged a loose ball to Bobby who rattled in a shot from 20 yards. It thudded against the underside of the bar, came out, and I nodded it past McFaul, the Newcastle 'keeper. I knew I'd scored. The local press credited me with the goal too. But Browny insisted Bobby's shot had been over the line. After that match, which we drew 1–1, Bobby's chest was puffed out. He could have been forgiven for thinking that the football world was his oyster. But within three years, Bobby had broken his leg not once, not twice, but three times. On the first two occasions he fought back valiantly but after the third break, the doctor told him he was finished. It was a heartbreaking tale, and by 1973, the year the rest of us would enjoy the fruits of our FA Cup run, Bobby had to quit the game, aged just 22. There's no time to hang around in football, because the average length of a player's career is just eight years, which means that many will be far shorter than that. Even at 20, I knew that I needed to keep pushing onwards.

As I became more of a regular in the team, I began to become more aware of what the club meant to its fans and the community, and how it was perceived by others. Sunderland has often been viewed as being out on a limb, both in a sporting and a geographical sense. I soon saw that outsiders often viewed them as a small club, in many ways, albeit with a potentially gargantuan support. Football matters to so many up in the North East, because it represents a means of putting yourself on the map, of showing the rest of the football world that you, stuck out in the provinces, matter – that you exist. In 1966, a few World Cup matches were played at Roker Park, and the Fulwell End had a roof added to it to mark the occasion. They talked about that with pride during my time at the club. But even as a youngster, it often seemed to me that simply having a vast reservoir of potential support, and perhaps finishing above Newcastle in the league table, was enough for the directors to claim that Sunderland was a "big club". As I'd see for myself over the next few years, crowds could dip alarmingly at Roker, only for the masses to return in their hordes when something bright appeared to be on the horizon. It could be a frustrating existence, both plying your trade and watching football, at Roker Park.

By 1970, there were whispers among the players – who in those days were often the last to know what was going on at the club – that the directors wanted Browny gone. We were relegated amid rumours that he'd gone to the board and asked for the money for two more signings. He often told us that the nurturing of young-sters, either from the youth team or having bought them in from elsewhere, filled him with pride. He had taken very seriously the word of his scouts, who had told him that Charlton's Billy Bonds, a rugged central defender, and a bright young thing in Scunthorpe's midfield called Kevin Keegan, were just what the club needed. The board begged to differ. "Billy who? Kevin who?" was the riposte, and the directors refused to back him. That famous Roker Roar was now barely a whimper, and relegation, understandably, brought a funeral atmosphere to the club and the town. It was absolutely horrendous. Crowds crashed to around the 11,000-mark.

Relegation was a huge blow for me and other youngsters breaking through, but I was getting some good reviews in the local news-papers. I enjoyed playing for Sunderland, gave it my all, and even had a fan club run by two young female supporters. A lady by the name of Dot McCabe was the secretary, assisted by Janet Martin, and membership of the Dennis Tueart fan club numbered 109, and cost four shillings per year. I received all sorts of letters, mainly ones wishing me all the best, and requesting signed photos, that sort of thing. I made sure that I responded to each and every piece of correspondence, because I understood the importance of the club in the community, and I was grateful for everyone's support.

My concerns were eventually proved correct. At Newcastle, there was a winger by the name of Stewart Barrowclough, and I felt I was a better player than him. But because he was playing in the First Division, he got into the England Under-23 team, whereas I didn't get a look in over the next couple of years. The selectors were far less likely to take a risk on a lower-division player. I was used to playing against the Chelseas and the Evertons of this world. Now, it would be about playing at Preston or Orient. The club was contracting at a time when I was becoming extremely ambitious.

The experience of our exceptional centre-back, Colin Todd, who was from Chester-le-Street, slap bang in the middle between Newcastle and Sunderland, came to symbolise Sunderland's problems at that time. Sunderland fans graffitied his name over the walls surrounding Roker Park, and sung songs in homage to him. You couldn't meet a more modest bloke, one who went about the art of central defending with such aplomb. When the team was relegated in 1970, Derby County, or rather Cloughie, came calling. Cloughie had coached Todd in the Sunderland youth set-up in the mid-Sixties. But Cloughie would have his revenge. "You'll never win any pots or medals with that lot," he told Toddy, and he promptly signed him for £175,000. That stuck a dagger right through the hearts of the Sunderland fans and already I began to wonder whether the club would ever have the ambition to not only attract, but also to keep hold of their leading stars.

I was always aware that I wasn't going to be able to make a living out of football forever. When I was at Sunderland, I took several PFA-sponsored courses, just in case I needed something to fall back on when I stopped playing football. I did a Conversational French course in Newcastle, and then a Recreational and Administrative Management course at Teeside Polytechnic. I also ran a mobile disco business with my then brother-in-law, Geoff Costigan, who had been a DJ at Greys Club in Newcastle. You could get hold of us if you dialled 650012. I bought a van, PA system, a playing deck and Geoff used his large collection of vinyl records. I was into soul – stuff like Marvin Gaye and Stevie Wonder – but we played everything that was popular at the time. The business was regularly booked by several venues across the North East and occasionally I would join him as a guest celebrity DJ. We never made a penny from it, but it was great fun anyway, and I enjoyed the entrepreneurial side of it.

Later, during my second period at Manchester City, I studied Business Management at St Helen's college. I guess I was different to most footballers of that era in that I was always looking to the future, and trying to prepare myself for whatever lay ahead. Another thing which sets me apart from many of my contemporaries is that I don't have any golfing stories to tell. In my younger days, I played some pitch-and-putt, and at my 21st birthday party all my gifts were to do with golf – a set of clubs, golf balls, golf trolley, shoes and gloves – but it was never really my bag. Neither was sitting and having a few beers in the clubhouse. I did get into squash, though, because I found it more dynamic, and it sharpened me up when it came to playing football.

Throughout all this time, I continued to live at home, sharing a bed with my brother and commuting from Newcastle. I remember on one occasion the local buses were on strike so I had to walk from Walker to Newcastle town centre, which took about 50 minutes, to catch my bus to Sunderland for training.

I was extremely single-minded when it came to playing football, and put everything into it. All footballers are different. Some conserve energy, and play within themselves. Not deliberately, and not in any sense taking it easy, but watching themselves on the pitch. My style was all action, and hard running for 90 minutes. Nowadays, the physical legacies from football mean I can't twist and turn anymore. I discovered later in life that my pelvis is out of line, which may well have contributed to the hamstring and Achilles tendon injuries I suffered from. These days I can't kick a ball about – not even for fun – whereas there are some guys my age who I played against and alongside, who are still playing, either on the Masters circuit or just a kickabout with friends. I can't play squash now, either. I visit the gym to keep fit these days, take a Pilates class every week and visit the Lymm Chiropractic Centre once a month to manage the injuries picked up from football. I wouldn't change anything, though, because I knew that I had to make the most of the opportunities I had in football. No matter which profession you are in, to be successful you have to be fully committed and focused, and keen to make the best of yourself.

By October 1970, a month into my first season in Division Two, I wasn't convinced that staying at Sunderland was the best thing for my career. I felt deflated and depressed, and I fell out with Browny. I wasn't the only one. Billy Hughes told Brown he objected

to his Sergeant Major attitude and was forced to train on his own.
Maybe I too was starting to rebel against his strict style of management. It was the usual type of thing. I'd got into the first team,
and I wanted the same money as other first-teamers. Clubs, wanting
to save money, make the lowest offer possible. At clubs across the
land, youth-team graduates are paid far less than imported players,
and this can lead to bad feeling in the ranks. It certainly did at
Sunderland. Brown wouldn't give in. He wouldn't give me another
penny. He told the press that, if necessary, he would take the whole
thing to the Football League Management Committee.

I found out from a journalist that Second Division Cardiff put
the feelers out for me. Their manager was Jimmy Scoular, who'd
played for Newcastle back in 1955 when they won the FA Cup,
and I remember calling him furtively from a public phone box to
try and set up the deal. I was so fed up with Sunderland's relegation and Browny's stubbornness that I was willing to jump ship to
another Second Division team. I wasn't thinking straight. Maybe it
was youthful impetuousness. It was my first act of rebellion as a
footballer, but Brown knew that he had me, because in those days
a club could hold onto your registration, and the move never came
about. Technically, George Eastham's High Court victory a decade
before had ended the era of players being treated like slaves by
their clubs, but in reality they still called the shots.

When Browny sold Colin Todd to Derby a few months later,
I knew that there was more money sloshing around the club, so I
carried on badgering him, telling him that unless I got a rise I
wanted out. To be honest, it wasn't even about the money. It was
my grudge against the club for their lack of ambition, which gnawed
away at me.

I kept on asking for a transfer for the next two years, as Sunderland
plodded along in Division Two, but the response was the same. I
was now in my early twenties, we'd been mired in Division Two
for two seasons, and I didn't want to be playing at that level, plain
and simple. I was getting high ratings from the local newspapers
and being tipped for big things, but the team had stalled. On one
occasion, Bob Cass, a local journalist, was walking with the players
prior to a game in London, and I said to him, "Bob, I feel as if
I'm on top of the world, but the world is passing me by."

By 1972, the chairman Keith Collings reported an annual loss of around £103,000, and with crowds shrinking by the week that figure seemed set to worsen during the next financial year. Two things highlighted to me the club's plight. Firstly, they resorted to advertising home matches in the local newspaper to try and encourage people to come and support the team, and then, over at St James' Park, Newcastle shelled out £180,000 for Luton's Malcolm Macdonald, a figure that Sunderland couldn't even come close to being able to afford.

There was some sympathy for Brown among some of the players, because he was being asked to perform miracles on a shoestring budget. You have to speculate to accumulate sometimes in football and business, but the board clearly hadn't grasped that concept and certainly didn't realise the potential of our players and the support. Given that Brown was reliant largely on homegrown talent, the team was doing as well as could be expected on the pitch. If the younger players' talents had been allowed to come to fruition, then maybe he would have stuck it out.

On November 1, 1972, Brown resigned. He would never manage a football club in England again. In some ways, his resignation was a shock to me, because he appeared to wield so much power, but in other ways, it was a huge relief. I often felt massively uptight in his dying days as manager, and the press and the fans were lambasting the club mercilessly. Grateful though I was to Browny for teaching me so much, I have to be honest that I didn't shed any tears when he left. You have to move on quickly in football. The question was, who would take the helm?

Among the fans and some of the players who'd been at the club a while, there was one man whose name was shouted loudest: Cloughie. The whole city was alive with rumour and counter-rumour about who would take over. We heard them all. Local journalists claimed they had it on good authority that Clough, who'd just won the title as Derby boss and who'd signed a new contract, was ready to walk out on his club and come back to the North East. There were tales that Leeds boss Don Revie was also locked in talks with Sunderland, and was seriously considering coming to Roker for a massive wage. Another story went that the Charlton brothers – Bobby and Jack – anxious for a crack at management, were being lined up as joint player-managers. I was sceptical.

I hoped that the next boss would have the tactical acumen and nous of Alan Brown, but that he would also allow us to express ourselves, and I tried to ignore the rumours that were doing the rounds. Exciting though it all sounded, I couldn't see how Clough or Revie would ever come to Roker Park, and I was proved right.

In the end, none of the favoured candidates emerged from the pack at all. The board plumped for a guy who'd hardly been pulling up trees during a rather chequered managerial career at places like Bury, Charlton and, latterly Blackpool: Bob Stokoe. Some of us local lads had heard of him, because he'd played for Newcastle in the 1955 FA Cup final team, whose homecoming I'd celebrated with my dad. But to me, it all seemed like a classic Sunderland botch job. The board claimed they were aiming for the stars with their next managerial appointment, and they got as far as the Blackpool Tower. Stokoe was not exactly Don Revie, and he hardly seemed to be a Cloughie/Svengali-type figure either. But there was much, much more going on behind the scenes, which none of us players knew about or realised until years later. The paths of Revie, Clough, and Stokoe, all of whom were born in the North East, were already inextricably entwined.

Ten years earlier, when Cloughie was plundering goals for Sunderland with frightening regularity, he'd played on Boxing Day against Bury on a frozen Roker pitch. Late on, he chased a loose ball, crashed into goalkeeper Chris Harker, and ripped his cruciate ligament in the process. Bury's player-manager, a rugged, no-nonsense former Newcastle central defender, was unimpressed. He towered over Sunderland's stricken striker, and told the referee that he reckoned Clough was "codding." Feigning injury. Even in the midst of his agony, Clough clocked the insult and never forgave Stokoe for it. The story goes that, when he heard that Stokoe was a front runner for the Sunderland hot seat, Clough decided to throw his hat into the ring. Clough had no intention of leaving Derby at all – he just wanted to make Stokoe squirm.

The same year that Clough's injury forced him to retire from the game, Stokoe alleged that Leeds United's new boss, desperate to avoid relegation from Division Two, had offered him £400 for his Bury side to "take it easy" against his team during a crucial end-of-season encounter. Leeds' hot-shot young manager was Don Revie. Nowadays, with the publication of *The Damned United* and the media's obsession with Revie and Leeds, Bob's allegations are common knowledge. I now know far more about the Machiavellian intrigue surrounding Sixties and Seventies football than I did at the time. Revie, uncomfortable that Stokoe knew all about his "dirty secret", also wanted to make him sweat for a while over the job, like Clough had. The vacant manager's job at Sunderland became all about personal vendettas. But it was Bob, balding, dressed in a sober suit, with that self-effacing smile of his, who ended up landing the job. When we met Revie's Leeds at Wembley in 1973, it's tempting to imagine that Stokoe urged us on with reminders of how Revie tried to bribe him, and therefore jeopardise his burgeoning managerial career. It's tempting, but the truth is that it never happened. Bob never spoke to the players about it at all, although he later told others that the lasting bitterness he felt towards Revie was a huge motivating factor on FA Cup final day.

If I analyse Bob, I couldn't really say what he did. When people ask me what gifts the man who would become known as 'The Messiah' possessed, or what magic he cast, they look disappointed when I shrug. The truth is I can't really say.

Stokoe certainly wasn't an innovative coach. He employed Arthur Cox as his right-hand man and allowed him to get on with the job, and he wasn't especially tactically astute either, as he was still making his way in the game as a coach. From the off, Bob simply told us to use our natural abilities. On reflection, his main strength was that he was able to relax us as a group, in a way which Alan Brown never did, and ultimately that was what sparked us into life. Bob was perfect for us at that particular time. He also understood how to communicate and connect with the local community.

On top of the Clock Stand at Roker Park, the clock which had been there since the glory days of Raich Carter in the Thirties had given up the ghost during the mid-Sixties. I'd never seen it work, and I'd been at the club for five years. No one at the club had bothered to fix it. It didn't take the most imaginative person to work out what that clapped-out clock said about Sunderland. Broken. Not working. Standing still. Not moving forward. No investment. No one bothering to fix what was quite a simple problem. Within a month, Bob saw to it that the clock was ticking once more. It showed me that he cared about the little things, which in turn showed the fans – especially the traditionalists – that he cared about them. Likewise, he insisted that the club's midweek fixtures were switched to a Tuesday so the shipyard lads, who often worked the night shift on a Wednesday, could get to midweek matches. Not only did it swell the crowds, it showed that Bob, the son of a miner, was in touch with the fellas in the shipyard and the mine. He also reverted the home kit's shorts back to black from white, which again appealed to the traditionalists. Clever, I thought. Bob could connect in a way which Alan Brown, consumed with tactics and discipline, never could. After all, he had to. He wasn't Clough, he wasn't Revie. And he'd played for Newcastle.

But it was how we as a group performed on the pitch which would ultimately make or break Bob. The first thing he did with us was gather us together for a photo shoot in front of the BBC cameras at Roker Park. There we were, a bunch of ragged, scruffy kids, with long hair over our collars, mutton chop sideburns, flares and butterfly collars, all grinning like Cheshire cats. I hadn't grinned for a long time at Sunderland. It was a pleasant change, I thought. I sensed a pleasant buzz, and the general consensus among the team was, "He seems a good bloke. Let's see what happens."

No one's grin was wider, or toothier, than Bob's though. He'd finally got a shot at a "big" job, and looking around the group, he would have been right in thinking that he had the nucleus of a good side. But I never had a private conversation with Bob about my role in the team, or my hopes and dreams for the future – not at any point. That wasn't Bob's way. The Messiah didn't possess the interpersonal skills to do anything like that.

Soon, the media would portray us as a collection of jovial no-hopers, and it partly suited us to perpetuate that image. But Bob had inherited a special group. Dave Watson and I went on to play for England. Jimmy Montgomery was always on the fringes of the England squad. Billy Hughes played for Scotland, Ian Porterfield and Dick Malone came close to playing for Scotland and Micky Horswill was called up for an England get-together. We had a good blend at the club, but we hadn't exactly done much over the last few seasons. I'd be lying if I claimed I could have predicted what would happen next. We all had good abilities, but Bob brought the next phase which was the freedom to express ourselves. As players, we were prepared to give Bob every chance, and he endeared himself to us more or less straight away. He was cheerful and warm and seemed pleased to meet us all. Straight away, I felt like a weight had been lifted off my shoulders. Despite the fact that he wasn't the "marquee manager" I'd hoped we might get, I had a good feeling about things after that initial meeting. I never officially withdrew my transfer request, but it certainly went on the back burner.

The crowd's reception to Bob for his first match in charge at home to Burnley was polite and generally fairly welcoming. Over 18,000 showed up, which was an improvement on the crowd figures in the latter days of Alan Brown. But it didn't go our way, and we lost 1–0, leaving us perched precariously above the relegation zone in Division Two.

As we trooped off at the end, I heard a couple of members of the crowd near the tunnel yell at Bob, "Bugger off back to your black-and-white stripes, Stokoe." If he didn't know it already, Bob had a big job on his hands.

However, all managers who achieve success need one crucial ingredient in their locker – luck. And Bob was about to have several slices of good fortune, not that it always seemed that way to me at the time. Within a couple of weeks of him taking over, a flu virus spread right through the city and the entire club, and put most of us flat on our backs for several days at a time. I got it, and simply couldn't move. It got into your joints and your muscles. It was the worst case of flu I've ever had. At one stage, there were only four players fit enough to train. As a result of the outbreak, the Football League postponed our entire Christmas programme, which allowed a period of settling in for Bob and Arthur Cox and for them to get to know us as players, as we filtered back to the training ground in dribs and drabs. The entire club, training ground and all, had been closed following advice from medical advisers, but we were able to regain our strength and began light training again. By the time the New Year, and the FA Cup third round, arrived, I felt refreshed and ready for the battles which lay ahead.

Bob was knocked out for a week or so himself, but with his enforced winter break he was able to ponder his options, put the feelers out, and do a bit of scouting during the busy Christmas programme. Having been around the block for a decade or so in the lower leagues, and played at the highest level with Newcastle, he had a vast array of contacts in the game.

The first thing Bob did was to go back to his former club Newcastle and chat to his former team-mate Joe Harvey, who was boss at St James' Park. Bob needed a left-back at Sunderland, as Richie Pitt was still a youngster learning his trade at Roker Park, and at the time Newcastle United had Ron Guthrie and Dave Young, both supporting left-backs, on the books. Dave Young was versatile and could play at centre-back as well, so Bob bought them both for a combined fee of about £25,000. It was strictly bargain basement stuff, and the supporters were hardly heralding the dawning of a new era when Messrs Young and Guthrie ("A couple of Toon rejects" appeared to be the general consensus) arrived at the club. I'd later come to realise that they were archetypal Bob signings. Safe as houses, and so low on the radar that they slipped in almost unnoticed. Dead cheap, too. But they settled in immediately, and were key pieces of the jigsaw.

Bob got lucky when his big-name signing from Crystal Palace – John 'Yogi' Hughes – got injured in his first game for Sunderland. Yogi was Billy's older brother, had won medals galore at Celtic, and had played in the European Cup against teams like AC Milan and Leeds. Although he and Billy were brothers, they were completely different in size – Billy was only an inch or two taller than me, while John was six foot two, and weighed around 13 stone. On the face of it, he looked like a signing who would add a touch of experience to what was a phenomenally young squad. But in truth, there was no way that Bob could have played myself, Billy and Yogi in the same side. You'd have needed three balls because we all wanted to get it down and play with it – it would have been like a traffic jam up front. I knew that from the moment Yogi arrived.

Arguably, he was the biggest "name" at the club, but within five minutes of his debut he slipped on the ball and injured his knee ligaments. He somehow got through the rest of the first half, but he never played football again.

It forced Bob to press ahead with Plan B. Billy and I needed a target man – someone who could hold the ball up and play off the pair of us, and I'd mentioned it to the coaches. I said that we needed someone who could also pose an aerial threat from corners and dead-ball situations.

In the interim between Browny getting the sack and Bob arriving, coach Billy Elliott had taken control of first-team affairs. One of the first things he did was to move Dave Watson from centre-forward to centre-back. It proved to be an inspired move for the team and for Dave, who went on later to play at Manchester City with me, and England. But Dave's move from the front to the back left a giant hole up front.

We heard that Bob had gone to Harry Haslam at Luton to try and sign target man Vic Halom on loan. Haslam told him to buy Halom, or forget the whole thing, so Bob duly complied. He got his man for £30,000, and Vic's style was absolutely perfect for both Billy and I. It allowed us to switch flanks, if necessary, and buzz around Vic, who was a real livewire character, and would then hold the ball up for us to run onto.

All the new signings – Guthrie, Halom, and Young – played at home in a match against Brighton early in 1973, with the wind howling over the Fulwell End. It was bitterly cold, but I remember that match as the game which suggested that Stokoe might just be onto something. We hammered Brighton 4–0. Admittedly, they were bottom of the league, but it was the manner of the victory which lives long in my memory. Before the game, in what became his customary style, Bob instructed Billy and I to "go and play in your natural style". I can't emphasise enough the degree to which that was music to my ears. I was off the leash and able to go at it. Billy and I ran hard and fast at the Brighton defence and ripped them apart. We got right in their faces, marauding forward. Billy, with his long dark hair flapping around the place, clutching his cuffs with his fingers, scored twice, and I got one when I linked up with him, and he slipped a great pass to me in the box. Suddenly, we were 17th in the table, with three games in hand on our rivals due to the Christmas flu.

But Bob knew that we needed something to distract us from the weekly grind of the league, and put bums on seats at Roker

Park. Only 12,000 bothered to come and see us play Brighton, and a quarter-full ground didn't exactly boost my morale. After the game, Bob was asked what he wanted in the new year, aside from avoiding relegation. "A cup run would do us fine," he replied.

CHAPTER THREE

OMENS

O mens, omens. In early January 1973, Sunderland supporters were insisting that we would win the FA Cup this year, because if you flipped the final two digits in the year you got 1937, which happened to be the year the team had last won the trophy.

Sunderland can feel like a small place, and I regularly bumped into older fans who'd remind me, if I didn't already know it, that the club had done nothing for too long. "When are things going to improve, Dennis?" I was asked, time after time. Not since goals by Bobby Gunney, Eddie Burbanks and local hero Raich Carter defeated Preston at Wembley in 1937 had the team won a thing. During that match, I was regularly reminded, the streets of Sunderland were utterly deserted, save for the odd stray cat, as the whole city gathered around radios and tuned in. On the trip back to the North East, supporters queued ten deep next to the rail tracks, and tugs and other vessels on the Wear tooted with joy as the team, now in open-top coaches, squeezed down Fawcett Street, also rammed with fans. Then it was on to Roker Avenue and Brand Street, heaving and tumultous, before the team reached Roker Park itself, a ferment of red-and-white striped joy.

As our own FA Cup run gathered momentum at the start of '73, I heard more and more about it, and more and more column inches were devoted to drawing comparisons. But I tried to ignore it. As far as I was concerned, going on about something which had happened 36 years before didn't have any bearing on me or Sunderland.

"We will win it this year," the fanatics insisted. "Just you wait and see."

I liked the sentiment, and the quirky sense of logic, but Sunderland in 1973 was a starkly different place than it was in '37. The club was mired in the nether regions of Division Two, and the talk was all about strikes and job losses. Unsurprisingly, the crowds were low. I was fully aware of what was unfolding around us in the city. The team was full of working-class lads, many of whose dads, like mine, worked in heavy industry. We didn't live in cloud cuckoo land. We were aware of the hardship which many of our supporters endured. There was a strike in the North Sands shipyard, and a dispute at Coles Cranes. The days of the coal mines were numbered, and unemployment in Sunderland was at its highest for over a decade. It may not have exactly been on its knees, but the city's legs were wobbly, no question of that. And so were the football club's. Raich Carter, his opinion always much sought after by our local journos, reckoned it was about time the football team galvanised the locals. I agreed with him, although, with the team hovering near the relegation zone, I couldn't see a great deal of hope on the horizon.

After 70 minutes of our FA Cup third-round clash away at Notts County in January, Raich Carter, watching us from the Meadow Lane stands, must have all but given up on his old team. We were already one-down on a mudheap of a pitch to a team a division below us, when County striker Les Bradd powered a header towards the top corner of Jim Montgomery's net. As he connected, I heard Bradd scream "Goal." From where I was standing, the ball, to all intents and purposes, looked in. I didn't think even 'Monty' would be able to save that. But then a miracle occurred. A footballing miracle, anyway. Monty, twisting backwards in midair, tipped the ball away for a corner. That astonishing save gave me heart – and convinced me that we could still save the game.

Monty was a phenomenal 'keeper, always anxious to improve his game. In those days, before goalkeeping coaches, he would get us to knock the ball to either side of him alternately, as he hurled himself to his right and left to keep his reactions razor sharp. Another training ploy he had was when he would ask us to hold the ball, and stand on the penalty spot. He'd then run out off his line, touch the ball, and then we'd throw it over his head, forcing him to backpedal, dive upwards and backwards, and claw the ball away. I helped him with these exercises on countless occasions, and was always astonished at his agility. There probably wasn't a 'keeper in the game who could backpedal like Monty. And it was all because he trained so hard and pushed himself to the limit. I think back to those kind of moments like at Notts County, when we were virtually dead and buried, and realise that on such moments, careers and reputations are forged. A minute later, up popped big Dave Watson for the equaliser. We'd got away with it, and escaped with a draw.

When we got back to Roker Park later that night, I peered out of the coach window and saw the crowds snaking round the ground, queuing for tickets for the replay, a novel sight, indeed. They were fired up by the fact that, if we nudged out County in the replay, we'd play Fourth Division Reading – managed by ex-Roker legend Charlie Hurley – in the next round. It got me thinking. If we could get past two lower-division sides, we could be in the last 16 without having faced any of the three pre-tournament favourites: Leeds, Manchester City and Arsenal.

A few days later, 30,000-plus turned out for the replay against Notts County. A rare treat, and we responded with gusto to their support. Dave Watson put us in front, then I robbed the ball from David Needham and shot past their goalie to give us a 2–0 win. That night, for the first time in a long time, I felt electrified and energised. I know it was only an FA Cup third-round replay, but now within a couple of weeks we'd beaten Brighton comfortably in the League, and we'd won in the FA Cup. I felt some of the gloom lifting.

Two weeks later another crowd in excess of 30,000 streamed into Roker Park for the return of Charlie Hurley, Reading boss and Sunderland icon from the 1960s. I found it very tough going. Reading took an early lead, but the star of the show was Reading's five-feet-seven shot-stopper Steve Death, who had an uncanny ability to twist himself in midair and deflect the ball away from goal. I thought that we'd never break them down, and I could picture the tabloid headlines as Death made save after save to keep us out, "Kiss of Death to Sunderland's Cup Hopes" etc…

He was everywhere. He charged down a shot from Dave Watson, tipped a goal-bound shot from Billy Hughes around the post and, as Ian Porterfield practically rammed a shot down his throat, Death still scrambled the ball away. Eight minutes before half-time, Death finally succumbed to our relentless pressure. Billy Hughes crossed from the left, Death fumbled it, and I tapped in the rebound. I was elated and confident that we could go on and win the game, but imperious service was resumed by Death after the interval, tipping one of my efforts onto the crossbar and denying Billy Hughes once more. 1–1. The *Sunderland Echo* suggested that we'd had a "Near Death Experience" and I wouldn't disagree.

In the replay, there was no such drama. Elm Park, shoehorned in between rows of terraced houses, had a reputation as being an intimidating place to play cup football, but we were three-up after half an hour. Dave Watson got the first goal, I lobbed Death for our second, and Bobby Kerr finished them off.

But now the cup run was about to go truly technicolor, and my profile as a footballer would change forever. Lights, camera, action! Next up was a trip to Maine Road to play Manchester City in a televised fifth-round match.

Bob had a number of little tricks he'd use to motivate us in the lead-up to these big games. He was never one for the Churchillian speech to the whole team, or the quiet, incisive comment, but he was able to personalise his approach with individuals in clever and quirky ways. He would go around to Vic Halom, Billy Hughes and I and offer us odds on whether we'd score in games. Then he'd go to the defenders and wager that they couldn't keep clean sheets. I'm not talking vast sums of money here – just a little wager between you and the boss, with the maximum bet being £1. But I liked the way Bob did it. Simple but effective. A private little thing between you and the manager. Not scientific or revolutionary, but he tapped into the footballer's psyche of offering us a challenge, and it broke down the barriers. When Bob paid out, he did so out of his own pocket too, which made the whole thing seem a bit more real.

He was also trusting when it came to players drinking. Bob's view was that the team was professional, and that those who wanted to drink would understand when to draw the line. As Newcastle were a division above us in '73, it meant that the only ground we played at within a hundred miles was Ayresome Park, so it was an arduous journey back from pretty much everywhere we played. We would stop off at a restaurant for a bite to eat and something to drink, and virtually as soon as Bob joined the club some of the lads thought they'd see if they were able to get a beer for the road. Bob clocked this, and walked towards Billy Hughes and Bobby Kerr. I think most of us expected that he might "do a Browny" and tear a strip off them, but instead he rummaged around his pocket, pulled out some money, and said, "I'll get these lads." As I wasn't a drinker at all, I didn't indulge, but I was impressed. It showed me that Bob had a human side, and that relaxes people. Again, simple, but effective man-management. That trusting and generous approach earned the respect of someone like Billy Hughes, who had so often been in conflict with Alan Brown's no-booze culture. You just couldn't expect 11 grown men, especially not in that era, to stay teetotal. Bob realised this and began to treat the team like responsible young footballers.

Bob's good luck continued during this time, because between January and May the team stayed largely injury-free and, despite the fixture list being so crammed with both cup and league matches, he only called on 16 players in that period. I always liked games coming thick and fast, because more than anything else I wanted to play. I always wanted to challenge myself, and the more times I could do that the better. Our league form began to pick up during this time as well, and we gradually clawed ourselves away from the relegation zone. I could see that, within the team, things were starting to fall into place. Dave Watson was playing really well in his new role at centre-half, and Vic Halom was beginning to connect well with Billy Hughes and I up front. I felt we could move more freely, and that Vic would hold the ball up effectively. I sensed that the pieces of the jigsaw were clicking into place.

By the time we faced City at Maine Road, the team had a much more settled look about it, something we hadn't had the luxury of for years. Bob took us to one of his old bolt holes in Blackpool during the week before the City match. I remember running along the beach, gulping down the fresh sea air and craning my neck to look at the Tower. There was nothing too high maintenance on the agenda. He even let us have fish and chips to get in the seaside spirit. It was good fun. Bob didn't give us the lowdown on City, it wasn't really his style, and we'd seen them enough on TV. To be honest, he didn't really need to gee us up and get us motivated too much, because Malcolm Allison did that for him when he began mouthing off in the press.

I wouldn't have missed what happened at Sunderland for the world, but our encounters with City in the FA Cup opened my eyes to what it must be like to play for a top club. We'd been in Division Two for three seasons by then, and it was joyful to be facing genuine quality opposition. And it was Manchester City, in their sky-blue shirts, that electrified me as soon as we went into battle against them. There was an aura about them. Playing for City during the late 1960s and early 1970s must have been wonderful. They won the league in 1968, the FA Cup in 1969, and the League and Cup Winners' Cup a year later. Malcolm Allison's partnership with Joe Mercer was perfect for City. Joe – wise old head that he was – could rein in Malcolm's enthusiasm and, as it turned out, fatal weakness for flair players. I rated the holy trinity of Colin Bell, Mike Summerbee and Franny Lee as highly as Manchester United's glamorous three of Denis Law, George Best and Bobby Charlton, and I was desperate to pit my wits against them.

By the time we came to play them, though, it had been three years since they'd won any silverware, and Malcolm was under pressure. In the papers that week, he boasted of what his side was going to do to us, and of how we wouldn't be able to live with City and their attacking force, but it seemed to me a bit desperate. I'd heard through the grapevine that the root cause of the discontent at City was Rodney Marsh. Malcolm had brought in Rodney from QPR during the latter stages of the previous season when City were charging away with the title. It was a costly misjudgement, and Malcolm and Joe had fallen out massively over it. Malcolm reckoned Rodney was the final piece of the jigsaw, but in my view in fact all Rodney did was disrupt the flow of the team and an already settled system. Within a year of facing City in the FA Cup, I would begin to see the effect that Rodney had on the team for myself, but for now, I could only base my judgement on playing for the opposition.

There were 55,000 inside Maine Road that afternoon, and I knew that this would be the biggest game of my career to date. The *Match Of The Day* cameras were there, and I felt that at 23, this was my big chance to perform on the big stage. Bob urged us to go out and enjoy ourselves, and to play our naturally attacking game. I don't think we could have played any other way. When we ran out, we could see swathes of red-and-white all around the ground. An estimated 12,000-odd Sunderland fans made what was effectively a pilgrimage to Manchester that day, which made the whole place buzz. I think we surprised City, because we really went for it.

Allison had said that because his team had knocked out Liverpool the round before, "little" Sunderland wouldn't offer too much of a threat. A few years before, he'd claimed that City would be the first football team to play on the moon. You couldn't knock him for trying to knock United off their perch and paint Manchester sky blue, but I later found out that the City players were often a bit embarrassed by Malcolm's comments and boasts. His "little Sunderland" jibes certainly fired us up. It was a freezing day and, just up the road in Salford, United's game had been called off, so a lot of Old Trafford regulars travelled to Maine Road to support us. You could hear the chants of "Sunderland United" all through the game.

City put us under huge pressure in the first few minutes. Mike Doyle fed Tony Towers, and he scored. Rodney Marsh was doing his usual thing, indulging himself with the odd flick here, the occasional nutmeg there, but his tricks came to very little, and when City failed to put daylight between them and us we got stronger and stronger as a unit. Several of our players really came of age that day, and our midfielder Micky Horswill was definitely one of those.

I went in hard on their goalie, Joe Corrigan, when I chased a loose ball. From the resulting free-kick Corrigan passed the ball to Derek Jeffries on the edge of the box, who didn't really want it there, and Micky steamed through and nabbed the ball before firing into the roof of Corrigan's net. City were rocked back on their heels.

Bob did his usual thing at half-time, urging us to carry on the way we were playing, and telling us that if we plugged away our just reward would come. When it did, the manner of it surprised everyone. City were trying really hard to press their home advantage, and carried on knocking it deep. When one of their moves broke down, Dick Malone quickly knocked the ball out to me in midfield. Maine Road had the largest pitch in the country in those days, and the space really seemed to open up for me. I spotted Billy Hughes galloping forward, and nudged it in his direction. We'd broken away so fast that no one was up to support Billy, although Vic Halom, desperately trying to keep pace with him, was steaming forward as quickly as he could. Billy twisted past City defender Derek Jeffries, teased him left then right, and unleashed a fire cracker into Corrigan's net. It was nothing less than we deserved, and I could see City players shooting each other nervous glances. They knew they were in a fire fight.

Late on, from a City corner, Monty struggled to get sight of Summerbee's cross. Marsh was standing in his way. Even in those days, when you could get away with a lot more on the pitch than you can today, I knew that Rodney was breaking the rules, and that the ref should have blown up with the ball in mid-flight. But he didn't, and Monty could only palm Summerbee's corner into the roof of the net. 2–2. City didn't celebrate too hard. I think they knew they'd got out of jail, and the ref blew up soon after-wards. In the dressing room after the game, the mood wasn't downbeat at all. It wasn't like we were thinking that we'd blown it at all. I knew that, if we played like that at Roker, we'd go through. No fear. Monty was actually laughing away after the error, claiming that he would be getting a cut of the profits from the Roker replay. No one had a go at him. We weren't that type of team. I was just delighted that we'd played so well, and that we'd given an indication of our potential.

After the game in Manchester, we headed north and went for a meal in Harrogate up in Yorkshire. The coach dropped us back at Roker Park just after midnight, and the sight that greeted us was unlike anything we'd seen before. This time, when I looked out of the coach window, I saw that the queue for tickets for the replay wasn't so much snaking around the block, as wrapping itself around the ground twice over. It was a freezing night, the coldest of the year so far, and fans, waiting for the tickets to go on sale at 9am the following morning, were huddled under the stands to get some protection from the cold. Burger vans worked through the night, and locals living around the ground opened their doors to make tea for the frozen fans. I was speechless. We all were. I realised that the whole community was behind us. Six weeks before, we'd struggled to get 12,000 to come to Roker to watch us. By 11.00 the following morning, all 49,000 home tickets for the replay had sold out. Now I knew that Bob Stokoe had unlocked something, however inadvertently. Roker Park was about to roar once more.

When City came to town for the replay four days later, there was a cold North Sea wind billowing in over the Roker End. I thought that I'd become hardened against the elements in the North East, but that night against City was more extreme than anything I'd experienced before. The wind howled – quite literally – around the streets surrounding the ground. Tiles were blown off the top of nearby houses. Dustbins were blown over, and all the paper rubbish, old newspapers and betting slips, swirled around in a gale. I felt like it might cut me in two, but that night the chill factor, the smell of that turf, the faint scent of the sea and the electricity from the crowd under the lights combined to produce the most vibrant and spellbinding atmosphere I ever experienced in football. They still talk about that night up in Sunderland today, and I'll certainly never forget it as long as I live. We also knew that the traditional Monday lunchtime radio FA Cup draw had given us Luton Town at home if we could beat City.

I'm not sure that anyone really knows how many fans were inside Roker that night. The gates were locked half an hour before kick-off, and officially there were just over 50,000 inside, but there were stories of turnstile operators letting more in than that. As soon as we walked out onto the pitch, I could see our fans crammed in on the terraces at both the Roker End and the Fulwell End. It was an incredible atmosphere. I couldn't hear myself think, let alone speak, and early on I saw guys like Summerbee and Bell, who'd played in Wembley Finals and Manchester derbies, shake their heads at the sheer ferocity of the place. Because of the wind and the noise we had to change our tactics. You couldn't hear, you couldn't think, and you had no time on the ball, because if you did dally around with it a City player would steam in on you. So from the off, we went straight for City's jugular, ran hard at them, moved the ball about between us as fast as possible and tried to get it forward as soon as we could.

Early on, City's class showed. Marsh hit the bar, and then Colin Bell rampaged through and put the ball just wide. Quality oozed out of their team, but nothing was going to stop us on this incredible night. I remember that the Roker floodlights seemed to give the green turf, our red-and-white shirts and City's sky-blue shirts a luminous, technicolor glow. I loved it. After weathering the City storm, we threaded a beautiful string of passes together which cut City apart. Porterfield to Guthrie out wide on the left. Square to Billy Hughes, and on to Horswill, and then to Kerr, with a smart flick out right to Vic Halom. Vic took a step back to give himself a bit more time and rifled in a 25-yard shot into Corrigan's net. Even through the din, I could hear Corrigan scream at his defenders to "Leave it!" He got a right mouthful from his team-mates afterwards. He probably didn't think Vic would do a whole lot of damage from out there.

There was no way we were going to blow it after that. After Vic scored, he was laughing his head off, Billy Hughes was cackling like a maniac, and we all screamed our heads off and disappeared into a forest of arms and heads as we mobbed Vic. A few minutes later, Billy Hughes rifled in a second after a fantastic interchange of passes between him and Bobby Kerr. Two up at half-time, and we were in dreamland.

During the interval, our dressing room was bouncing with excitement. I felt like a kid let loose in a sweet shop, because this was the kind of night that I'd always dreamed of, but which had been sorely lacking at the club during my time at Sunderland. Bob told us to stay calm and not to get carried away, and reminded us that City still posed a threat. He was right, too. Ten minutes in, Franny Lee slid in to pull a goal back, and for the first time that night a hush fell inside Roker Park. I got a little nervous, but I knew, and we all knew, that we could finish it.

Red-and-white shirts were flying around everywhere in our penalty box to block Summerbee and charge down shots from Colin Bell, and then we'd try to hit them on the break. I made a couple of block tackles, and dropped back a bit to help out the defence.

Ten minutes from the end, I received the ball out on the right, cut into the area, took aim, and fired. Joe Corrigan palmed the ball out to Billy Hughes, who slid in and scored. It was pandemonium, absolute pandemonium. We were through.

In the bath afterwards, Billy Hughes, his long black hair plastered to his face, stood up and shouted, "We're gonna win the cup. We are gonna win the cup." Bobby Kerr, always a realist, always controlled, reminded everyone that we were only in the quarter-finals, and that we shouldn't get carried away. I was shouting my head off after the best night of my career so far and, like everyone else, told Bobby not to be so bloody miserable. Even though he was right.

'Big Mal' stuck his head around the dressing room door. "You fully deserved the win," he said, before adding drily, "Next time, it might be better if I keep my gob shut for once!"

'Crash – Out Go City!' ran one tabloid headline. I loved reading it, and our odds were cut from 250–1 to 100–1. But we were still rank outsiders. As Malcolm Allison pointed out, Leeds and Arsenal, the two previous winners of the competition, were alive and very much kicking. And what hope did little Sunderland have against those two, even if we did beat Second Division Luton Town at Roker Park in the quarter-finals? Few, it seemed, believed we even had half a chance. Except for us, of course.

The season was moving at breakneck pace. Because of the flu attack at Christmas, and the FA Cup run, we had a huge number of games in hand on our nearest rivals in the league, but confidence was high and our league form improved. If we hadn't begun the season so abysmally, we'd have been in the promotion race, no question. By the season's end, we would shoot up to sixth place, and around March time we played five matches in 15 days. I had no time to think about what was happening to us, or the impact of the cup run on the local community.

I was firing on all cylinders, and couldn't wait for the next game to come. Like everyone else in the team, I was flying by the seat of my pants, and this reflected the way in which we played our matches. Bob was always telling us to hurry up in games.

"Dennis, use your pace. Keep moving all the time. Don't give the opposition any time to settle," he would tell me.

Again, not highbrow stuff, but it showed that Bob knew what my strengths were. Whether it was throw-ins, corner kicks, or goal kicks, he believed that the quicker we moved the ball upfield, the more likely we were to penetrate the opposition. It paid dividends on the cup run, although I knew that we couldn't play that way over an entire season, because you sometimes need to slow games down. Bob's tactics were ideal in the short term though, and especially in one-off FA Cup matches.

Luton Town, sixth in Division Two, arrived at Roker in their flashy new kit, paid for by the legendary comedian Eric Morecambe. They wore orange shirts, with a blue-and-white vertical stripe up one side. A massive Luton fan, Eric's involvement with the club meant they were seen as quite glamorous opposition, although he decided to stay away from their FA Cup games, believing himself to be an unlucky influence. They had two quick and clever wingers in John Aston and John Ryan.

On yet another blustery day, with rubbish swirling around all over the place, Roker expected. The crowd of 53,000 was bigger than that for Manchester City, but the match was far more like a game of chess than the City replay, which had been really open. Dick Malone kept Aston quiet, and Ron Guthrie did likewise with Ryan, so the play was all squeezed through the middle. Our breakthroughs came from dead-ball situations. Dave Watson headed home from a corner, and then Ron Guthrie swivelled and smashed the ball home for a second. The match was lower key than I might have expected, and would have liked, but it was very satisfying, because it showed that as a team we could slow the pace and be patient, rather than simply going gung-ho and looking to break at every opportunity. To be successful, I knew that we had to adapt our play when the occasion demanded it.

We were now into the semis to face Arsenal and, off the pitch, things really did start going crazy. We received invites to car showrooms, supermarkets, bedding centres, the whole caboodle. The whole town was in on the act, and I found it all thrilling. It's a good job Bob Stokoe didn't keep tabs on us, because he'd probably have had a heart attack if he'd known how much we were gallivanting around, attending this and that. My attitude was that I only had a limited amount of opportunities to be successful in my career and I was going to enjoy it. But I never lost sight of the ultimate goal of winning the FA Cup.

As the cup run gathered momentum, Ian Porterfield and I found ourselves in charge of the players' pool. Any TV appearances we made, articles we wrote, or personal appearances were taxable, but donations weren't. Some of the donations made me think. The shipbuilders on the Wear donated a lump sum of £650 for getting to the semi-final, and £1,300 for the final. They said that absenteeism was at an all-time low and morale at an all-time high, because the lads couldn't wait to get in on a Monday morning to talk about the weekend's game.

The whole thing was so innocent, really. I was on £60 a week at that time, and the majority of the first-team squad were on roughly the same apart from Micky Horswill who, as the youngest player in the team, was on a paltry £25. It wasn't bad money, but not one of us was in football for financial gain. No one drove flashy cars, or owned huge mansions, or gambled their money away in casinos. There were those who enjoyed a drink in the squad, but there was never any pressure on the likes of me, who didn't really go for the drinking scene, to partake. That's why I think the whole unit blended, because we all accepted each other for who and what we were, and that's why we all remain friends to this day. No one tried to bully anyone else into doing anything which they didn't want to do. The squad was ego-free. If there had been any big-time Charlies, I doubt they would have lasted all that long. There was a real innocence, a purity, about it all. I went into football to win medals and trophies, and to enjoy playing the game. And at Sunderland, where life had been a bit depressing before Bob arrived on the scene, I was aware that good performances on the pitch brightened up the lives of our supporters, although it was only years later that I came to realise just how much. I was fiercely ambitious, but above all I loved playing the game, and couldn't wait for the next big cup match to come along.

I always think that in order to win the trophy you are aiming for, sometimes you need a stroke of good fortune in order to help you along the way, and we got that before we faced Arsenal. We'd had such a long run of league games to catch up on, and four days before the Arsenal game we were due to play Blackpool at home, but it snowed up in the North East and the game was postponed. So we had the rare luxury of a clear week to prepare for the semi-final. Bob took us to a hotel in Buxton, in the Peak District. During the day, we played on snow-covered pitches at the local sports centre. In the evening, we played snooker. Some of the lads went out for drinks, or went shopping, or slipped out to the cinema. I was happy preparing for the game, and winding down on the snooker table. We didn't spend a great deal of time thinking about Arsenal.

It was probably a good thing that we didn't, because when it came to FA Cup semi-finals in the early Seventies the Gunners were always the brides, and never the bridesmaids. Arsenal had a settled, tight system which worked for them. Tough, physical strikers in Kennedy and Radford, a midfield enforcer in Peter Storey and a mean defence marshalled by their skipper, Frank McLintock. But McLintock was ruled out of the semi due to a hamstring strain, and this changed their dynamic. His replacement was Jeff Blockley, who'd cost a lot of money from Coventry but wasn't match-fit. It ended up costing Arsenal, who were chasing their second Double in three years.

We ran out at Hillsborough under a bloated, grey Yorkshire sky. It felt like it might teem down with rain at any minute, but the minute I saw our supporters, stacked up as far as the eye could see in the Kop stand, I felt my heart race. It was one of the most incredible sights of my career. That huge bank of terracing arched upwards and upwards, chock full of 25,000 hysterical Sunderland supporters, clad in their parkas and their red-and-white scarves, literally bouncing up and down with excitement, screaming "Sunderland, Sunderland." That was what I had gone into football for, to experience and feed off passion like that. Such had been the demand for tickets back in Sunderland that I could see some supporters had climbed the trees at the back of the Kop in order to get a better view. The crowd really was our 12th man that day.

Vic Halom set about Blockley from the off. He was all over him. I saw him barge him, nudge him, snap at his heels, not giving him a second to breathe. After 30 minutes, as Vic snarled in his ear,

Blockley tried to pass the ball back to his goalkeeper Bob Wilson. It fell woefully short, and Vic intercepted it, strode on, and slotted the ball into the net. I felt that we had Arsenal from then on. I was surprised to see their defenders arguing among themselves and, as the recriminations flew about, Vic took off towards the Kop and our supporters. Arsenal had no room to function, as our 4-5-1 formation effectively meant we flooded them out in midfield and they became open to our quick counter-attacking.

At half-time, sitting in the dressing room in our muddy all-white away strip, we were like a bunch of naughty, excited schoolboys, because we knew that we were edging closer and closer to the FA Cup final.

Early in the second half, Bob Wilson went down injured in the Arsenal area, clutching his leg and rolling about in agony. It took a while for their physio to fix him up, and when he did get up to carry on he was limping heavily. A few minutes after that, Bobby Kerr bombed in a throw-in from the right, and I stretched my neck backwards to flick it on into the six-yard box. Billy Hughes threw his head backwards before nodding the ball back towards goal. The ball looped upwards, as if it was in slow motion, heading towards Arsenal's goal. Bob Wilson was frantically backpedalling, his movement hindered by the injury he'd just received, and all he could do was palm it into the back of his net. We went ballistic.

Arsenal, despite a late Charlie George goal, couldn't muster an equaliser. For the last three minutes of the game, I don't think any of us crossed the halfway line as we repelled Arsenal's desperate attempts to draw level. But there was to be no late glory from the Gunners that year. Not in 1973.

The outpouring of emotion at the final whistle was unlike anything else I experienced in football. I was in tears as we saluted our fans, as were many of my team-mates, because whatever happened from then on, I knew that we had put Sunderland back on the football map. No one remembers the losing semi-finalists. If we'd lost to Arsenal at Hillsborough that afternoon, this team would have been consigned to the dustbin of football history. It would have been an example of Sunderland failing to achieve anything of note since 1937. I'd probably have ended up forgotten. Guys like Vic Halom, Bobby Kerr, and Billy Hughes would have been known to Sunderland fans of a particular vintage, and that would have been it. Instead, Sunderland now mattered. I mattered. We mattered. We were in the final to face the mighty Leeds.

Bob Stokoe was granted full icon status by our fans. After the final whistle, partly at the prompting of the photographers who swarmed onto the pitch, he held his arms aloft to our fans in the Kop. "Stokoe, Stokoe, Stokoe," they sang. Bob was in tears. He couldn't leave the pitch, because our supporters wouldn't stop chanting, and it would have looked disrespectful for him if he'd have walked away before they'd finished. He was now officially The Messiah.

After the match finished, we boarded the coach and stopped at the Hallam Towers Hotel for a meal. We had a massive celebratory dinner for all the staff in a private room, with Billy Hughes, Ian Porterfield and I standing on the tables and orchestrating the singing. "We shall not be moved" and "Sunderland, Sunderland" never sounded so sweet! The beauty of it was that everyone in the squad, the physios, and even Bob himself, joined in the singing.

As players, we were a bunch of naive kids. None of us had ever played at Wembley before, none of us had won any titles or cups, so there was no one who could put a dampener on the whole thing, pull us back, and say, "Cool it lads. Let's think about this." Obviously, Bob had won the FA Cup with Newcastle, but he kept his opinions and thoughts to himself and let us enjoy the whole experience. If, at any point, we had started to analyse teams like Arsenal or Manchester City, and thought about what and who made them tick, I think that fear and tension would have set in. I believe that this team had a unique dynamic, especially when you add in the ferocity and passion of our fans, many of whom had never seen a Sunderland side challenge for trophies. For me, it was a thrilling journey into the unknown.

CHAPTER FOUR

THE FINAL

Raggedy-arsed Rovers in the FA Cup final. In Sunderland, there was almost a sense of disbelief at what we'd achieved. Not among the players and staff at the club though – we didn't have a care in the world, and we knew that we'd deserved to beat Manchester City and Arsenal. If anyone did have any nerves about facing Revie's Leeds in the final, they certainly weren't showing it.

The demand for tickets was absolutely incredible. Everyone wanted to be at Wembley. But first and foremost I wanted to take care of my family's ticket needs. Even though my dad and brother were passionate Newcastle fans, and ribbed me about playing for the 'enemy', they were delighted for me. Also travelling down to the game was my fiancé Joan, whom I'd met when I had just turned 18. Our wedding was set for June 16, just a few weeks after the final, and Joan still reminds me that she barely saw me at that time, and dealt with most of the wedding preparations on her own, because I was so wrapped up in Sunderland's FA Cup run. I think my brother couldn't wait for me to be married and out of my parents' flat (I was still living there up to the wedding) because it meant that finally he'd get the bed to himself. Until I got married, the only time he had it to himself was when Sunderland were playing away or were on tour.

We continued to take full advantage of all the publicity opportunities which came our way. We were fortunate to have one of the most successful and innovative commercial managers in football at that time – Corny O'Donnell, a great friend of the players. Over many years his commercial department generated a tremendous amount of cash which the club reinvested in the youth set-up. Corny produced a semi-final brochure for the players which contained pictures and comments by us about the cup experience. He then organised many local signing sessions and visits to local factories and department stores, and the proceeds from the sales of the brochures went straight into the players' pool. That was a fantastic experience, because I was able to get right out into the local community to speak to the fans. I really got a feeling of what reaching the final meant to them. Some of them had tears in their eyes, and they were shaking my hand or hugging me so hard that I thought they would never let go. The whole experience was extremely humbling. I'm so glad that Corny gave us the opportunity to do it, because it was a brilliant reminder that a club really is nothing without its supporters.

Billy Hughes, Ian Porterfield and I travelled down to King's Road to do some publicity for the Lord John fashion group, and we were photographed outside their shop wearing their latest gear. We were kitted out in classic Seventies garb: flares, butterfly collars and lapels, and platform boots. It was fantastic fun, and when I wore those boots, for the only time in my life I discovered what it was like to be six feet tall!

The team also released the obligatory FA Cup final song called *Sunderland All The Way* which was recorded in Stockport's famous Strawberry Studios where The Beatles recorded some of their songs. I felt a bit sorry for the producer who was trying to get a gaggle of footballers to sing in tune. Suffice to say, *Sunderland All The Way* didn't make it to the top of the charts.

Billy Hughes, Micky Horswill and myself also appeared in London on the Emperor Roscoe radio show, which was one of the most popular programmes in the country at the time. We also met Rod Stewart, who had been performing in concert in Sunderland, and when the three of us were in London we were invited by Rod and his PR man, Tony Powell, to join him at Tramp Nightclub. At the end of the evening Rod invited us back to his mansion near Ascot. We all jumped into his chauffeur-driven limousine, drove down to his place and then finished up in his private snooker room, its walls adorned with framed football photographs and its floor covered with a tartan carpet. We played until the early hours of the morning and talked all about football, which was Rod's other passion. He really knew his stuff. I was impressed. The model Dee Harrington, his then girlfriend, actually popped her head into the snooker room and asked Rod to come to bed. Rod replied, "Not yet, I'm playing snooker with the lads."

Rod was very commercially aware, and he reckoned that footballers were underpaid. He said that we played in front of forty or fifty thousand people and received 100 or so pounds a week, yet he played in front of three or four thousand people and made thousands. The comparison was tenuous perhaps, but I could understand his thinking. It never occurred to me until later how crazy it was that Rod Stewart should be interested in rubbing shoulders with a bunch of young footballers from the sticks. I was living inside a surreal bubble. If we'd ever had the time to peek outside that bubble, we'd have realised that the entire nation was becoming gripped by Sunderland's FA Cup heroics, even Rod Stewart.

On the Monday before the cup final, we played down in London at Orient, but I had been kicked on the knee on the previous Saturday against Blackpool which put me in doubt for the final against Leeds. The nature of that season meant that we'd played games at such breakneck speed that bumps, bruises and strains were inevitable due to the small size of our squad. However, it also meant that most of us were forever shrugging off injuries because we wanted to play in all the matches. Bob left myself, Ian Porterfield and Monty out of the game against Orient, so that we could recover in time for the final. To have missed out on it at that stage would have broken my heart, but luckily it was a soft-tissue injury and there wasn't any ligament damage. I was passed fit, and I was able to enjoy the lead up to the final.

These days, the week we had before the game would be considered completely unacceptable because of the amount of socialising we did. We stayed down in London after the Orient match and headed straight off to the Selsdon Park Hotel in Croydon. Bob gave us the Tuesday off to recharge our batteries, although he allowed the Milk Marketing Board to come and take some publicity shots of us on the training pitches drinking pints of milk. We also had a company from the North East called Northern Autoport who agreed a deal to follow us in that last week and produce a photographic diary, which they then bound and presented to each member of the squad after the final to keep as a souvenir.

On the Wednesday, the team visited Wembley for the first time. It was quite unreal, being there with no one else inside the ground, and it was actually rather eerie hearing our shouts echo around the old stadium. My first impressions were very disappointing as the old stadium was in its raw state prior to being prepared for the big game on the Saturday. It really did look tired, and even the pitch had some bare patches. But I tried to get used to the stadium, familiarise myself with the dressing rooms and layout, and imagine what the atmosphere was going to be like on that Saturday with 100,000 fans inside. That made the hairs on the back of my neck stand on end.

Our preparations didn't stop Ian, Billy and myself from going to the BBC studios to see *Top Of The Pops* that night – if you can find a recording of the show, you'll see us dancing at the back! We'd been invited as guests of Rak Records, who were promoting our FA Cup final record. The company was owned by a guy called Mickey Most, and that night his new act, Suzi Quatro, performed live on TV in the UK for the first time along with the glam rock group, Sweet, who were there to promote their new record *Hellraiser*. Suzi, clad in her black leather jacket and trousers, was really bubbly and full of life. She didn't know an awful lot about English football, but she was having a great time as she made her way in the music business.

I had quite a long chat with Brian Connolly, Sweet's charismatic lead singer. With his blond feather cut, and all his glam gear, Brian looked every inch the performer, but I found him a really reflective character. He talked about the trappings of success, and his concerns about having too much, too young. Brian loved football, and it was clear to me having met Rod Stewart and Brian that many pop stars would have loved to have been footballers, and vice versa. With the increasing amount of money and exposure for footballers and musicians in the 1970s, there was a strong crossover between the two industries. Both groups enjoyed one another's company. I felt really sad that Brian died so young because in the conversation

I had with him he was obviously aware of the possible pitfalls of the rock and roll lifestyle, but clearly he couldn't stop himself.

On the Thursday night, we had another social engagement when, as a squad, we attended the Sportswriters Dinner in London. We didn't stay for too long though, because the final was less than 48 hours away. Finally, it was time to fully focus on the game, and to think about Leeds United.

We knew all about Leeds. They were a marvellous team, in their pristine white tops and drilled to precision in almost military fashion by Don Revie. They could get in your faces too. From my one previous experience of playing against them, I remembered how Bremner and Giles snapped at my heels for the whole game, and in Norman 'Bites yer legs' Hunter they had arguably the hardest defender of the day. Their reputation was of a hard, ruthless team, but they were also one of the most successful teams in Europe. As we'd been in the Second Division for three seasons, not many of the team had any experience of playing against Leeds. Everyone knew what Leeds were about, though, and such was our confidence that their reputation did not faze us.

To be honest, the physical threat from Leeds didn't really scare us because we were used to facing hard and cynical teams each week in Division Two. All sides got stuck in during that era, and players were able to get away with far more back then. Leeds became notorious for their "hardness" because they were the best and most high-profile team of their day. In truth, I knew that they would probably beat us seven or eight times out of ten but, as we were finding out on our run to the final, that didn't really matter on one-off occasions. Anything could happen.

Bob had a steely determination about him in the days leading up to the final. I could see it etched on his face and in his eyes. He was business-like and fully prepared which set an example for the team. I also felt that he got his match tactics spot on by continuing with the flexible 4-3-3 to 4-5-1 formation which had served us so well. This was the best way of countering the threat from Giles and Bremner, who were the best midfield duo of the day. We knew we had to snap at them and suffocate them – get in their faces, and not allow them to boss the game, or the referee. If we could swamp the midfield, we could also cut off the supply line to Jones and Clarke. We'd have to play the game of our lives though, and have luck on our side.

It helped that our approach was the opposite to that of Leeds. No dossiers, no superstitions, no lucky suits. A lot of people at the time in the game suggested that if Revie had allowed his players to relax a bit more on the big occasion, they wouldn't have choked as much when it came to the business end of the season. They were holed up in London for a week training, eating the right things, and going to bed early. Being right and proper about everything. Meanwhile, I was out dancing on *Top Of The Pops*. The contrast couldn't have been greater.

This was also manifest in what we would wear on final day. We had a commercial deal, organised by Corny O'Donnell, with a clothing company for the obligatory FA Cup final suits, but the lads and I wanted to do our own thing, so I chose a grey tweed suit with wide lapels, and a lovely brown and white kipper tie. I was always interested in fashion and liked to wear what I wanted. Bob was fine about that – after all, the entire cup run had been all about doing things our way, in our own unique style.

Another example of that came on the morning of the match, in our team hotel. BBC's Barry Davies interviewed the whole team, which went out live to millions of viewers around the country. In the middle of the interview, Billy Hughes pulled out a laughing policeman which he'd bought from a toy shop from inside his jacket, pressed the button, and suddenly, the airwaves of the nation were full of "Ho-ho-hos". So all of us were sat there laughing like a bunch of degenerates, and Barry Davies looked a bit bemused by the whole thing, probably thinking, "This lot will get battered in the final if they're not careful." I was later told that John Motson spoke to the Leeds team, in what I understand was a very sober and focused atmosphere, with Don and his men wearing their expensively tailored suits, talking seriously about the job in hand.

I slept really well the night before the final, and when we boarded the coach at Selsdon Park to go to Wembley we were all really relaxed. It felt like a school outing. ITV had decided that the Sunderland team would be used as guinea pigs, and they rigged up a camera at the front of the coach to beam back images to viewers as we went along the route. The problem was, it kept breaking, and the technicians spent most of the journey trying to fix it. It was on the journey to Wembley that the enormity of what we'd done really hit me. The route was lined both with our fans, twirling their red-and-white scarves, and neutrals who were happy to wave at us and give us the thumbs up. Leeds fans aside, everyone wanted Sunderland to win the cup that afternoon. Our supporters had been our 12th man throughout the FA Cup run. I felt an unbelievable sense of pride, as I looked around the coach and saw all my team-mates happy and excited about what was coming. I'd come through the youth team with many of the players, and six months before, when Bob had taken over, the critics reckoned that because our morale was so low we were even candidates for relegation. The transformation had been incredible. As the coach nudged closer to Wembley, my sense of expectation grew.

We were such a tight-knit unit, and everything was so exciting and fresh, that a feeling of nerves never hit me. We went out for a pre-match stroll on the turf and, glancing across, I caught sight of the Leeds players. They were regimented, upright, and correct, suited and booted, walking in formation. To me, it seemed they were almost on a military route march, rather than a pre-match walkabout. We were wandering in small groups, hands in our pockets, laughing and joking and waving to our supporters. I could see that the crowd was at least 70 per cent Sunderland fans. The demand for tickets up in the North East had been unbelievable and, apart from small pockets of white, the whole place was a sea of red-and-white stripes.

I got collared by John Motson for an interview on the pitch and he asked me what the mood was like within the camp.

"Just really relaxed," I told him.

He seemed rather perplexed, and asked me how Bob Stokoe was.

"Just the same. Really relaxed. I don't know what's wrong with us — is it wrong?"

John said there was nothing wrong with that at all, but then he asked me for a prediction. "I'll see you later," I responded. I didn't really want to say something that might be seen as a bit cocky, but inside I knew we could win.

Few of the pundits shared our optimism. Up in the TV gantry,

Brian Clough, working for ITV, was watching the live feed. I was told that he turned to Brian Moore and said, off camera, "Young Tueart is far too cocky. Just look at him." On air, he modified his comments slightly and said, "Sunderland are so relaxed that if Leeds catch them in this mood, it could be over in 20 minutes."

In the dressing room, as we got stripped and ready, I could hear the distant noise of the crowd, but I couldn't pick out specific chants. Our group was calm and focused before we went out onto the turf. There were no ghetto blasters pumping out music, which I know a lot of teams have these days. We didn't have any daft superstitions within the team, either. No one insisted on going out first, no lucky suits, no one insisting on silence. Just calm and quiet, except for occasional jokes from Billy Hughes and Vic Halom to lighten the mood. Bob gave us a few words about keeping it tight, monitoring Bremner and Giles closely, and cutting down their space. There were no words from him about his experience with Newcastle in the FA Cup final 18 years earlier. He wanted us to enjoy it and experience that unforgettable feeling for ourselves. I did a bit of stretching to keep myself warm, and then the bell went, and off we went. Into the lion's den.

In the tunnel the roar of the crowd created an atmosphere you felt like you could reach out and touch. Leeds filtered in alongside us, but unlike today when the players shake hands and exchange pleasantries, there wasn't so much as a look or a greeting swapped between the two sides. At least not directly, anyway. There were a few furtive glances shot in both directions. I sensed tension in the Leeds players. I noticed that our players had their arms loose by their sides, whereas the Leeds players were more rigid, more upright. As hard-bitten pros who'd won so much, I had a feeling that Leeds felt we didn't even belong on the same pitch as them. It was almost as if they were looking down their noses at us, and yet they were tense as well.

The contrast between us and them was also evident in the clothes worn by the two managers. Traditionally cup final managers always wore a suit for the big occasion, but not Bob – he wore his red Sunderland tracksuit as usual whereas Revie was immaculate in his blazer. I felt that Bob's fashion choice that day added to the feel that a collection of urchins were playing the aristocrats, as I can't recall a manager ever walking out on the Wembley pitch on cup final day in anything other than a suit. I could see that the vibes between the pair, who led the teams out, were mixed. Initially, Don tried to engage Bob in small talk, and Bob blanked him, but then Bob appeared to have a rethink and did have a bit of a chat. It was strictly small talk, I imagine, and it was all a bit strained. Years later, I heard Bob claim that he felt sick every day of his working life about Revie's offer to "take it easy" back in his Bury days, so I often wondered what exactly was going through his mind as he walked alongside the Leeds manager out onto the pitch. Bob being Bob, he never let on to anyone what he was thinking.

The first thing to hit me when I came out of the tunnel was the wall of noise. The Leeds fans were shoehorned around the tunnel, but the rest of the crowd was all candy-striped red-and-white, chanting "Sunderland, Sunderland," in unison. It was deafening. I could barely take it all in. Funny things play on your mind as you walk out onto the pitch, like where you're supposed to be headed once you get out there, for one thing. We snaked out onto the pitch, and I hoped that those ahead of me knew where they were going. It makes me laugh when I look back on the footage now and see Bobby Kerr striding out there, looking like a man possessed. After a few seconds, Jim Montgomery, second in the line, called to him, telling him to cool it, and not get too far ahead of Billy Bremner, who ambled along like he was in his own back garden. At the time, I focused on some of the little things. I remember Richie Pitt, with his gigantic afro, bouncing the ball on his head as he walked out. We had been given tracksuits with our names printed on the back of them, so I can clearly remember who was ahead of me in the chain.

The two teams lined up near the halfway line, waiting to meet the Duke of Kent, after they'd played the national anthem. First, he was introduced to the Leeds team, the FA Cup holders, standing dead still and upright. Then he met Revie, who knew all the protocols – unlike us, of course. When he was introduced to the Duke of Kent, Bobby Kerr told me he tried to speak "posh", and, like the rest of the lads, I couldn't stand still in the line. I was between Vic Halom and Dave Young, who was our substitute, and I was jiggling about, chewing gum, jumping from foot to foot, looking back at our fans who were behind us. I was trying to drink in the atmosphere, but in truth I just wanted to get on with it. The Duke simply said "Good luck," shook my hand, and moved on.

In those days, so few footballers ever got to play at Wembley, that all I could think was, "I've made it." I was playing at the ground where England had lifted the World Cup just seven years before, and great players like Stanley Matthews and my boyhood heroes like Denis Law and Jim Baxter had starred on the grandest stage of all. Of course, there were things that happened on the day that I was unaware of at the time. It was only when I saw the footage that I noticed Billy Bremner's refusal to look Bobby Kerr (they are the two smallest captains in FA Cup final history) directly in the eye as they tossed the coin to decide who would kick off. I felt it was sheer arrogance on Bremner's part. He actually looks a bit bored by the whole thing, probably thinking that it wouldn't matter what the call was anyway, because Leeds were sure to win. What did jar with me at the time was when Leeds did their group wave to the whole crowd, which was their party piece. Again, it looked like cockiness to me, and it was all a bit misplaced, because most of the crowd was rooting for us.

After what seemed an age, the game finally began. Those early minutes were telling. Eight seconds in, Norman Hunter thumped a clearance into my midriff, and I scampered towards the Leeds goal. I took a shot, and Hunter cleared. Normally, I'd probably have taken another touch and given myself a bit more time, but when it's that early in the game, you've not had a chance to settle into it. But it suggested that Leeds could be rattled, and that if we got in their faces we had half a chance. In the follow-up to my chance, Micky Horswill and Bobby Kerr fell flat on their faces, showing just how slippery the pitch was. Leeds quickly broke down the other end, and Allan Clarke cut in and was promptly scythed down by Richie Pitt. These days, that would have been a yellow card, no question. But Ritchie was let off with a ticking-off by the ref, and within the first two minutes Leeds knew that not only could we threaten down at their end, but we could also look after ourselves physically.

Revie would have sent his scouts to watch us several times before the final, so our tactics wouldn't have been a mystery to him, but Leeds couldn't get the better of us, although they certainly showed glimpses of class in that first half. Twice Dave Watson blocked Clarke's efforts, and in midfield Micky and Ian Porterfield got so tight on Giles and Bremner that Bremner in particular got rattled. You could tell that because the foul tally increased as the half progressed. Leeds knew they were in a battle and, with Bobby Kerr doubling up with Dick Malone on the right to shackle Eddie Gray, they couldn't breathe. Our flexibility was paying dividends. At every opportunity, Billy Hughes and I ran straight at Hunter and Madeley, trying to pick out an opening. We were always switching positions to keep them guessing. I think they were a bit surprised because we didn't show them any respect. We just played our natural game and went for it, and I think if we'd stood off them it would have been an invitation for them to come and get us.

To be honest, the cup final wasn't my best performance. Not all of my runs came to much, and things didn't go quite as swimmingly as I would have liked. But along with Billy and Vic, we kept their defence busy, and got back to defend when necessary. Everyone in our team ran their hearts out from box to box, and when our breakthrough did come it summed up the random, off-the-cuff nature of our cup run. Thirty minutes in, Bobby Kerr, who was usually so accurate with his right peg, spotted me and Billy moving to the near post, but ended up skewing his cross so badly that David Harvey in the Leeds goal had to palm it over the bar. Because we wanted to get on with it, Billy Hughes, who didn't normally take our corners, ended up taking it because Bobby Kerr, our usual dead ball specialist, was jogging into the box. Incidentally, Bobby got a bollocking off me because his cross was so awful. So Billy's corner hit Vic Halom on the thigh and bounced its way through to Ian Porterfield. Ian's left foot was unerringly accurate, but he'd admit that his right was useless, a "dead leg" which he tended to use as little as possible. So what did he do? He flicked the ball up with his left and volleyed in magnificently with his right foot.

It had been a bizarre chain of events which led to Ian's goal. An awful cross palmed over by a goalie who should probably have held it. A corner taken by a fella who was usually in the box on the end of one. A poorly-controlled ball by our striker. And a shot thrashed in by the right peg of Ian Porterfield who is probably the most left-footed player I've ever seen.

As we headed for Ian, screaming with joy, I was thinking, "This has to be our time. It has to be now." But such was the nature of the team dynamic, that no one was telling each other to "cool it" or "take it steady until half-time". As we had done since we played Notts County in the third round, we flew by the seat of our pants and carried on going at Leeds. No grand plan. No killer scheme. But we had deserved the goal. With the pressure we had been putting Leeds under, it had been coming. Just before half-time, Billy and I interchanged a couple of back heels, and I could see the Leeds players' battle-weary faces darken. They realised that they had a big problem because we were showing no fear.

At the break we were buzzing. We were a goal to the good against probably the best team in Europe, so you wouldn't expect much else. Bob's half-time talk was precisely what I expected. He told us simply to keep going and play the way we had in the first half. Later, I'd come to realise that Bob's skill set was limited, so he wouldn't have been able to come up with some new tactical formation had things been going wrong, but on that afternoon his talk was perfect. Given the opposition, I don't really see how things could have gone any better, and in that situation I felt that everyone needed a pat on the back and a spot of reassurance, not to start fretting about minor things which might not be quite right. And Bob got his talk just right. Certain managers are good in certain situations, and Bob was at his very best that afternoon.

In some ways, Bob was a smart cookie. A few days before the final, he had told a journalist that he hoped the referee would actually get on with the job and referee the final, rather than let John Giles and Billy Bremner boss him around. I read the piece, and could see what Bob was trying to do. Revie's team was infamous for pressurising referees and trying to influence their decisions, but at Wembley, the referee, maybe conscious of what Bob had said, was very strict with Leeds. As the second half wore on, the "Leeds streak", as I call it, kicked in. They got nastier. Bremner whipped my legs away, and I crashed to the deck. Nobbled. But then, he tried to nobble Ian Porterfield too, and Ian not only kept the ball, but he beat Bremner, ruffled his hair like Bremner was his naughty little brother, and then winked at me, as if to say, "He won't get the better of me." I thought that was a defining moment. Ian was playing brilliantly in midfield and allowing us to retain a fair amount of possession. He was in his element.

Leeds did have a lot of the ball as well, but often it was what I call "negative possession" in that they were knocking the ball around in areas where they couldn't do us any damage. With half an hour left, they did penetrate, though. Monty's double save – firstly from Trevor Cherry's diving header and then from Peter Lorimer's follow-up – is still ranked up there with Gordon Banks's save from Pele in 1970. Rightly so. That second save was absolutely breathtaking. I couldn't believe that he kept it out, although I did later kid Monty that if he'd actually held onto Cherry's header then the stop from Lorimer wouldn't have been necessary!

Monty told me later that it was pure instinct. He gambled, and threw himself in the spot where he guessed Lorimer would place it. Monty guessed right, twisted his body, and deflected it onto the bar. There's no doubt about it that Monty was a super, super goalie, and that double save was extraordinary, although if you'd have blinked, you'd probably have missed it. Doug Weatherall, a journalist we knew well, came into the dressing room afterwards and admitted he thought Lorimer had hit the bar directly, and in those days, before instant replays, even the TV commentators had taken a while to fathom exactly what had happened.

With a few minutes to go I was standing on the halfway line next to Norman Hunter. His shoulders and his head were slumped, and through the din he said, "It looks like it's going to be your day, Dennis."

When Revie took off Eddie Gray – their most creative player – and brought on Terry Yorath, it convinced me that we finally had them, because I just couldn't see where the spark was going to come from. By the end, we were totally knackered, but we still kept going at Leeds. Me, Ian Porterfield and Ron Guthrie had successive cracks, and at the death Vic Halom's shot was tipped away by David Harvey. I felt that by the end we made Leeds look like old men, as we were so much more full of energy than they were. My dad told me later that he couldn't stand the tension. He thought his heart was going to pack in, so he disappeared into the Wembley concourse to listen for the final whistle.

When the referee blew for full-time, there was a deafening explosion of joy from our fans. I hugged Norman Hunter, and then took off. Our supporters were bouncing up and down in sheer ecstasy, a rolling sea of red-and-white. I had an overwhelming desire to take the cup, that beautiful silver pot with the big ears, now bedecked in red-and-white ribbons, to our supporters. I think that went back to when I was a kid, when I spent more than my fair share of time at the Leazes End at Newcastle, and I understood the strong connection between players and fans.

I was one of the last players up to the Royal Box to receive my medal, and by the time I got back down to pitch level, the team was already congregating in front of the massed ranks of photographers. I was right at the back and, being one of the smallest, felt that I was in danger of being missed out from the team shots. So I ducked down, stuck my head between Bobby Kerr's legs, and lifted him onto my shoulders. All the photos next day showed me hoisting Bobby upwards, but it was a close-run thing.

That almost spiritual link between club and fans in the North East was never better illustrated than when we went on our lap of honour. I didn't want it to end. We lapped it up. No silly faces at the cameras, no on-pitch interviews, no staged team shots, loud music or fireworks. Just us running around with Sunderland hats and scarves on, and celebrating with our supporters. As it should be.

Unsurprisingly, given the pandemonium, there was plenty that went on which I wasn't aware of. I never saw Bob, dressed in his tracksuit, raincoat and natty plastic hat, dash off towards Monty when the final whistle blew and it wasn't until we got home that we realised the effect the game had had on those back in Sunderland. Tyne-Tees produced a wonderful documentary called *Meanwhile Back In Sunderland* which showed how, from midday onwards, the whole place had ground to a halt as everyone tuned into the final and the build-up. It's a fantastic piece of social history, and when I watch it back now it's poignant because so many fans, a good proportion of whom are no longer with us, were totally wrapped up in the whole thing.

The dressing room afterwards was strewn with the detritus of the game; socks, shin pads, shirts, boots, all our Sunderland regalia, and the spoils of war – our medals and that lovely silver cup in pride of place on the side of the bath. We were one big happy family. We threw Bob Cass, a local journalist who'd been with us all the way during the cup run, into the bath with us.

We went on to a reception and dinner at the Park Lane Hotel, via our own hotel where we met up with our families. It was insane. In my excitement, I'd left the lid of the trophy in my hotel room, so when I got to the reception there was a real panic on and I had to rush back and get it. Mickey Most laid on all the entertainment, and Alan Price and Suzi Quatro did the honours. There were so many gatecrashers that there weren't actually any seats left for the players, so when I'd finished jabbering away to all the fans and journalists who wanted a word (or several) I ended up standing up to shovel some food down. I was still alcohol-free, though – I wanted to remember the night forever.

We were then taken off for an interview on *Match Of The Day,* with David Coleman, recorded at the hotel. Some of the lads like Monty and Dick Malone never got around to eating at all, so they ended up in a Wimpy Bar at around 2am. I think I finally crawled into bed at around four in the morning.

Then it was off to Cardiff to play a game on the Monday. We still had a couple of league matches to play, and this one was important to the Bluebirds because they needed a point to stay up. I don't remember a thing about the game itself, except that Vic Halom scored in a 1–1 draw, but the City directors laid on more champagne afterwards because they were chuffed that they'd avoided relegation.

Finally, on the Tuesday, three days after beating Leeds in the final, we headed back to Sunderland to parade the trophy to our fans. The whole thing was planned like a military operation. After the events of the previous few days, and all the celebration, most of us looked and felt like death warmed up. We got a wash and a brush-up at the Scotch Corner Hotel, and I caught a sight of myself in the mirror. I had huge bags under my eyes and looked like I needed to sleep for a week. But still, I couldn't wait to take the cup back to our supporters and then onto Roker Park. As soon as we got close to the turn-off for Sunderland, the red-and-white army started to appear along the motorway bridges, at first in ones and twos, and then in their droves, all singing, dancing and waving. Before we got onto the A690 into Sunderland, we transferred onto an open-topped double-decker bus and trundled our way into town. It was all red-and-white. In fields, some farmers had put Sunderland rosettes on their sheep and cows. Supporters lined the bridges which criss-crossed the roads. As we reached the city, bedridden hospital patients were wheeled out onto balconies. Firemen tooted their horns as we passed, and shops and banks shut for the afternoon to welcome us home. Schools closed as well so all the kids could see the FA Cup come back to Sunderland. I don't know about my team-mates, but I started to think that the sky could be the limit for us, such was the overwhelming level of support in the area.

Then it was onto Roker, where 52,000 were present and correct with their songs and their "Stokoe" and "Sunderland" chants. That night, I'm sure that if he'd wanted, Bob 'The Messiah' Stokoe could have walked across the Wear. Walking around the ground, looking up to the hordes of red-and-white stripes, I just didn't want it to end. I'd have been happy if it had gone on forever, and my emotions were sky-high, stratospheric. Sooner or later, I knew that I'd come down to earth, but right now that was not going to happen.

Anyway, I couldn't switch off quite yet because, unbelievably, we had yet another league game to play against already promoted QPR on the following night at Roker Park. My head might have been foggy after all that had gone on, but I could see what a class act Rangers were. They'd been in the top two right from the start, and had quality players like Stan Bowles, Gerry Francis and Terry Venables in the side. It was a team built to withstand the rigours of a marathon season and push onwards. Bob Stokoe should have taken note. By now, we were practically crawling on our hands and knees, totally spent. QPR tonked us 3–0 and we could barely move. Running on empty didn't begin to sum up how I felt. The fans didn't turn up to see the game as such, they showed up to see the silver pot, which was on display pitch side on a bench. Just before half-time, Stan Bowles booted a ball towards the bench and sent it crashing to the floor. I heard later that, true to form, he'd done it for a bet. Our fans erupted. I thought there would be blood spilt. But none of us players sought retribution against Stan, because our heads were still in cloud cuckoo land.

At the end of the season, Pyrex, who were based in the city, presented every first teamer with a dinner service, because as their official letter stated: "Our customers in Europe now know where we are in England." I later found out that during March 1973, Wearmouth Colliery, where the Stadium of Light now is, enjoyed a new production record. Of course it couldn't all be down to our FA Cup run, but I doubt that any other club in the country could have had such a galvanising effect on the industries and communities around them. It was only in the summer after that season that the enormity of that fact hit me, and it just showed the effect our success had on the city.

As soon as the season was over it was off to Magaluf, and an all-expenses paid holiday laid on by the club as a thank you for winning the cup. I say that, but we did have to fly midweek to Nice to play a friendly game with Cannes to pay for the whole thing. There were no free excursions at Sunderland.

The whole holiday was like a *Carry On* film. One night in Palmanova we all went clubbing, and Ian Porterfield boasted to us that he could get into a club for free. Up he strode towards the doorman.

"We are Sunderlando," he said.

The doorman looked unimpressed.

"Sunderlando," Porterfield said again.

"We win FA Cup. We a famous football club. Me – Ian Porterfield."

The doorman simply rubbed his fingers on his right hand together, and growled, "Pesetas" at Ian.

We weren't that famous after all, but finally we could start to reflect on what we'd achieved. I think if I'd stayed in Sunderland all summer, I'd never have got that kind of head space. What was great about it all was that we took the entire backroom staff and journalists Bob Cass and Len Shackleton with us. One big happy Sunderland family. That summer excursion was brilliant. Sunbathing and basking in the reflective glory, and looking forward to my forthcoming wedding to Joan.

Yet even in my zen-like state, I did have one thing gnawing away in my mind. What would Sunderland do next?

CHAPTER FIVE

IN AND OUT OF LOVE

I'd met Joan when I just turned 18, and on our first date I took her to see *The Nutty Professor*, the original version starring Jerry Lewis. I had a tough time trying to convince her side of the family that I was a good catch for her, because it was very much female dominated, and I found that yapping about football, as I did with my dad and brother and friends all the time, didn't cut too much ice with Joan's side. Joan was one of three sisters, and her father had five sisters. "What does he really do?" asked Joan's mum when she told her I was a young professional with Sunderland. "When's he going to get a proper job?" I think that by now I've probably convinced my mother-in-law that it wasn't such a bad trade to go into, but in the mid-Sixties your bog standard footballer didn't earn a great wage, and a large number never really made it in the game, so I can understand her scepticism. She was looking out for her daughter's best interests.

We were married at St John Vianney Church in Newcastle on June 16, 1973. Even after some of the furore surrounding the FA Cup win had subsided, there had been an added complication because I'd spent five days in hospital having a varicose vein removed, leaving Joan to continue organising it all herself. The wedding was, to all intents and purposes, another football do. I was surrounded by pretty much all of my Sunderland team-mates, and Derek Foster, whom I'd progressed through the ranks with, was my best man. By then, my best mates in the game, Derek, Paddy Lowrey and Brian Chambers, had all left the club, but we've stayed very close for over

40 years. When we meet up, we still talk about our early days at Roker Park, when we were just young hopefuls dreaming of the future.

Joan was perfect for me from day one, as she has always had a very balanced view on life and was never affected or overly interested in some of the nonsense which surrounds the game. I'm very quick to make decisions and quite impulsive – quite black and white in some ways. But she would always speak from a common sense point of view, and sometimes help me to see that there are two sides to every argument. I remember that, later in my career, I'd just signed a new contract at Manchester City but decided to hand in a transfer request. I stomped home, told Joan what I'd done, and all she said was, "Well let's talk about whether that's best for you or not." Very calm and rational, and no histrionics. Being the wife of a footballer isn't always easy, and Joan, who was manager of a branch of Northern Rock, was always willing to put my career first. She was always conscious of managing finances and from her own savings she even lent me money to buy my first car.

Joan is just like her father Tony was, who always spoke with sincerity and honesty, and he was pleased when I joined the family because finally he had another bloke to talk about football with. He was a constant source of support to me, especially after I hung up my boots. One day, he had his head under the bonnet of his Ford Anglia, messing about with the engine and I said I would never be practical like him. He turned to me and said two things: firstly that good companies would always need good people and secondly that it was always important to get a fair day's pay for a fair day's work. I remember one Christmas in Newcastle when everyone was exchanging presents, he walked towards Joan and I with a gift of a tool box in his hand. Everyone looked in amazement as if he was going to give it to me but then he said, "Don't worry, this is for Joan, Dennis does what he is good at!" I admit that I'm not at all practical and, in that sense, not especially domesticated, but Tony's pieces of advice remained with me and I called upon them many times during my business career. Sometimes, you have to know what your skill set is, and what you're good or not good at.

It was around the time of the wedding that I had my first

experience – and it wasn't a good one – of the sharks who swim around footballers hoping to raise their profile at the same time. During the cup run, a London businessman by the name of Barry Gout was brought in by the sponsors of our cup final record to help with the production. He began to ingratiate himself with the team. I suppose that Barry was pleasant enough. He wore a suit, spoke nicely, and talked a lot about the commercial deals that might come our way if Sunderland continued to be successful. But I wasn't entirely convinced by him, and wondered if he might be a little bit "wide." He spent a lot of time up in the North East with the team, mainly with Billy Hughes, whose house he stayed in on occasions. In the lead up to the final he promised the players that he could get publicity and commercial deals for them. In some cases, he delivered, but there were several nasty stings in the tail.

I didn't have that much day-to-day contact with Barry, but he told me that he could arrange an all-expenses-paid honeymoon in Miami for Joan and I through a commercial deal. I have to say that I was a little uneasy about the whole thing. I still didn't fully trust him, but I went along with it all the same. I didn't let on to Joan where we were going, as I wanted to surprise her, and when we got to the airport and she found out we were headed to Miami she was excited, but she wanted to know why I was being so cloak and dagger about it all. We both got more than we bargained for. While we were out there, staying at the Dora Hotel, we met up with a photographer from the *Daily Mirror* to have some pictures taken of us on Miami beach. It seemed fantastic at the time, and I presumed that the whole thing had been sorted out between Barry, the airline, the Miami tourist authority and the *Mirror*. I didn't ask any questions. Lovely, I thought. Trans-Atlantic travel, in an era when it wasn't common, drinks on the beach, and all that sunshine. And all free. Or so I thought. It all seemed too good to be true.

I presumed the whole thing had been arranged in exchange for publicity shots and interviews, but when it came to settling up at the end of the honeymoon we found out that the deal he'd done was that Gout was supposed to be picking up 50 per cent of the tab. He neve████████, but by then he had disappeared, and I realised I'████████. So half the bill for the honeymoon was still outstanding. I was in a desperate state, and furious that I'd been caught out like that. I found out from the Miami Tourist Authority what had happened. I felt like a fool. Joan and I had got on really well with a guy called Hal from the MTA, and he wouldn't accept that any of it was my fault. In a funny way, this made me feel even worse, because not only had I been conned, but I was also left feeling embarrassed as Hal would not allow me to settle any of the costs. So we did get our free honeymoon, but I felt utterly awful about the entire thing. But the question was, where was Barry Gout?

When we got back to the UK, I discovered that he'd also deceived Billy Hughes. Gout had got Billy a new car, which Billy thought was heavily discounted until he was asked for the £3,500 outstanding balance – roughly 90 per cent of the cost of the car. When Billy went on holiday to Spain after the final, Gout had had his new bungalow painted, decorated and fitted out with furniture. Billy had been led to believe that it would be done for free, but he was landed with the complete bill. Gout was arrested and charged with fraud, and Billy and I ended up having to spend three days at the Crown Court in London. Gout was obviously a bit of a fantasist – a Walter Mitty character – who wanted to live a more glamorous life. I found out that he'd also chartered a plane from Biggin Hill and ran up many hotel bills but never paid any of them. Standing in the dock, I was terrified. In my best suit, my knees shook so badly that I had to hold onto the rail just to stay standing up. With all that was about to unravel at Sunderland, it was an experience I could have done without.

Gout was jailed for two years for fraud. It was strange really, because as it turned out he never actually made any money from all his scams. He pulled all these stunts simply for the kudos of rubbing shoulders and mixing with footballers who were suddenly nationwide heroes. I'm not entirely sure what ever happened to him after he came out of jail, but it opened my eyes to the fact that footballers are easy targets for freeloaders, piranhas and spivs, something which is becoming more prevalent in modern times. This was in an era when, by current standards, footballers didn't earn an awful lot. It brought me down to earth after the FA Cup final victory, but to be honest the club's inactivity in the transfer market was already giving me a sense of unease. I'd had it before on several occasions, when the club had sold Colin Todd in 1971, for example. It had only been seven months since I had asked Alan Brown for a transfer. I know a lot had happened since then, and I'd put the request on the back burner after Bob arrived, but I never officially withdrew my request and, just a couple of months after winning at Wembley, I was feeling uneasy again.

I was absolutely ravenous for another crack at the top flight. After all the euphoria of beating Leeds, the reality, when I looked at the fixture list for the 1973/74 season, was that we were facing Orient, Notts County and Cardiff in the opening fixtures in Division Two, not Liverpool, Leeds or Arsenal. The cup run and all that went with it reminded me of the thrill and the buzz of the big occasion against top clubs, but now it was over. It had confirmed to me that I wanted to be playing in those kinds of matches all the time. I wanted to be competing for major honours. As soon as the fixture list was released, Sunderland were tipped as favourites to win promotion. But I always knew that just because we'd won the cup, it didn't necessarily mean we'd get promotion. We'd finished sixth in the league in the previous season, and I felt that Bob needed to drive us on. We needed some more top-quality players, and that was where Bob was found wanting. All his managerial career, he'd been used to working in the lower leagues and picking up a few bargains here and there. He'd got lucky on the FA Cup run to some degree, because he just kept things going and didn't change anything tactically. I felt that approach wouldn't work over the course of a whole season, when you get injuries, suspensions and loss of form. Our FA Cup run was a breathless sprint, but a nine-month league campaign is a gruelling marathon. Having won the cup, we were there to be shot at, and I knew that our opponents would raise their game against us. I didn't think Bob would have had any trouble attracting good players to Sunderland after our cup success, but it never happened.

There was a lot of talk about him signing Alan West, an up-and-coming central midfielder from Burnley. He was a talented player, but when he had his medical at Sunderland the club doctor reckoned his knee looked suspect and told him that if he carried on playing he'd end up in a wheelchair. So he was never signed, although he did move to Luton, where he enjoyed an excellent eight-year career, despite what the medics had said. In the end, the only addition to the squad was Rod Belfitt, a utility striker who'd been a squad player at Leeds under Revie and then drifted on to Everton and Ipswich. He was a nice enough lad, but to be brutally honest he was no better than what we already had.

We played Orient at Roker Park on the opening day of the season and drew 1–1 in front of nearly 30,000. After the unforgettable atmosphere at Roker for the QPR game at the tail end of the previous campaign, it was all a bit flat. We drew three of our opening four matches, and then we went down to Oxford, where I scored one of the best goals of my career. Bobby Kerr floated in a cross from the right, and I launched myself at the ball 12 yards out, volleyed it, and it flew into the top corner. It proved to be the winner. A while back, it popped up on YouTube, and I was delighted to hear that Brian Moore, commentating for ITV, declared it to be a possible Goal of the Season, even though it was only September. But as for the season as a whole, it wasn't going our way.

Ritchie Pitt injured his knee a week later at Luton. The fella who'd outmuscled Allan Clarke just a few months earlier never played for Sunderland again, and we missed his physical presence in defence. Then Billy Hughes damaged his hamstring, and his effectiveness was reduced. Problem was, we didn't have anyone in the squad who could come close to replacing him. We weren't anywhere near the promotion chase, and our Cup Winners' Cup adventure was brief. We lost to Sporting Lisbon in the second round. I could feel things slipping away, and I was quickly getting disillusioned with the whole situation and, possibly due to the state of mind I was in, I lost the plot after we'd beaten Swindon 4–1 in November. I scored a classic hat-trick, with right foot, left foot and my head. After the game we were all in the Black Cat Social Club at Roker Park and I spoke to Bob Cass, our local journalist, and made a comment about being his Man of the Match. I thought that it was inevitable I would be. To my astonishment, Bob Cass awarded Vic Halom the prize because he had scored the other goal and Bob considered that his all-round approach work had been excellent. I know it sounds big headed and all that, but I thought,

"If I'm not star man after a performance like that, then I never will be." I felt that it reflected the difficult job which homegrown players can have in gaining their deserved recognition at their respective club.

My sense of gloom was deepened by the refusal of the board to make good their promise and "look after us" after the FA Cup win. The Government had imposed a national wage freeze as a response to the economic crisis, so the directors said they couldn't increase our pay. They neglected to mention that there was a rule which stated that you were entitled to a raise if your status changed, and if winning the FA Cup didn't change our status then I don't know what would. It was typical of the club at that time. They weren't prepared to have a go and reach for the stars. None of this sat well with me. We had qualified for Europe and had a wonderful supporter base, but I felt there was an inherent fear, a small mindedness, that stopped the club trying to push onto the next level. Keith Collings, our chairman at the time, has since admitted a regret that the club didn't do more to look after our team. I had ambition, but felt that the club didn't, and that it would be forever stuck within its own limited paramaters. I felt that small-town syndrome was at the heart of it all, yet we were pulling in around 30,000 a game at the start of that 1973/74 season, even when we weren't really playing too well. It showed what could happen if we could gain promotion.

I felt that a major part of the problem was Bob himself. Here was a guy who'd lived through the depression of the 1930s, whose dad was a miner, and whose managerial career had always been in the lower leagues. I sensed he felt uneasy sanctioning the spending of big bucks. It went against the grain of his personality. But then, by the same token, Stein, Shankly and Busby all came from similar backgrounds, and they knew when to spend money on the right player. I often felt that Bob feared managing more famous players, bigger stars. Perhaps that was why he never gambled and signed one, or at least tried to tempt bigger names to Roker Park, because, with all due respect to him, Rod Belfitt, who'd go on to score three goals during that season, was not a big star or a name to get anyone salivating.

Joan and I had bought a detached house in Washington new

town and paid £5,500, with a £5,000 mortgage. Rod Belfitt was looking to buy a house in Durham almost three times that value without any mortgage. Good for Rod, but it made the rest of us think, and we realised that if we stayed at Sunderland we would be unlikely to ever be in his fortunate position. I wasn't the only one who felt let down by the club's approach to looking after the cup-winning team. I understand that Bob often worried about the effect which football management, all-consuming career that it is, was having on his family life. He was very close to his family, and liked nothing better than a quiet night in front of the television with a beer. Around this time, he started getting really bad migraines, which indicated to me that he was feeling the pressure of Sunderland misfiring at the start of the season. It had all been plain sailing before for Bob, but now I felt he was struggling to move us on.

We played away at Bristol City in October and lost 2–0. I didn't play well, I accept that. But neither did the entire team. It didn't stop Bob from lambasting me in the press and telling them that I'd let both him and the team down. I wasn't best pleased. Looking back, I feel this was probably the point of no return for Bob with me. He hadn't managed the situation well at all. If he'd pulled me aside and given me a bollocking, I'd have accepted it. Even better, he could have spoken to me about how I felt things were going, and allowed me to voice my opinions. Instead, he'd shown that he didn't have the people skills or the man management skills. I don't quite know what I expected Bob to say when I asked him for a transfer in November 1973. Maybe I hoped that he'd sit me down, tell me that he was actively seeking some top-class players, and that the club really was reaching for the skies. Perhaps I wanted him to look devastated, implore me to stay, and win me over with his passion for the club. I got the precise opposite. I'd walked into his office, and Bob was sat there doing some paperwork. "What can I do for you?" he asked. So I explained that I felt it was the right time to move on, and that I'd like a transfer. Bob moved back in his chair slightly, looked at me solemnly with his big, brown eyes, and in that deadpan Geordie accent of his said, "I'll put it to the board." End of discussion. No Churchillian speech about the soul of the club or his ambition. I got nothing back from him at all. He seemed to give the impression that he thought that by ignoring the issues at hand, they'd simply go away. That doesn't work in any walk of life, and especially not at football clubs, where bad feeling will only fester.

The following week, Bob, yet again, went to town in the papers, labelling me unprofessional. He dropped me from the team and then, to compound his problems, Billy Hughes also asked for a transfer, and the team's form continued to veer between the average, the occasionally good, and the sometimes awful. We slipped out of the promotion race. Bob's 'Messiah' veneer was fading, but a few weeks later he asked to see me and offered me a deal. He said that if I came off the list and knuckled down while he tried to get the spirit back in the side, he'd let me go before the March deadline. I felt that I owed it to the club and the supporters – not to Bob – and so I did as I was asked. Then we hit another ridiculous problem. We'd been named as Team of the Year at the BBC *Sports Personality of the Year* awards, and at the presentation down in London I wore an open-necked shirt. Six months earlier, our unwillingness to conform to stereotype showed how off the cuff we were, and was considered a virtue. Me not wearing a shirt and tie, along with many of the team, showed that we weren't afraid to be different. Suddenly, not wearing a tie became a big issue. I could feel Bob glaring at me throughout the evening, and on the way back home he told me that my lax dress code reflected poorly on Sunderland Football Club. On the evening, with the press in close proximity, Billy Hughes once again pulled out his laughing policeman. But the FA Cup Final win now seemed an age ago, and our laughter and smiles were forced. Bob dropped me from the team – again – but told the press it was because I had a sore throat. I was getting to the stage where I was convinced that Bob's communication skills were nil. He did, nonetheless, make one last-ditch effort to keep me at Sunderland.

Just before the deadline, the club made me an offer. I'd been on £60 a week plus £30 appearance money, and they offered me £120 a week to stay. Good, but not great money. I still felt let down. If they could offer that to me in early March, why couldn't they have offered it to me and the rest of my team-mates earlier? I thought it was a poor way to treat players who'd brought so much success and finance to the club. A great Sunderland supporter and local property developer and builder, Matty Roseberry, met up with me at a local supporters' event and even offered to give me a house worth £15,000 if I stayed at Sunderland. When I'd first asked for the transfer, I was at a sportsman's evening in Newcastle and bumped into Freddy Shepherd senior, the father of the former Newcastle United chairman. Shepherd was a local scrap dealer who had made good and a massive Newcastle fan. He asked me if I would be interested in signing for Newcastle and said that if I did he would look after me with a house. It shows how much passion there was among the fans in the North East to keep hold of their local young players. Of course I was interested, but Newcastle never made a formal approach.

For me, too much water had gone under the bridge at Sunderland, and by this time money was not even an issue; I'd made my mind up to leave. We were still nowhere near the promotion race, and even if we went up the following season I knew that I'd be 26 before I was back in the First Division. My last game for the club was against Portsmouth at Roker, on a dismal foggy midweek afternoon in front of just 8,000 fans. It was at the time of three-day weeks, as the Government tried to save on fuel. As the mist rolled in off the North Sea, I could barely see 20 feet in front of my face, but I scored twice in our 3–0 win. As I trotted off at the end, I have to be totally honest and say that I had no idea what was about to happen to me, not an inkling. Clubs had total control of player movement by holding their registration, so I knew that if Sunderland refused to sell me I'd be going absolutely nowhere.

CHAPTER SIX

SKY BLUE

As the transfer deadline approached, I heard plenty of rumours about the clubs that were interested in signing me. There was speculation in the press that West Ham had offered £150,000 for me and then another story said Spurs topped that with a bid of £200,000. Bob Stokoe never told me a thing, and I didn't have an agent, so in a way I was in the same boat as the Sunderland fans – listening to tittle-tattle about my possible future moves. To be honest, though, I'm not sure that I'd have been overly keen to move to London. It never really appealed, and I saw myself always playing in the north of England. In any case, neither West Ham nor Spurs were in especially rude health in those days, and both clubs were relegated in the next couple of seasons, so I never felt that I missed out. Moving to a northern giant like Liverpool would have been a different matter, though. Not that I thought they were interested in me at the time. Years later, though, when I went to a football dinner at the Hilton in London, I caught a taxi with the Liverpool chairman Sir John Smith. He told me that Bill Shankly had been really keen on signing me from Sunderland, and that apparently Bob had given him first refusal on me if and when I left. When the time came, though, Bob reneged on the deal, and Shanks was apparently so furious that he never spoke to him again. What might have been...

As the fateful deadline day drew nearer, it seemed that I might be stuck at Roker Park for another season. I spoke to my good friend Corny O'Donnell, who had done the most to try and persuade me to stay at Roker Park. I mentioned to him that I felt torn. Corny sensed my doubts about the ambition of Bob and the club. I looked him in the eye, and said to him, "Okay Corny, so Sunderland has a fantastic supporter base and huge potential, but do you honestly believe that they will get promotion under Stokoe?"

He was stumped and admitted that he wasn't convinced that Stokoe was the man to lead Sunderland back to Division One – at least not any time soon.

Corny grinned at me, and said, "Well Dennis, I guess that answers your question."

It wasn't an easy time. I'd always had a marvellous relationship with the Roker Park faithful, especially those in the old Clock Stand. The Clock Stand was full of really knowledgeable supporters who knew their football, and had watched the club for years. They knew all too well the vagaries of supporting the club, but they stuck with it through thick (sometimes) and thin (mostly). They'd let us know if they were disgruntled, but I'll never forget the support they gave me during my five years in the first team. The supporters were eternally grateful to us for winning the FA Cup, and it would have been easy for me to stay, live on the memories of '73, and remain a small-town hero for the rest of my career. Strangely, the fact that we were commonly referred to as FA Cup "giantkillers" (although we crashed out of the competition in the third round against Carlisle the following season) highlighted to me that, although we had been successful once, we were still perceived as "little Sunderland" despite that massive potential. Falling into a comfort zone at the age of 24 would have been fatal for my career.

My situation was about to change dramatically. On the Saturday evening before the Thursday, March 14 deadline, I got a call to go to a meeting at Roker Park the next day. When I arrived, the chairman, Keith Collings, was there, as was Bob, and Micky Horswill, who'd also asked for a transfer. Micky had the same feeling as Billy and several of the players in the squad that the team was going backwards. Transfers in those days could be ludicrously cloak and dagger, and there was nowhere near the level of media interest and speculation that there is today.

I honestly had no idea where we were headed when we jumped

into the chairman's car that day. All Bob and Keith would say was that another club was interested. It was one of the strangest car journeys I've ever had. Micky and I were full of nervous tension and could barely sit still. We kept glancing at one another furtively, and tried to make small talk with Bob and Keith, but not a great deal came back in return. I looked at the countryside flying by, and my mind was racing. Bob said little, and looked a bit gloomy, and Keith, as I recall, said nothing at all. I was excited, though. On reflection, it seems incredible that transfer deals were ever conducted in such a way. It was mine and Micky's careers, and yet even on the day we were about to leave Sunderland we still had no clue where we were headed. Even though the maximum wage had been abolished 13 years previously, and players were now free to move at the end of their contracts, the clubs still held all the aces. But when I strolled into the Wetherby Hotel and saw Manchester City boss Ron Saunders, his assistant Tony Book and chairman Peter Swales, puffing on his cigar, sat in a huddle in the lobby, I had a pretty good idea what was going to happen next.

We made a little bit of chit-chat with Swales and Saunders, and then I was ushered away to a room with Ron. We sat on two chairs facing one another square on. The conversation didn't last too long. In his broad Brummie brogue, Ron was typically straight-talking and direct.

"I'm looking to freshen up the squad, Dennis, and bring in some good young players," he told me. "You'll be the first of many."

He had only just been appointed manager and was keen to stamp his authority on the club by bringing in his own players. Ron, with that steely look of his, said he was looking to turn the club into the major force in English football. He told me that he wanted me to stay out on the left and play my natural game, and that he believed that by cutting in from that side I could offer City another dimension. I liked his forthrightness.

He offered me £150 per week, and I couldn't wait to put pen to paper. It's not quite the £150,000 per week that modern City players command, but I was more than happy with the deal, as I was desperate to join a major First Division club.

I was thrilled at the prospect. Even though we'd beaten City on the way to the FA Cup final a year before, I knew they were a class outfit. They epitomised the kind of football I loved to watch and play – all creativity, flair and aggression. Over the previous four or five years, they'd been arguably the most consistent team in the country, and could genuinely claim to be the best team in Manchester. The team had won the First Division Championship, the League Cup, the Cup Winners' Cup and the FA Cup in that magical period. But in the 1973/74 season they were floundering around in mid-table, an almost unthinkable state of affairs for City in those days.

Micky went in to see Ron after I came out. I had a brief conversation with Peter Swales, as he puffed away on his customary cigar. He was brief and to the point:

"Welcome to the club, Dennis. We're hoping that soon City will be back to winning trophies."

Over the years, I came to have a huge amount of respect for Swales, a genuine City fan who'd made his money in TV rentals. I know that he wasn't everyone's cup of tea, not by a long chalk, but I always admired his devotion to the club.

The only stumbling block was the fact that Joan had been promoted to be one of the first female branch managers of Northern Rock in the North East. As she was an employee, she had been given a preferential mortgage rate, which as newlyweds was very important to us. If we moved to Manchester and she had to give up her job we could lose that. That this was even a consideration shows how modest player wages were in those days compared to today's massive salaries. I rang Joan from the Wetherby Hotel. Her view was that a move to City was far too good an opportunity to miss, and so she would enquire as to what vacancies there were elsewhere with Northern Rock. Fortunately, there were vacancies available in both Manchester and Liverpool, so in the end we didn't have to worry about the mortgage after all.

There were still a few things to sort out, because part of the deal was that, as Micky and I headed to Manchester, the City midfielder Tony Towers would head in the opposite direction. Micky and I travelled to Maine Road the next day to finalise the deal, but we had to wait around for ages until Tony Towers agreed his salary with Bob. After everything was sorted, Bob opened up to me a bit, and told me that he was frightened to death of going back to Roker with just money. He knew that selling two players from the FA Cup-winning side less than a year after landing the trophy was hardly a statement of intent, so he had to return to the North East with a decent player, otherwise he would have been roasted by the press and the fans. I think that is why he didn't do the deal with Bill Shankly for me alone and preferred the combination that City were offering, with Towers going to the North East. I could see his point, but I can't say I felt much sympathy for Bob's plight, because I believed that he and the club had brought much of it on themselves. The one disappointment of the deal was Tony Towers leaving City, as I rated him highly. I'd seen what he could do on the pitch in our games against City in the cup run, and he was the right age to develop into a top-quality player.

With Towers in the team, Sunderland did actually have a decent end to the season, but they still tailed off in sixth place, which effectively meant there had been no improvement since the cup run. I felt vindicated in leaving, but it was a shame that Micky and I didn't even have a chance to say our goodbyes to the players at Sunderland. I knew that the Sunderland cup run with Bob Stoke and that team of 1973 would go down in North East football folklore and that no-one would ever forget the memories of those magical few months, but I could not let that distract me from my own future.

There was absolutely no time at all to settle in at City. When Micky and I finally signed all the papers on the Monday, we learnt that we would be pitched in at the deep end on Wednesday night, at home to Manchester United no less. If ever I needed a reminder that I was no longer the local boy made good, the big fish in the medium-sized pond, and that I'd stepped up to a higher tier, it was when I reported to the main entrance at the Maine Road ground on the afternoon before the game, and the doorman wouldn't let me in. He looked me square in the eye, said, 'Sorry son, I don't know you, where is your pass?' and he had to go and check that I was indeed City's new record £275,000 signing. In fact, the problem was down to a lack of communication. There was a players' entrance just beside the main door, but no one told me about it. Still, it put me in my place a bit.

Straight away I loved the feel of Maine Road, located deep in the heart of Moss Side. In some ways, it reminded me of Roker Park, as it was surrounded by terraced houses, right in the centre of the community. On match days, I parked my car right outside the ground, and if I got there early enough I'd see locals going about their everyday business – shopping, pushing prams, going out for the day.

City and United weren't exactly enjoying vintage seasons. City had been shot-shy. Even with Denis Law, Francis Lee and Colin Bell in the side, they'd averaged less than a goal a game that season, and the fans were less than impressed. United were in a hell of a mess under Tommy Docherty and were in the bottom three. Both sides desperately needed to get something out of the game to salvage some pride, and United needed points to try and stave off the threat of relegation.

Ron was as good as his word, and put me on the left-hand side. My mind was whirling. I looked around the dressing room and saw players of the calibre of Mike Doyle, Mike Summerbee and Colin Bell. Legends of the game. I couldn't fail to be inspired by that. City had some injury problems, though, and Lee, Law and Rodney Marsh sat this one out. Immediately, I noticed subtle differences between the City players and those at Sunderland. Even on derby night, the City players had a coolness about them.

Mike Doyle was a veteran of games against United and was publically vocal in his dislike of City's red neighbours. I remember well his calm, controlled aggression before the match, urging everyone to do their job, and not get carried away. From the moment I arrived at the club, Mike made it clear to me that he expected me to do my job effectively, and that City winning games was all that mattered. He treated me like an experienced professional from the off. A firm handshake when we first met, a welcome to the club, and the comment, "Right, let's get to work." He knew exactly what it took to win games and trophies.

As soon as I pulled on my sky-blue shirt that night, I knew that I'd made the right choice in joining City. It felt absolutely perfect from the moment I first wore it. Ron Saunders didn't need to say an awful lot to anybody, just something along the lines of "up and at 'em". As I'd discover, City players never needed much geeing up when it came to derby games. Then we trotted onto the field, to an absolute racket. I jogged over to the giant Kippax terrace which ran the whole length of the pitch. As far back as the eye could see, it was rammed with City fans. The dim lighting on the Kippax gave it an otherworldy atmosphere, and from my first kick in front of them the fans who stood there gave me an electric bolt of energy every game. I couldn't fail to be inspired by that huge mass of City fanatics. They gave their new boy a generous reception, and I gave them a little wave.

Talk about a baptism of fire. There were over 50,000 fans shoehorned into every corner of Maine Road that night, and the din was unbelievable throughout. But even through the racket, every time I ventured near the United dugout I could hear Tommy Docherty and his assistant Tommy Cavanagh urging United defenders Jim Holton and Alex Forsyth – in fact any United players who got near me – to "break his legs". They were obviously trying to intimidate me. After all, I was the new boy thrust into the ferment of a local derby. At one point Forsyth went straight through me and left me spreadeagled on the deck, but I still loved every minute of the game. It was what I had come to City for.

The match was more of a war of attrition than a game of football. Jim Holton, United's massive defender, a Scot with a Desperate Dan jaw line, spent the entire first half trading kicks and shoves with our centre-forward, Mike Summerbee. There were private battles, in an age when lunging, two-footed tackles were deemed fair game, going on all over the pitch.

I felt that I played well over on the left and, when I did get a few seconds of space, linked up effectively with Mike Summerbee and Colin Bell. I headed narrowly over the bar in the first half, and United goalkeeper Alex Stepney parried another of my efforts away. I could tell that Colin Bell's touch and vision was – quite literally – in a different league from what I had come across in the Second Division, and Mike Doyle, as well as being a fearsome physical presence, could play a bit too. But the ferocious, unrelenting pace of the game took my breath away, as well as the crash, bang, wallop side of things.

Just before half-time, Lou Macari and Mike Doyle squared up to one another, and the referee Clive 'The Book' Thomas came over all dictatorial and sent the pair of them off. I didn't think what they did justified being dismissed, and neither did anyone else. Doyle and Macari refused to leave the pitch, insisting that their "handbags" encounter happened all the time in local derbies. The players refused to budge, so Clive, in his authoritarian way, ordered both teams off. After ten minutes or so, we all trooped back on, without Macari and Doyle, and battle recommenced.

Overall, I felt I acquitted myself well during the match, but it was nigh on impossible to do anything constructive in that war zone. I left the pitch with my ears ringing and my head spinning, glassy eyed from the encounter. The match ended 0–0, with one newspaper headline memorably proclaiming: 'Point Each – Nothing For Soccer.' Ron Saunders and Mike Doyle each said a cursory, "Well done", and I hopped into my car and drove back to the Brook House Hotel on Wilmslow Road, where City housed all their new signings.

Joan had stayed up in the North East while we put our Washington house on the market, and she sorted out her move to the Manchester Northern Rock branch, so I was holed up in the hotel for the first few weeks. Despite the fact I was living out of a suitcase, I knew I'd made the right move. After the United clash, I had a chance to reflect on life at my new club, and I felt sure that I could adjust to the step-up in quality.

The early training sessions at City were also a real eye-opener. Ron Saunders, a former striker at Portsmouth, ran a very disciplined training programme and he used to love joining in the shooting practice routines. Aside from Jim Baxter, my other hero as a kid had been Denis Law, and now, although he was in the autumn of his career, he was my team-mate. 'The Lawman' was in his thirties, but he was still a class act. He wasn't at the club long enough for me to get to know him well, but he was very clued up about the fact that Manchester, in his opinion, was England's prime football city. "There isn't another place like it," Denis reckoned. In time, I'd come to agree with him completely. In Europe, only Milan can rival Manchester when it comes to football. Both cities, industrial and economic powerhouses, have two giant clubs which both claim to represent the soul and spirit of the place, and the passion for the game permeates every strata of society.

I soon detected that Denis wasn't overly impressed with City's poor season, but nonetheless his attitude remained second to none. In training, his shooting prowess was still awesome, and he could rifle them in from any angle. The same could be said for his heading ability – Denis was always sensational in the air. I used to love the training sessions when Ron Saunders put me alongside Denis for individual shooting practice. Bang, bang, bang. Absolutely lethal.

All the City players were extremely welcoming. The triumvirate of Bell, Summerbee and Lee was a total contrast of personalities. Colin was very much an introvert with a dry sense of humour, but once on the field of play he was a highly tuned athlete. He had the complete range of skills for a midfielder, with a unique ability to ghost into the box and score goals both with his feet and head. Years later, when I became a director at City, I recommended Colin as an ambassador for the club, and it was sometimes very difficult to push him to attend club events, on account of his introverted nature. Mike was an aggressive team player with an ability to penetrate defences down the flanks and give great supply to his team's goalscorers. His aggression towards full-backs rubbed off on myself, and he always told me to get my retaliation in first. In my first few games with him, he played at centre-forward and, as I had been taught by Alan Brown, I would track back to assist our defenders. Mike turned to me on one occasion and said, 'Don't defend all the time, you stay up here with me, they don't effin help us'. I only spent a couple of months with Francis Lee, a very extroverted character, who was very aggressive on the field, an out-and-out goalscorer who did so with great effect. He was not the best athlete in the world but had great explosive pace over short distances, especially when he was around the penalty area, something which I took notice of.

At first, I found Manchester a big, big place, although over the years I've learnt that you can make what you want of it. There is the commercial and corporate side and the big-city feel, but it can also feel quite parochial, like a large village. Manchester is roughly as big as Newcastle and Sunderland put together, and the City players were spread all around the area. Most of us were married or had girlfriends, so we tended to have our own friends and families who we mixed with away from the club. Ever since my time at Sunderland, I never felt the need to be "one of the lads" and part of a social set. I like to think that I got on well with the vast majority of my team-mates over the years, but ultimately I was being paid to play football, not make friends, and I was anxious to prove myself at Maine Road.

My initial form at City fluctuated, as I hadn't quite adjusted to the pace and extra intensity of the top division. We lost our next two games against Arsenal and Sheffield United, and then won at home to Newcastle. We were taking one step forward and two steps back. City had a few injuries at the time – Lee and Law were in and out of the team – and we were hovering on the brink of the relegation zone. I scored my first goal for the club in my fifth game, a 1–1 draw at home with Everton. It was a massive relief. Mike Summerbee cut the ball back, and I rifled it in from just inside the six-yard box. I felt a weight lift off my shoulders, although I still knew I was some way off the form required at this level of the game.

It was also taking me a little while to get used to life in the big city. Joan came down for a weekend to help look for houses and I asked Mike Summerbee to recommend a good restaurant. He suggested Mario and Franco's restaurant, which was one of the best in Manchester. When we arrived we looked at the menu and realised the prices were far higher than we'd been paying in Newcastle, but we decided to give it a try. In those days there were no credit cards, so Joan and I were regularly looking at the menu and adding up the prices as we went along to make sure we had enough cash with us so that we wouldn't end up washing dishes at the end of the evening.

Another reason for my fluctuating form, of course, was that the team as a whole was labouring. It wasn't a happy camp at City when I joined. Many of the senior players in particular didn't take kindly to Ron Saunders' direct approach. Ron decided that he wanted to rebuild the club, and that some of the experienced professionals like Francis Lee and Rodney Marsh were too set in their ways. Saunders could be very cutting, even to the likes of Denis Law and Mike Doyle who had achieved so much in the game. Maybe it was his way of trying to keep them on their toes, but it suggested to me that he was inexperienced at the highest level. Ron was never too harsh on me, though. I think he was targeting players whom he felt were coming to the ends of their City careers. City had lost to Wolves in the League Cup final in February 1974, and that was the catalyst for several of them to rebel. You need certain skills to deal with a group that has seen it all and done it all, and Ron was found wanting in this area. He clearly was a good manager, demonstrated by the fact that he went on to win the title with Aston Villa five years later, and that same team then won the European Cup under Tony Barton, but this wasn't the right time for Ron.

The mood in the dressing room was flat. It would take time to sort things, and it was clear to me that a fresh injection of talent was needed, but I was confident in the knowledge that I was part of the new breed. I tried to stay out of the griping among the senior professionals, but it was often uncomfortable. After the match against Newcastle at Maine Road, the former City coach Malcolm Allison met up with us at the hotel where I was staying. Many of the players and former players were there, including Law, Summerbee and Marsh. All were discussing the state of City, and I was slightly in awe. They were grumbling and grizzling about everything: the quality of players; the financial state of the club; the coaching… moan, moan. You name it, they whinged about it.

After several minutes, Malcolm spotted me listening in, came across and sat next to me. We engaged in a little small talk, and he asked how I was settling in. Then he looked back at the huddle of dissatisfied players and raised his eyebrows. He turned to me and warned, "Don't you get mixed up with this lot." I think that Malcolm realised many of the guys in the room were coming to the end of their Manchester City careers, but I was just starting mine. There's nothing more destructive in a dressing room than a clique of unhappy and vocal players, and he felt I would be better off not getting involved in all that.

On the Tuesday before Easter, after training had finished, the manager told the team that there was to be a meeting in the players' lounge, a square room with green seats and sky-blue wallpaper. When I arrived, I noticed that all the big names were there – Marsh, Doyle, Lee, Summerbee, Bell and the rest – but one face was conspicuous by his absence. Ron Saunders was missing. Peter Swales strolled in with City director Ian Niven and proceeded to go around the group and ask the players what they thought of Ron Saunders. As blunt as anything, "Mike, how do you rate Ron Saunders as a manager?" "Rodney, what's your opinion of him?"

I was astonished. I'd never seen anything like this before. Their responses were equally as blunt. Ron was overly critical, they said. He was a bully. He couldn't man-manage. He couldn't handle the players. He simply wasn't good enough for Manchester City. From the moment they laid into Ron, I could tell there was only going to be one outcome. There was a real feeling among the players that if something didn't change, then City could shortly be joining United in the relegation zone.

When it came to my turn, I was guarded. "I don't really feel qualified to comment," I said. "I haven't been at the club long enough." Thankfully, they moved swiftly on to the next person. It was a really uncomfortable feeling to be in that meeting. It felt like a military coup.

Three days later, on Good Friday, Ron was fired. His right-hand man, Tony Book, was promoted from assistant to full manager. Football is a ruthless business – and it was even back in the 1970s. I always wondered if Ron was ever given the right of reply by Swales. Somehow I doubt it. It was my first real experience of dressing room player power, something I'm sure modern-day managers are used to.

Although I saw for myself the full ferocity of the senior players' dislike for Ron Saunders, I was struggling to get my head around how such a multi-talented side like City were struggling so badly. I didn't understand the full reason for City's slump, at least not initially. When I arrived at Maine Road, Mike Summerbee had taken me under his wing, and begun to talk to me in a bit more depth about life at City. Mike owned a shirt shop in the middle of Manchester and, one day, after he managed to sell me a couple of shirts made from Swiss Voile without any discount, we settled down to a coffee and he really opened up about Rodney Marsh. He confided in me that many of the team felt that Rodney Marsh was a liability, and that his arrival in the spring of 1972 under Malcolm Allison had cost City the title. Mike's view was that Rodney, who was undoubtedly an entertaining player to watch, disrupted the flow of the team, and that he was purely interested in furthering his own interests, rather than that of the team. From my observations of Rodney during Sunderland's matches with City, I'd already begun to notice that the ball-juggling, the dummies and the feints were all pleasing on the eye, and made him a fans' favourite, but had little end product.

Rodney was injured at the time I arrived at City, and I wouldn't link up with him until the following season, but I was already forming my impressions of him. Socially, Rodney was okay in that he could dish out the one-liners and spin a good yarn, but he needed to be at the centre of attention the whole time. I wouldn't say that any of the City players openly disliked him at the time, but some mistrusted him.

He had a penchant for not wearing socks with his shoes. I didn't have a problem with that, but Rodney would always seem to make a big thing about it. It was as if he needed constant attention. If that was his fashion thing, then fine, but I didn't see why he had to make a big deal about it all the time. He'd hold court and try and dominate the conversation on any topic – politics, holidays, cars – whatever. I could see the other players glance at each other. They weren't really sure how to take Rodney. Little things about him like that began to stack up and grate on everyone, I think, me included, but it happened gradually. Mike Doyle told me that after City had lost in the League Cup final to Wolves a few weeks earlier, Rodney had stormed off, rather than do the right thing and shake hands with the Wolves players. Things like that made him look like a *prima donna*. I know that Rodney's view is that a kind of northern mafia made life uncomfortable for him at Maine Road, but my experience was always that he brought problems on himself.

I had been suspended over the Easter period when Ron Saunders was fired. It was a three-game ban which had been held over from just before I left Sunderland, when I'd got myself into a confrontation with the referee after he had sent off Bobby Kerr against Middlesbrough, and so I was sent off as well. I got permission to go back up to Newcastle and see my family during my suspension. Things didn't go well for City over that period. We got a solitary point at home to Liverpool, but were hammered away at QPR and Liverpool.

When I arrived back at the club after just a few days away, I could see how dramatically Tony Book's mood had changed. Within the space of a long weekend, it was suddenly Tony who was feeling the pressure, and his previously relaxed demeanour had evaporated. It's amazing what the rigours of football management can do to anyone. He was now personally responsible for all first-team matters, and that meant City winning games. I liked Tony, and I liked his ability to man-manage different players. He'd only retired from the playing side at City earlier that season, and had skippered the club to their triumphs in the early Seventies. His lack of managerial experience might have been a problem, but he countered that by dealing with his players as individuals, and encouraging all of us to play to our strengths. I sensed that his ex-team-mates were very respectful to him, and Tony was fine by me because he encouraged positive tactics which City crowds demand, and gave me the freedom to wreak havoc on the left. "Dennis, just go and play your natural game," he told me. I also felt that, because he'd played the game at the highest level, he knew what to look out for and was adept at making sound tactical points at half-time.

Other results went our way at the tail end of the 1973/74 season, and so we travelled to Old Trafford on the last day knowing that we were safe, but that anything less than a win for United would see them go down. It was a surreal experience, because I felt there was such an "end of empire" feeling to proceedings. United seemed unsure whether to attack us or sit back and try and hit us on the break. I played fully committed, the only way I could, but with just a few minutes left there was still no score. I felt they were giving Colin Bell too much space in midfield, and late on he floated towards the United area. I was out on the left and yelled at Colin to pass it to me so I could push forward. Instead, he went right to Francis Lee. Lee miskicked his shot and it went to Denis Law, the ex-United legend, who backheeled the ball past Alex Stepney. I've never seen a footballer look so horrified after scoring a goal. He virtually went into a stupor afterwards and, although Colin Bell slapped him around the face to try and get him to raise a smile, Denis, once the King of the Stretford End, was in his own little world, realising that United's relegation was now confirmed. I was just delighted that we'd won at Old Trafford, one of the world's most famous grounds, but I could tell that the atmosphere was simmering so I didn't celebrate too hard.

Within a few seconds, I was running for my life to the tunnel when some United fans invaded the pitch. Hordes of young fans with long hair, flares and stack-high boots made a beeline for us, and for a while it seemed like it might turn nasty. Denis, his league career over, simply disappeared after the match. He didn't even come back to the dressing room, he just vanished. The rest of us clambered back onto the team bus, and the driver took the longer route back to Maine Road through town, much to the delight of the players. Me being new around the place, I didn't understand why he'd done that, but pretty quickly I got the message. Every time we drove past someone wearing red scarves or rosettes, the driver beeped the horn and everyone laughed at them. In those days, there were no blacked-out windows to hide behind, so United fans knew exactly who was tormenting them, and they replied with V-signs and banged the side of the bus. The game confirmed the fact that City were top dogs in Manchester, as they had been for a few years by then, but our final league position – we ended up in 14th place – was hardly a reason for wild celebration.

Even though City's indifferent form in the league had been a massive concern for us, I was called up by the England manager, Alf Ramsey, to the Football League representative squad to play against the Scottish League at Maine Road a few weeks after I joined City. He selected me to join a very strong team which included my former Sunderland team-mate Colin Todd (Derby County), Ray Clemence (Liverpool), Trevor Brooking (West Ham), Stan Bowles (QPR) and Roy Macfarland (Derby County). Here is a classic example of how perception counts for everything in football. I was still exactly the same player I had been at Sunderland. I hadn't been at City long enough to develop yet, but now outsiders *perceived* me as a bigger name, and a more proficient player. It's how football works, and it's loaded against players at smaller clubs. If you really want to push yourself forward and gain international honours and be noticed, it helps massively if you play on a bigger stage. My profile, within a few weeks, had become that much greater, simply because turning out for City in the First Division put me in the spotlight more than playing for Sunderland in Division

Two. We won the game 5–0 and I scored my first goal at Maine Road from the penalty spot. During training Alf had asked for a volunteer to take penalties, and my hand shot up as I had taken all the penalties at Sunderland and always enjoyed the challenge. It was a delight to score in front of the supporters at my new football "home".

I then spent the summer decorating our new house in Sale (incidentally, all that running up and down ladders meant that I got myself down to my lowest-ever playing weight of 10st 12lb) and watching the 1974 World Cup. How quickly life had changed for Joan and I over those last few months, and I couldn't wait for the start of the new season.

CHAPTER SEVEN

THAT GOAL

Bit by bit, Tony Book began to build his squad at City. I hoped that he was gradually assembling a team which might win the league, but that is never easy, because what often happens is that one exciting new player comes in and another experienced professional leaves. So out went Francis Lee to Derby County, and Book nabbed Asa Hartford from West Brom, which I thought was a fantastic deal. Asa was a combative Scot. Direct and tenacious, he added a lot to the team in terms of quality and aggression, which we definitely needed. Later in the 1974/75 season, Joe Royle signed from Everton to add a more potent physical threat up front and, although slow to settle initially, he became a terrific target man for me.

I felt that it would probably be a three-year project for Tony to build a title-winning squad. The balance still wasn't right. Although our home form was outstanding – we only lost to Derby and Carlisle at Maine Road – away from home we were shocking. We actually topped the table in mid-September, but our away form was our Achilles heel. It was difficult, because although our displays showed a marked improvement on the previous season, players like Mike Summerbee and Alan Oakes were coming to the end of their City careers, and it was clearly a period of transition at Maine Road.

At the beginning of the campaign, the fit-again Rodney Marsh came back into the team as our main striker, and I played alongside him for the first time. I now saw for myself how much he unbalanced our team. He wasn't an out-and-out goalscorer, and we needed a target man alongside him. Sometimes, he could look the part, especially when the opposition gave him licence to roam. On the first day of that 1974/75 season, in blazing sunshine against West Ham, we won 4–0, with Rodney scoring a brace, and I weighed in with one of the others. On days like that, you'd think Rodney was a world-beater and a leading talent. But in my opinion it was an illusion. Even on a day like that, he frustrated me. My job, and that of Colin Bell, was to storm forward and use our pace to damage the opposition. Rodney slowed us up massively. West Ham weren't known for being defensively solid, so he could show-boat to his heart's content, performing a few of his circus tricks. I watched on with bemusement as he dummied and juggled the ball. The crowd loved it, but I was frustrated as I could now see for myself what Mike Doyle told me about Rodney was true.

It concerned me that he was our main front man and, as the season wore on, his inconsistency frustrated me more and more. I saw that he often did little that was effective with possession, and his self-indulgent tricks were often in areas of the pitch where he couldn't inflict any damage. When the conditions suited him, he could delight the crowd, but the opposition knew that if they stuck tight to him like limpets he would disappear from games. So in the really big games, when it came to the crunch, I felt that he would invariably let you down. He was consistently inconsistent, and I felt that he was letting down our supporters. I know that these are strong words because Rodney remains a big City hero, and I risk incurring the wrath of some fans who are reading this, but I felt that he was very much a square peg in a round hole. His style didn't suit City, and I couldn't understand why the club had bought him.

As a senior professional at the club, I felt that Rodney should have set the younger players at City a better example. Micky Horswill became part of Rodney's social circle and began to enjoy the night life a bit too much. Rodney was a big part of the Manchester scene, and Micky was in awe of him because, if nothing else, Marsh was extremely charismatic. It was to the detriment of Micky's football career, no question. He only played a handful of matches at City, and never broke through as he should have done.

He lost his focus, and ended up at Plymouth. He could have done so much better, and I know that we all make our own choices in life, but I do feel that Rodney held a lot of sway over Micky and should have been encouraging him to be more professional. However, I was aware that I was still very much the new kid on the block, and that until my form became more consistent I was in no position to preach to others how to live their lives, or voice my concerns to Tony Book. Rodney and I never had words, as such, but he knew, and I knew, that there was a tension between us. Glances during games. Hands being thrown up into the air – mine mostly – as our possession broke down. The tension simmered for the next year or so, before I had finally had enough of Rodney.

In total contrast to Rodney's attitude was Joe Corrigan, who when I signed was virtually a joke figure in the squad. He looked terribly overweight and was the butt of many supporters' jokes after a game against West Ham in the early 1970s when he kicked the ball from his penalty area and Ronnie Boyce knocked it straight back into the net as Joe was getting back to his goal. By the time I arrived at City, his approach to training was relentless. Joe would warm up with the rest of the squad and then go off with Glyn Pardoe for a one-to-one session – Glyn was an ex-City star on the coaching staff who had become one of the first specialist goalkeeping coaches. These sessions were extremely intense, and Glyn would put Joe under extreme pressure, practising all sorts of goalkeeping techniques. Joe eventually cemented his first-team status and went on to represent England in a long and successful career, as well as later becoming a goalkeeping coach himself for many top clubs including Liverpool and West Bromwich Albion. A Manchester boy, Joe was very similar to Mike Doyle in many ways. All that mattered to Joe was City winning matches, and it was great to see his confidence increase throughout the 1970s. I always felt that a local boy in any team is worth their weight in gold, as it increases the affinity that supporters have with the players.

My form at the time was steadily improving. Against Arsenal in October, I scored twice in our 2–1 win, but ended up with an ankle injury which still gives me trouble me to this day. The ball came back off the bar and I stole in with a header, but their goalkeeper, Jimmy Rimmer, landed on my leg and damaged my deltoid ligament. A couple of days later, it was so swollen that I thought it must be broken, but as it turned out I only ended up missing three matches. Without doubt, the highlight of that season was my hat-trick against Newcastle on Boxing Day in a 5–1 win. I loved playing in the free role on the left that Tony Book had given me, and the huge Maine Road pitch meant that Colin Bell and I could get away from opponents in the attacking area of the pitch. That might well have been the reason for our fantastic home form, and that day against Newcastle, every time I received the ball I seemed to rip through their defence. I scored two from outside the box, and rounded things off with a penalty.

I always used to play well against Newcastle. Subconsciously, I suppose a little voice at the back of my head must have been reminding me, "Dennis, they rejected you as a teenager," but in all honesty I never wanted to punish Newcastle any more than I wanted to punish any team. I'm told that was the afternoon when fans on the Kippax first chanted the song, "Dennis Tueart, King of all Geordies," but in truth I don't remember hearing it. I was probably more concerned with what my dad and brother would say to me when they saw me after the game. They were fairly tight-lipped and not best pleased, it's fair to say.

I was feeling very positive about the future. Back in September of 1974, I'd been invited to London's plush Piccadilly Hotel by England boss Don Revie, along with 80 other leading English players. The ex-Leeds manager, who'd taken over from Alf Ramsey that summer, wanted to set out his vision to established internationals like Kevin Keegan and Alan Ball, and hopefuls like me who wanted to become an established part of the international scene. I was utterly thrilled to be asked to attend. Of course, it was partly off the back of my good performance for the Football League at Maine Road back in May, but it was further proof that moving to City had raised my profile. This get-together was the start of the so-called "Revie Revolution", the blueprint which would supposedly take England to the 1978 World Cup. The newspapers labelled the 80-strong group '£20 million worth of talent', but when I walked into the meeting room that day and saw the sea of faces – not all of whom would ever get near the England squad, as it turned out – I had mixed feelings. There was some superb talent in the room, like Kevin Keegan and Peter Shilton, players I dreamed of playing alongside. And there were also some players who I thought had no real chance of making it at international level.

I felt that the gathering was a Revie riposte to the generally held consensus that Alf Ramsey stayed loyal to his trusty lieutenants for too long. Revie wanted to come across as more transparent, more meritocratic in his work. But I felt this get-together pushed that philosophy a bit far. There were guys there like Alan McDowell and Graham Paddon from West Ham, and Alan Stevenson and Paul Fletcher from Burnley. Obviously good professionals, but with the best will in the world they weren't going to be at the forefront of any World Cup squad. I agreed that Revie needed a gameplan to try and sort out the mess left over from England's failure to qualify for the '74 tournament, but the message would have been better delivered had it been targeted at a core of maybe 30 or 40 leading players. Revie gave false hope to many of those present. The fact he called in so many players seemed to emphasise the fact that from the outset he was unsure of who should really be in the frame, and who could lead England on to further glory. It ended up being more of a PR exercise than a real strategy for the future.

But I also noticed quickly that players tended to be divided into camps. As I'd eventually see, it was very difficult for Revie to get all the players to gel effectively, partly because he saw us so rarely. Like many of the others who stuck with their club colleagues that weekend, I spent most time with Colin Bell and Mike Doyle, but I was very interested to hear what Revie had to say. My impression of him was that he was incredibly professional and intense. Don called us "gentlemen", not "lads". I felt that he was a little nervous, though – perhaps slightly unsure of himself.

Certain things he talked about were positive developments, and forward thinking for their time. He informed us that all players would receive a £250 appearance fee, which was great in an era when players weren't on huge wages. Don, perhaps mindful of his own working-class background, was adamant that 'a man should receive a good wage for a good day's work'. He talked about the need for us to have a good diet, in an era when fry-ups and stodgy food were often the order of the day in many club canteens. He also talked about our biorhythms. Unfortunately, as soon as Don began speaking about our 'physical, emotional, and mental cycles', I got the feeling that half the room switched off there and then. That's a bit much for footballers to take on board. He spoke of our 'positive mentality' and the 'need for a good mindset' to be a top player.

I found what he had to say interesting, yet he never looked comfortable with the group. Don, who stuck firmly to a blazer, tie and trousers throughout the weekend, had us sat in rows, while he gave us a 45-minute presentation at the front. It felt like a school teacher speaking to his pupils. He was a good, charismatic speaker, and yet I noticed he had a nervous furrowed brow when he wasn't talking. I'd seen that haunted look spread across his face on the Leeds bench when his team was on television, and when things weren't going so well on the pitch. It added to my perception that Don was a bit of a worrier.

The players were not too enthusiastic about the prospect of playing bingo and carpet bowls, as Revie's players had at Leeds. It is still the subject of derision amongst several players of my era who ply their trade on the after-dinner speaking circuit. Players like Alan Hudson, Stan Bowles and Rodney Marsh thought the whole concept of grown men playing these games in the evening was ridiculous, and according to legend they later nipped out on the town for a few drinks. Whether or not that happened, I don't know – these things tend to be exaggerated over the years – but from my point of view, I'd just been given a chance to become part of the England scene and I wasn't prepared to jeopardise that, so I got on with it. I seem to recall that Colin Bell and I shot each other slightly bemused looks, but I suppose there were worse ways to try and get the players to bond. I was used to a tight-knit collection of players at Sunderland, where we'd tended to play pool or snooker in the evenings on away trips. The dynamics are different at international level, and Don couldn't suddenly expect to transpose all those "family" elements he'd deployed at Leeds over a decade or so to a collection of players from a range of different clubs. I sensed tension in the room, but everyone did as they were asked. I came away from the weekend feeling optimistic that I would soon play a bigger role for my country, but despite my excitement at being asked to attend, I did question the point of the whole exercise.

The season tailed off disappointingly, and we ended up mired in eighth position. It was a massive improvement on the previous campaign's 14th, but that year Derby won the league title with a really low haul of 53 points from 42 matches. With more attacking options, I see no reason why City couldn't have challenged for the title that year. Tony Book was aware of the weaknesses. He had already added Joe Royle and also began to push through youth-team players like Gary Owen, Kenny Clements and Peter Barnes. I was thrilled to see them emerge, because from my experience at Sunderland I knew that a local core was vital.

I always did my best to give something back to the local community, and became President of the Junior Blues, an organisation set up by City director Ian Niven and Malcolm Allison in the early Seventies. Along with several of my team-mates, we began to visit local schools, attend local events and set-up training days for local kids at Maine Road, years and years before other clubs began to forge their links with their communities. It was always in the back of my mind that those kids would be part of the next Kippax generation, and that taking for granted that 30,000-plus crowds would always roll into Maine Road was dangerous.

To be honest, I was just putting into practice all the good things that happened to me at Sunderland, when I'd enjoyed mixing with the local people. I'm convinced that those grassroots programmes which City laid down in the mid- and late-Seventies with school-children served them well when things got tough in the Eighties. It was that generation of fans who stuck with the club through thin and thinner. I also became PFA representative at City, as I had been at Sunderland, and through Joan's work with Northern Rock I set-up savings accounts for the young City players as I had done for Sunderland youngsters before. Even nowadays, few players really consider what they will do when they retire, and don't plan for the future at all. Top Premiership players earn vast sums, and yet my son Mark, who handles the personal financial planning for several leading footballers in the North West, tells me stories about a scarily increasing number ending up almost penniless when they finish in football because of the poor financial advice they received. Football gives a springboard to the rest of your life, and a successful career in the game should give players the ability to make future career decisions from choice, not necessity.

I'd completed the first part of an Administration and Recreational Management qualification at Teeside Polytechnic before I moved to City, and was always looking ahead to the future. I know that's very unusual for a footballer, and it especially was in those days, but given what had happened to former colleagues of mine, including Ritchie Pitt and Bobby Park, I knew that footballers' careers could be painfully brief.

Our form at the beginning of the following season (1975/76) was decidedly mixed. I scored two great goals against Norwich in the opening game, but the blend up front still wasn't right. My ex-Sunderland colleague Dave Watson had joined us to add some more steel at the back. Joe Royle had started to settle in to his central striker's role, but my doubts about Rodney Marsh re-emerged, especially when he didn't score until the seventh game of the season – our four-goal romp against Middlesbrough. Rodney was given every chance by Tony Book at City, he really was. He'd consult him on team affairs, and for a while even appointed him as captain. But Rodney was never captain material. As a front player, it's very difficult to get a handle on how the game is developing across the whole pitch, and I believed he was too wrapped up in himself to cajole and command the respect of the whole team. The other problem was he never seemed fully fit to me. When he first arrived at City, I heard that he used to be physically sick after training because it was so much more strenuous and demanding than at QPR. He was always slightly overweight, and hence his effective-ness was blunted. I never quite understood what made him tick. He went on to forge a career in punditry, and prided himself on being outspoken, which is how he was all the time at City. Whatever anybody said, did or thought, Rodney would do the opposite, just for effect, and that had a negative effect on our morale. It didn't surprise me when he got sacked from Sky a few years back for that tasteless Tsunami joke because, knowing him, he would have said anything for a wind-up, without thinking through the consequences.

Eighteen months into my City career, I finally plucked up the courage, went to Tony Book and told him exactly what I thought of Rodney. "He's not right for City, and he's letting down his team-mates and the fans," I told him. I'm sure that Tony knew all about the mechanics of what made a successful team, having captained City to several successes, but I felt I had to get things off my chest. I used the example of the team at Sunderland when we had a group of players with a great team unity which won the FA Cup final. We were successful because everyone fought for one another. I've never felt the need to be great friends with my team-mates off the field, but when they are committed to winning on the field they would always have my lasting respect. I finished by telling Tony that I wasn't willing to allow "a court jester to affect my career", and I wasn't overly keen on us being mired in eighth place every year either. I kept remembering what Mike Summerbee had told me, that Marsh had already cost City one league title, and now I felt he was preventing us from reaching our potential again. Tony listened to me and told me that he'd think about what I'd said.

I found out later that Dave Watson, Joe Corrigan and our captain Mike Doyle had also been to Tony and told him that something had to be done. I hasten to add that there was no mass uprising against Rodney, and all of us acted independently, which shows the depth of bad feeling which there was towards him.

I think Rodney must have guessed that I'd been to see Tony about him, or maybe someone told him. Maybe he felt aggrieved that I'd undermined him at the club. I don't know, and I don't really care. We were never each other's cup of tea, and there was no love lost between us. We both knew it. A few days after I went to see Tony, my patience with Rodney, already wearing thin, ran out. We'd beaten Norwich 6–1 in a League Cup replay at Stamford Bridge in September 1975. We'd drawn the first two matches, at Carrow Road and then at home, and so we traipsed off to West London to try and settle it. I scored a hat-trick, with two of the goals coming from the penalty spot, but it was a magnificent all-round team performance. Rodney played well that night, but then so did the whole team. After a game he was usually one of the last to get changed because he spent so much time preening himself. This time, he was out of our dressing room like greased lightning, and went up to the press room because he knew all his London journalist pals would be there waiting for him. Sure enough, the vast majority of quotes in the 'paper the next day were his. I felt that Rodney Marsh was in it for Rodney Marsh, and this was another case of him maximising a situation to his advantage.

Within a few weeks, Tony Book offloaded him, and Rodney headed across the Atlantic to the Tampa Bay Rowdies, claiming that English football had become "a grey game played by grey people on grey afternoons." A very catchy quote, and it wouldn't be long before I too felt the lure of the North American Soccer League, but I felt his parting shot was his attempt to justify his failure at City. Quite simply, he never took responsibility for his lack of consistency.

It might surprise people to know that I went to Rodney's leaving do at George Best's club in Manchester, Slack Alice. Not because I liked him, nor him me, but because I felt that by attending I'd be able to draw a line under the whole thing, and both the club and Rodney could move on from it. I didn't stay too late, and before I left I stuck my hand out to him and said, "Good luck, Rod."

"Fuck off," he replied.

His statement didn't surprise me, and it didn't overly bother me either. I certainly never lost any sleep over it.

I didn't bump into him for a while after that, but I saw him years later at one of the road shows he and George Best did in the 1990s. He didn't seem that pleased to see me, but at least he tried to inject a bit of humour into the situation by telling me, "You're a bastard, but I can't remember why, anymore." Again, his comment didn't bother me too much. "You couldn't criticise me as a player, we just didn't get on," I said. I left it at that, and walked away.

These days, Rodney's loosely defined as a Seventies "maverick", but what exactly does that mean? I always had far more respect for players like Best, Cruyff, Beckenbauer, and in the current era, Messi, Rooney and Ronaldo, who could do the unexpected, play off the cuff, but do so within the parameters of the team, and took responsibility on the pitch for their actions. I preferred my mavericks to be winners, not losers.

My actions probably did him a great favour, as his move to Tampa Bay Rowdies came at a time when the North American Soccer

League (NASL) was still developing, and showmen like him helped lift the profile of the game. He became a Rowdies star, albeit at that lesser standard, and this allowed him to enjoy many more playing years, but not surprisingly he won nothing. Professionally speaking, I hadn't quite seen the last of Rodney, and our paths would cross again in the States. What happened out there only reinforced the opinions I had formed of him at City.

Without him, we were a far more cohesive unit, and we played as a team. Our form, especially in the League Cup, probably not coincidentally, got better and better. Peter Barnes, a great young left-footed talent, began to add more width to the team, which allowed me to play more of a roving role as I had done at Sunderland, and Joe Royle now started firing in the goals.

In the fifth round of the League Cup we played Manchester United at Maine Road, and I think it was on that night that I finally understood the depth of passion for the game in Manchester. With hindsight, it was also a bittersweet night, because it was perhaps one of my best performances for City, and showed what we could become if we maintained our progress, but as it turned out one incident during the game had serious ramifications for City for the rest of the Seventies and prevented us from fulfilling our potential.

United had been promoted in the previous season and were beginning to rebuild under Tommy Docherty. But that Wednesday night, we played out of our skins. I loved the feel of midweek games in Manchester. The Kippax was swaying and heaving that night. I never used to look at individual faces in the crowd, rather the whole terrace. It made me realise that, out on the pitch, I was living and breathing every fan's dream of playing for City. I know that some City players down the years shrivelled away in front of that terrace, but I loved to rise to the challenge.

We had United under the cosh within 35 seconds. Dave Watson and Colin Bell scrambled the ball into the area, and it got stuck under my feet inside the six-yard box. My ability to play with both feet stood me in good stead. I quickly shifted the ball from right to left and flicked it home past Paddy Roche, one of the quickest goals ever scored in a Manchester derby. With respect to Paddy, he's never going to figure high on the list of great United 'keepers, although there was very little he could do about our second from Asa Hartford. A few minutes before half-time, Asa robbed Martin Buchan on the half-way line, and I found myself in a one-on-one race with Stewart Houston. I bore down on United's goal, and noticed that Roche had left a gap between himself and his left-hand post. When I was just outside the box, I unleashed a shot which arrowed past him.

The ground was in uproar, and as we trooped in three goals to the good at half-time the Kippax serenaded us with *Blue Moon*. It was an amazing feeling, and Joe Royle grabbed a fourth in the second half to send United home with their tails between their legs. After the game, I went to the Cellar Vie, a wine bistro in town, with Joan and some of our friends. The owner, Max Brown, was a City fan, and when I walked in many of the punters, who were also Blues, stood up and gave me standing ovation. If ever I needed reassurance that moving to City had been the right thing to do, this was it and now I knew what a successful City team meant to the fans. Everything. I would say that City really got under my skin that night and became a part of me. I felt that I'd now really connected with the fervour and passion of the supporters.

However, the thrill of victory would ultimately be overshadowed by the long-term consequences of an injury sustained by Colin Bell during the game. Martin Buchan had caught him square on the knee as Colin was attempting to drag the ball back. It looked fairly innocuous from where I was standing, and the initial thinking was that he'd be back within a month or so. But the tackle had snapped Colin's knee ligaments and severed blood vessels and, despite several aborted comebacks, he was never the same player again.

At 28, Colin had been the engine of the team and the instigator of many of our attacks. His injury stopped that City side going on to become a major force. We never really replaced him. Tony Book tried different options, bringing in Jimmy Conway from Fulham, and Paul Power would also play in Bell's position. In the short term, Tommy Booth was used as a quick-fix replacement from within the existing squad, but it was a big ask for a centre-half to convert himself into an attacking midfielder. Tommy did his best, but it was nigh on impossible to replace the best player in the country in that position. With Peter Barnes settling in on the left, Colin's energy and attacking prowess from midfield had enabled the team to settle into a flexible 4-3-3 or 4-5-1 formation, very much the same as I'd been used to at Sunderland. It was tragic, really, and Colin isolated himself from the rest of the team in a bid to regain his fitness over the next couple of years, and to re-build the strength and flexibility back into his knee. He pounded the streets around his home and tried to let his natural fitness do the work, but ultimately it was to no avail. I felt desperately sorry for him.

But despite Colin's dreadful injury, that win against United had still given us the belief that we could achieve big things. I scored a couple against Mansfield in the next round of the League Cup when we beat them 4–2, then we drew Middlesbrough in the semi-final, with Tottenham facing Newcastle. I had a problem, though. I'd got myself sent off for headbutting Hartlepool's George Potter, whom I'd known from my days at Teeside Polytechnic, in a third-round FA Cup clash. I'd got on with George really well – off the pitch, anyway. What happened in that FA Cup game in 1976 was ridiculous. Especially because we were 3–1 up, and I'd already scored two. I could have filled my boots if I'd stayed on, and the team went on to win 6–1 without me anyway. I'd dribbled in from the left, but the ball got away from me and I slid in again to try and regain possession. George was still standing as I was on the ground, and then he kicked me across the back of the legs while I was lying there. A red mist descended on me, and I got up and headbutted him. Down he went like a sack of spuds with a depressed fracture of the cheekbone. I remember that Joe Royle, who couldn't have seen the full incident, tried to protect me by going to the referee and saying that George had faked his injury. I had to calm Joe down and tell him it wasn't worth appealing. I knew what I'd done. The referee, Mr White, sent me off, and then he sent off George as well as he was carried off the field on a stretcher.

The press up North went nuts. So I locked myself in the house, and took the phone off the hook. The Hartlepool chairman wanted me suspended. I fully accepted responsibility, but felt it was important that people remembered that George had also been sent off, and that I was the retaliator, not the instigator. I wrote a statement that was printed in the *Manchester Evening News* apologising and expressing regret for the incident. I also wrote a letter to the Junior Blues of Manchester City expressing my apologies and telling them that what I did was not acceptable and they shouldn't copy that behaviour. I went to George in the hospital on the Sunday morning to see how he was. We'd both calmed down by then, and he was at least civil to me. Then I jumped in the car with Joan and drove up to the Northumberland coast, and we stayed in a small hotel in Bamburgh. I needed to calm down, and I accepted that I'd taken the competitive spirit a bit far. We spent a couple of days up there out of the way – no TVs or phones – just to get my head straight again.

The incident impacted on the League Cup run, because I'd gone over the top of the disciplinary points limit, so I had to appear in front of the disciplinary committee in London. I was fined, and suspended for two games. The disappointment was that one of the games I would miss would be the second leg of the League Cup semi-final against Middlesbrough at Maine Road (we had been beaten 1–0 in the away leg at Ayresome Park). Before my suspension, though, the headbutting issue blew up again in a league game at Stoke.

I'd had regular exchanges with Mike Pejic, their left-back, down the years. We were fine with one another off the field, but on it we knocked seven bells out of one another. Once, he'd grabbed my shirt as I tried to go past him, and ripped it off my back. I pulled it off, and threw it straight in his face. This time, he lunged at me with his head after we clashed, and caught me on the bridge of my nose. My eyes started to water, and I went straight down, so I got slaughtered by the press again. The papers all said I'd taken a dive, which I hadn't. Tony Book was great about the whole thing, but I was worried about another ban because that would have threatened my participation in the League Cup final, if we managed to get past Boro at Maine Road.

I couldn't bear to watch the second leg, so I sat in a restaurant in Altrincham with Joan. We had the chef listening to the radio in the kitchen and coming out and giving me updates. In the end, the boys excelled themselves, and beat them 4–0. What made it

Dad, Mum and the new arrival, me, outside Nana's house in Newcastle in 1949.

Me and my brother Paul, who later died from cot death. And that's Nana in the background.

Me in the famous black-and-white stripes of Newcastle – my first-ever football kit.

Manor Park Under-13s. The rest of the players were a year older than me and a lot bigger. (That's me, front row, second left). The teacher on the right is Bob Maddison, my football coach and a huge influence on me.

It was always my dream to score at St James' Park, but I never imagined I'd be doing it for the Sunderland youth team against Newcastle Juniors.

Aged 17, in the famous red-and-white stripes after signing for Sunderland.

A publicity photo during my early days at Sunderland.

Happy days! Mucking about with Billy Hughes, left, and Jimmy Montgomery.

Having a shot against Arsenal in the 1973 FA Cup semi-final at Hillsborough in front of the massed ranks of Sunderland fans.

Celebrating reaching Wembley in the traditional way, in the bath with the lads and a cup of tea!

Looking good! Me, Billy Hughes and Ian Porterfield doing some modelling for the Lord John fashion boutique on the King's Road.

We recorded our cup final song, *Sunderland All the Way*, at Stockport's famous Strawberry Studios, following in the footsteps of The Beatles.

Then we appeared on the same *Top of the Pops* bill as The Sweet, and here I am with their lead singer Brian Connolly, along with Billy Hughes and Ian Porterfield.

We were so relaxed before the final as Bobby Kerr introduced us to the Duke of Kent, whereas Leeds seemed tense.

We shocked Leeds by showing no fear and attacking them and they never recovered.

Leeds skipper Billy Bremner waits to shake hands, but I only have eyes for Ian Porterfield...

... and Ian clearly feels the same way as we parade the cup round Wembley!

Joan and I leave the team hotel to go to the club's celebration banquet. Unfortunately I'd left the lid of the cup in our room, so I had to go back for it later.

If you think I look tired in this picture, that's because I hadn't slept a wink the night before!

The homecoming parade, with the streets lined with Sunderland fans in their thousands, was something I will never forget.

Just me and the FA Cup!

Joan made an honest man of me just a few weeks after the cup final. Pictured with us are, from left to right, Billy Hughes and Brian Chambers, my best man Derek Foster, David Young and Ian Porterfield.

We then went on honeymoon to Miami.

It was great until we discovered the holiday wasn't quite as "free" as we'd been led to believe.

Scoring a volley against Oxford which was quite possibly the best goal I ever scored. Unfortunately I'd realised for some time, however, that the club did not match my ambition.

On March 11, 1974 I signed for Manchester City and Ron Saunders, centre, along with Micky Horswill. I had bought this leather coat a few weeks earlier for £60 which was a week's wages. It was purple!

Baptism of fire! My first game for City was v United at Maine Road. I remember Tommy Docherty screaming at his players to "break my legs". Pictured next to me is the City legend Colin Bell.

I was always good at volleying. This was against Coventry at Maine Road.

At first I didn't have a problem with Rodney Marsh, but as time went on we rarely saw eye to eye.

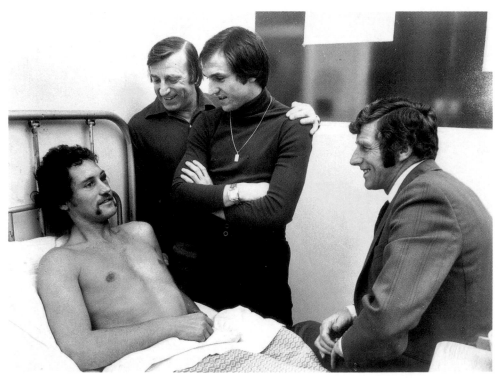

When we played Hartlepool in the FA Cup in 1976 I lost my head, headbutted their full-back, George Potter, and fractured his cheekbone. The next day I went to visit him in hospital.

My overhead kick against Newcastle in the 1976 League Cup final is probably the moment for which I am most remembered.

Scoring at Wembley was an incredible feeling.

I swapped shirts with Newcastle's Alan Kennedy after the game out of respect for my hometown club, so in all the photos I'm wearing black-and-white stripes instead of sky blue.

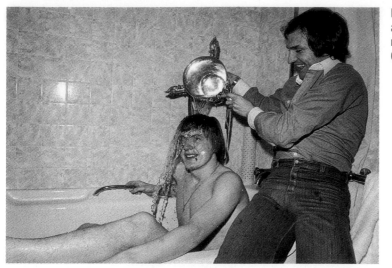

Peter Barnes gets a shower from the newly won League Cup.

The base of the cup made for suitable post-match headgear.

Tony Book, left, and I celebrate in the three-piece suits I'd sorted out for the final along with City chairman Peter Swales.

I missed the cup final parade in Manchester the day after the League Cup final because of the PFA Awards dinner – I'd been selected for the Team of the Year alongside Kevin Keegan.

In action against Jimmy Nicholl of Manchester United in March 1977.

even better was that Newcastle beat Spurs, so as a Newcastle supporter it was a thrilling prospect that we would be meeting them at Wembley.

In the weeks leading up to the final, I had so many requests for tickets from friends and relatives up in the North East – I couldn't oblige in most cases – and I knew more people in the crowd that day from Newcastle than I did from Manchester. I can't deny that it was a different sensation at Wembley second time around than it had been with Sunderland three years earlier. Several of the other lads, like Joe Royle, had played in finals for other clubs, and the fact that we had internationals at City with big-game experience meant there was a feeling that we knew what we were doing, and what was expected of us. It was still a huge game for the club, because I firmly believed that if we could win this could be a launch pad to greater things.

One day after training, Peter Swales arranged for us to go up to the players' lounge to meet up with a great City supporter, Leonard Rosenfield, to get measured up for our Wembley suits. I have always been fashion conscious and after the measure I spoke to Peter Swales and told him that I was far from impressed with the staid style of the suit Len was suggesting. "If you can do better, then go and do it," he said. I then contacted Phil Black, who had his own menswear shop in Manchester. He contacted an agent working for Castletex, a fashion house in Leeds. We selected a mid-blue, wide pin-striped three piece suit and Phil selected a shirt with a white collar along with a matching tie. I then sourced a Portuguese shoe supplier in Manchester called Zapatta and purchased boxes of shoes for the boys to try out. I must have looked strange driving around in my MGB GT sports car with show boxes stacked up so high that I couldn't see out of the back window. Still, Peter Swales was so impressed he bought a couple of pairs for himself.

We spent the week leading up to the final in the Champney's Hotel in Tring, which at that time was very unusual. We ate calorie-controlled snacks, with our great physio Freddie Griffiths monitoring our fitness levels, and we were also able to indulge ourselves in various spa treatments. There was none of the hullabaloo there had been with the Sunderland, no trips to *Top Of The Pops*, or fashion shoots. It was far more focused. This time, I was in the position where my side was expected to win the final, rather than being with the underdogs who were set up as sacrificial lambs.

You still can't beat that feeling when you come out of the Wembley tunnel, though, and the sight of the sea of sky blue still made the hairs on the back of my neck stand on end. I was as focused on the game as I had been in the FA Cup final, so much so that I missed the Newcastle fans serenading me with the song "Dennis Tueart is a poof" throughout much of the match – my brother Kevin filled me in on that particular detail afterwards!

It was a very open and attacking game. Newcastle were scoring plenty of goals at that time. They had some great players like Alan Gowling, Tommy Craig, Malcolm Macdonald, Tommy Cassidy and a young Alan Kennedy, so we knew it was going to be a real test. They were a gigantic team, who could dominate the opposition in any part of the pitch, so we worked really hard on set-pieces before the match, and on one move in particular. I think a lot of people forget what a fantastic goal our first strike was. We worked it so that Watson, Royle and Booth went to the back post for any free-kick. Peter Barnes and I went to the near post and Mike Doyle took up a position in the 'D' at the edge of the box. Ged Keegan and Asa Hartford stood over the ball, and Ged would run as if to take the free-kick. At the same time, the three big players at the back would run to the near post, drawing the tall Newcastle defenders with them. As Ged dummied, Doyle would spin round to the back post, into the space vacated by our three big players and their markers, so he would be up against Alan Kennedy. It was all planned, and it worked. Asa delivered the ball to the far post where Mike jumped and headed the ball back across the face of goal, where the three tall players, plus Barnes and I, turned to face the ball coming back across goal. Sure enough, Barnes got to the ball first and put it into the net. It was a great goal, and Peter took it really well. It was just as we'd planned it, and yet it almost didn't happen. In the heat of the moment Barnes, who was very young at the time, actually went to stand at the back post. He probably lost his head in the din that afternoon. You can see on the DVD of the match that Barnes is walking across late because I've shouted to tell him that he's in the wrong position – otherwise he'd just have been in the way and would never have had the glory of scoring that first goal.

Just before half-time Newcastle equalised from a very well-worked goal from Alan Gowling. And then, a minute into the second half, I had my moment, the moment people remember me for more than any other. It was so soon after the restart that a lot of people missed it because they were still coming back from the toilet or from getting a drink. Again, it was a real team goal. Joe Royle got possession and gave it to Alan Oakes in the centre of midfield. He played it to Willie Donachie, who was always attack-minded. He put in a high cross, and Tommy Booth, at the far post, headed it back across the area as I broke into the centre of the goalmouth. I'd gone in slightly too far and the ball came just behind me, so I had to adjust my position and perform an acrobatic overhead kick. Right off the laces, as they say. I knew I'd made good contact, but I didn't actually see it cross the line. It was only when I landed and saw the ball bouncing back off the stanchion that I realised it was in. Maybe that goal was partly down to me playing a lot of cricket, tennis and squash. I was good at judging the flight of the ball in midair. I think that if Asa Hartford hadn't grabbed hold of me afterwards, I'd probably still be running around Wembley now.

I'd always been a good volleyer of the ball. I've been told by City fans that the overhead kick I scored in an earlier league match that season against Sheffield United, when I caught the ball plum centre in midair at Maine Road, was even better. Sadly, that one was never shown on television, but my winning goal against Newcastle has been repeated many times. During my career, I scored goals from four overhead kicks. I suppose that it became my signature skill. It was always an instinctive thing. I had a split second to make up my mind to do it and, as I flipped my body horizontal, I went into my own zone. The noise of the crowd, the proximity of the opposition defenders – all that disappeared. All that counted was my own personal battle against the laws of gravity. Then, as I crashed to earth with a bump, I'd have an anxious glance at whether or not I'd been successful. I knew when I'd caught it right, though. The noise of boot on ball had to be true, and the ball had to rocket away at precisely the right trajectory and velocity. It was always a great feeling when I knew that I'd got it spot on.

Even now, fans in their 40s and 50s come up to me and talk to me about the goal. They tell me that, over the following few months at school, they practised overhead kicks and flying volleys on the school playgrounds around Manchester. I hope that I didn't inadvertently cause too many injuries. I landed on grass after the goal. Many of those kids would have landed on rock hard concrete.

After the game, when I was being interviewed by ITV, I was busy explaining how thrilled I was, and in the background all I could hear was Mike Doyle yelling, "Ask him about the two chances he missed. Ask him about those." Mike had had a bit of a go at me at half-time, and it shows what a demanding skipper he was. As I basked in my glory, he was reminding me that I hadn't played the perfect game. Mike Doyle was not someone who I was friendly with off the pitch but his desire to be a winner was obvious and something which I respected. His death earlier this year was a sad loss to Manchester City.

After the goal, Newcastle came back at us strongly, and in the last quarter of an hour we were pegged back inside our own half. The atmosphere was raucous, but there was a superb rapport between both sets of fans, and it was a genuine pleasure to play in a game in which both groups displayed such a love of football. I wanted to show my respect for Newcastle as a club, so after the final whistle I exchanged shirts with Alan Kennedy and went up to collect my medal wearing a Newcastle shirt. I was almost refused a medal. Somebody up in the Royal Box had to point out to a dignitary that it was me – City's Dennis Tueart – and not a Newcastle player.

We celebrated at the Grosvenor Hotel that evening. I rang my good friend Corny O'Donnell at Sunderland, and I reflected with him about how my career had progressed since I'd left Sunderland. Three years after I left the club, Bob Stokoe had finally taken them up to Division One. I'd now won two out of the three domestic trophies. But I wanted far, far more, and the fact that we had qualified for the UEFA Cup meant I now had the chance to test myself against Europe's finest and, as it turned out, most intimidating opponents. On top of that, all of us at City believed that the League Cup win would act as a springboard to our ultimate ambition of winning the League.

I missed the return to Manchester on Sunday and the open-top bus celebration with our fans, which I regret, because opportunities like that are few and far between. Tony Book had given me permission to stay in London and attend the PFA awards dinner as I had been selected in the First Division Team of the Year.

I never realised at that time how significant that goal would be and what it came represent for Manchester City. It was a huge privilege to score the winning goal in a Wembley final, and for a while being known as the last player to score the winning goal for City in a showpiece game was a badge of honour. Down the years, as the '76 final became more and more of a distant memory, it demonstrated just how unsuccessful City had been down the years. By the time I became a director of the club, being introduced as "Dennis Tueart, scorer of *that* goal in '76" had long since lost its lustre, and like all City fans I became increasingly frustrated at the dearth of silverware the club had secured down the years. It was strange when City-supporting dads introduced their sons to me, lads who were far too young to recall 1976, and talked them through the goal and told them who I was. The son would look at me with a mixture of surprise and occasional disinterest. I could tell what they were thinking, "That's so long ago. It happened before I was born." I became a painful reminder of how unsuccessful we'd been as a club.

For that reason I was delighted when Yaya Toure grabbed the winner for City in the 2011 FA Cup final, and when I saw the City players on their open-top bus procession through Manchester I was absolutely thrilled for all of them, as I knew from my memories how special it is to lift silverware with City. Now, I can look back on '76 with pure enjoyment, not a lingering sense of regret that the club have won nothing since. Yaya's goal lifted that curse.

CHAPTER EIGHT

BLUE MOON SINKING

At the end of the 1975/76 season, we went on tour to South Korea and Japan. Although we'd qualified for the UEFA Cup having won the League Cup, the club hadn't played in Europe for the previous couple of years, and needed the extra revenue. End-of-season tours are curious beasts because if the games aren't truly competitive the whole thing can sometimes feel like a waste of time. The '76 close-season tour was memorable for the good, the bad and the ugly of foreign jaunts with football teams, something I'd also experience when I moved to the New York Cosmos.

It took forever to get there, travelling through numerous time zones – first, we flew up to Anchorage to refuel, before jetting off to the Far East. We were due to play a South Korea national team three times and a Japan national team four times – three games in Korea and four in Japan. Those mini-tournaments are often tricky affairs, because grudges can often build between the sides. And that was certainly the case on this particular tour.

In our first game in Seoul, we stood around before the game, frying in the mid-afternoon sun, and waited around for a presentation and the national anthems. The game was a bad-tempered affair, and one of the South Korean players went in studs up on my knee – I've still got the scar today. We both fell to the ground, and when I saw three holes in my knee spurting blood I lost it and kicked him in the head and fell to the ground in agony.

There was uproar around us as the crowd exploded with rage. I was still prostrate on the ground as the referee showed him the red card, but I had to be stretchered off. My mood wasn't helped when Asa Hartford, who helped take me off the pitch, proceeded to drop me off the stretcher. There really did seem to be the threat of a riot in the stadium, and eventually two American GIs, who were there to keep order, came and escorted me to hospital in their jeep. The wound, although deep and bleeding badly, actually only required two stitches, so I was fit and ready for the next match.

I was delighted to see that my old foe was in the South Korean line-up for the rematch, and within a few minutes there was a 50–50 ball, and I went over the top on him. As he rolled around in agony, their bench emptied onto the pitch, and the Korean coaches urged the referee to dismiss me. I stayed on, but it demonstrated to me one of the perils of close-season tours. You'll often come up against a player who will do anything to get his name in lights, for good or bad reasons.

Aside from that altercation, I thoroughly enjoyed the experience of visiting Japan. We visited Peace Park in Hiroshima, and travelled from Tokyo to Nagoya on the bullet train. The sight of Mount Fuji, covered in snow at the top, took my breath away. I look back with fondness on that tour in some ways, because at least we were given the chance to sample the local culture, which didn't often happen on football tours. My old passports are littered with foreign stamps but, as a footballer, I was paid to play the game abroad, not go sightseeing.

When we arrived back in Manchester for the start of the new season, I couldn't help but think that the Blue Moon would be rising for a good few years. That Wembley victory had ended a seven-year hunt for a trophy, and now Tony Book was beginning to mould the team in the way he wanted. In the close season, Tony had brought in Brian Kidd from Arsenal. Kiddo was a target man, adept at having the ball fired into his feet, and with him playing alongside Joe Royle, who was excellent at holding the ball up, in attack we had a far more robust look. Ever since I had arrived, scoring goals with regularity had always been City's problem but now, with Peter Barnes out wide and me acting as a free runner, I felt we could match the very best. That year, I weighed in with my best-ever tally of 18 goals in 38 games – not bad for a player who wasn't an out-and-out striker. The problem was that Kiddo took a while to settle – he didn't actually get a goal for us until the 12th league game of the season in late October – and we made a slowish start, with one or two draws too many, so we were always playing catch-up with Liverpool, who were cruising at the top.

With the team unbeaten, I returned to Roker Park for the sixth league game of the season. I'd been looking forward to the game from the day the fixtures came out. Bob Stokoe had finally taken Sunderland up to the top tier the season before, and it was an opportunity for me to go back and thank the Sunderland fans.

On the eve of the game, I wrote an article for the *Sunday Mirror* warning Bob not to make the same mistake as he did after the 1973 FA Cup win and to be ambitious and improve his squad. I was delighted that they were back in the First Division, but once more they hadn't invested in a better standard of player and they were yet to win a game that season. I hoped that the fans wouldn't hold that article against me. I was only being honest, after all and, as it turned out, I was right.

There was a 37,000-strong crowd, and as ever Roker Park looked fantastic when it was full. I scored a goal eight minutes from the end when I met a right-wing free-kick from our right-back, Mick Docherty, and slid the ball in from close range. I didn't over-celebrate my goal, although, as much as I loved my time there, it was nice to go back to Roker and rise to the challenge. Four minutes later, I dashed forward on a run from the half-way line and set up Joe Royle to make it 2–0. The fans gave me a fantastic ovation at the end, and I applauded them back.

I've always had the ability to move on, and not be overly senti-mental about things. I think that you have to be that way as a footballer, and accept that sometimes it's just time to go. But I know full well that it was breaking through at Sunderland and winning the FA Cup there which made everything else in my life possible.

We had a fantastic draw in the UEFA Cup – Juventus. The game was a real eye-opener, and highlighted to me the huge differences between the European and British styles of playing the game. We pipped them 1–0 at Maine Road with a Kidd goal, but I knew that we'd be really up against it away from home. At the Stadio Communale, we walked out to an inferno, with the Roman candles belching out purple, red and orange smoke. Juventus had the core of the Italy team which would go on to lift the World Cup in 1982, with Gentile, Zoff, Scirea and Tardelli in their line up. As I walked out onto the pitch, I glanced across at Marco Tardelli. He was completely focused and hyped-up with adrenaline. I'd never seen a look quite like it on a footballer's face, and it proved to me that the level of intensity had stepped up a notch.

The Italians played their usual defensive format, with Cuccureddu man-marking me all over the pitch, and I found it very difficult to shrug off his close attention. He pulled my shirt, trod on my feet and made grunting noises throughout the clash. It was certainly over and above anything I was used to in Division One.

The referee seemed to be affected by the whole intimidating atmosphere in the stadium and we received very little protection. The whole team was battered and bruised. Our midfielder, Tommy Booth, came off with six stud marks between his shoulder blades. He'd been defending the back post at a corner, went for the ball with a standing jump and Scirea just jumped into him with his foot up. I'd never seen anything like it but that was the vicious, uncompromising side to them which had traditionally served them so well in Europe, and would provide Italy with a backbone of steel during the 1982 World Cup. We ended up losing 2–0. It was so frustrating to go out so early in the competition, and I came off feeling that we had missed a great opportunity as European football involvement was a fantastic experience.

Gradually, Kiddo's form picked up and his strike rate improved as the season wore on. We hit a purple patch during December and January. Traditionally, they had been months when City faded out of the picture, but this time the team really was firing on all cylinders. In particular, there was one match against reigning champions Derby at Maine Road which was just incredible to play in. Tony Book was excellent at telling us to go out and express ourselves. He knew that Joe, Brian and myself were experienced at this level, and he could trust us to play the kind of buccaneering style which we all enjoyed, and which the City fans lapped up. On the day, Derby's Leighton James was a thorn in our side, scoring twice, but Brian Kidd weighed in with a double, which lifted a lot of pressure off his shoulders, and with a couple of minutes left I stormed forward, latched on to Joe Royle's back-flick, and leathered in the winner from 25 yards. I loved that kind of do-or-die atmosphere, and with the new attacking options I had been given licence by Tony to switch wings if I sensed that I could probe for a weakness there. That afternoon, I operated on the right as the game wore on, and after I blasted in the winner ran straight over to the fans, gulping down that lovely cold Manchester air. They had urged us on and on, and often I found that Maine Road crowd would be galvanised when it got tight in matches.

On afternoons like that, I felt that anything was possible for City because, with the emergence of Peter Barnes, we now had four top-class attacking options – myself, Peter, Brian, and Joe. Defenders really struggled to cope with Peter and I operating in tandem out on the left, and for that Christmas period it seemed that anything I fired towards Kiddo would end up in the back of the net. We pulverised Leicester 5–0 and he scored four, all courtesy of passes from me and substitute Peter Barnes, and the press began to suggest we might even be good enough to land the title.

We only lost one home game all year, but we couldn't quite grab onto Liverpool's coattails and overtake them. They edged us out in a fantastic match at Anfield when Kiddo grabbed our only goal in a 2–1 defeat, but overall they had more bite and weight in midfield. We didn't take the initiative in enough away matches, whereas Paisley's side ground out more than their fair share of 1–0 away wins that year. Ultimately, we ended up a single point behind Liverpool. It shows what a monumental effort the team put in without Colin Bell, and I couldn't help but think that if he had been fit we would have won the title.

It was an excellent achievement, of course it was, and it suggested we were still on an upward trajectory, but I felt hollow. I felt that if we were to make that final step, and surpass Liverpool, we needed more variety in midfield as Asa Hartford was our only experienced player in the middle of the park. In our league match at Anfield, I could see that Liverpool had the bite and drive of Kevin Keegan and Jimmy Case. If we were to challenge, Asa Hartford needed another top-class player alongside him to complement his skills.

My form at City meant that I was now becoming a regular in the England squad. Don Revie had given me my debut in May

1975, as a substitute in a European Championship qualifier away in Cyprus. I only came on for the last few minutes, and didn't really have time to do an awful lot in our grim 1–0 win, but I remember saying to Peter Swales, who was part of the FA travelling committee, in the dressing room afterwards that at least now in magazines like *Shoot* and *Match*, it would say Dennis Tueart: Manchester City and England.

Don awarded me my full debut against Northern Ireland in a Home International a few days later. The game could best be described as a scrap between two tired teams, whose players knew each other very well. Nondescript is the best word for it, although of course I was thrilled to have finally broken into the international team.

I have to be brutally honest and say that my experience with England was the biggest disappointment of my football career. Colin Bell once told me that you need 10–11 games to get used to international football. He explained that there was a big difference between playing with the same group of players week by week and playing with a different group of players four or five times a season. I could see exactly what he meant, but I never came close to being given the kind of run of games he was referring to.

The two mainstays of the England side at the time were Mick Channon and Kevin Keegan. They were both top-class players, very articulate, and very influential within the camp. I felt that they had the ear of the manager. Kevin, in particular, had an aura around him, and made himself into a superstar at Liverpool through sheer guts and determination. I saw that when I was in the England squad. He was always on the go, wanting to play squash or tennis in-between training sessions, and was very knowledgeable about the game, thinking about it in a tactical manner. He could hold court, and players liked to listen to what he had to say, me included. Revie awarded a huge number of caps during his three years in charge, but he was always loath to drop Mick or Kevin. It goes like that in football. All managers have their favourite players. None of that was good news for me. Both of them were very mobile and liked to make darting runs all around the opposition half, so they needed a big centre-forward to play off, rather than somebody like me. It's why players like Stuart Pearson, Joe Royle and Paul

Mariner got their chance under Revie, and why I was always up against it. To fit in to the team, I had to play as an out-and-out winger, and that wasn't my natural style at all. I felt that my game was just too similar to Mick and Kevin's, and in the following three or four years I won only six caps, with four of those as a substitute.

So the trait which made me stand out from the crowd at Sunderland and Manchester City – the fact that I played on the left but was right-footed – turned out to be my Achilles heel on the international scene. I wasn't a wide man and I wasn't an orthodox front man – Joe Royle called me a wide striker. I was unorthodox in a sense and, although Tony Book and Bob Stokoe had been happy to give me a free role in club football, I never had that luxury with England. In that roving role up front, Mick and Kevin had their positions almost guaranteed, and Peter Taylor, Dave Thomas, Gordon Hill and Steve Coppell were ahead of me in the pecking order out wide. But it went back to the problem that I was neither a winger nor a striker, so I was always falling between two stools. In training and get-togethers, I saw myself as equal in terms of ability and, I hasten to add, was always treated that way too, but I was always up against it.

Trips with England squads did help me develop my business skills, however. A friend of mine had introduced me to an Italian casual wear supplier, L'Uomo, in Hebden Bridge, Yorkshire. So when the squad met up on England duty, I used to take an extra large suitcase packed with the latest 'in' fashion, flared trousers. Several of the players would purchase pairs, in particular, Kevin Keegan and Mick Channon. My profit for each pair would be £2, not exactly a booming business, but I enjoyed the entrepreneurial experience.

After a year's absence from the squad, Don Revie gave me my chance in a World Cup qualifier against Finland at Wembley in October 1976. I received mixed messages. Don Revie had said to me, "Go out and play your natural game" in the dressing room, but just before I went out onto the pitch his trainer, Les Cocker, said to me, "Don't forget to give us width down the left." The problem was, that wasn't my natural game. I was used to drifting in behind the forwards and spotting openings. What compounded the situation was that the left-back was a young Kevin Beattie, who was naturally a centre-back, and he was short on confidence too. Every time I started to drift into the middle a little more, he screamed at me in his broad Cumbrian brogue, "Hold your position," because he didn't want to be exposed. In the middle was a young Ray Wilkins, and I thought that I might be able to link up with him, but he kept wandering off to the right, so I was left feeling totally isolated, and I always had the impression that the other players weren't entirely clear on their roles either.

We ended up winning 2–1, but it was one of those dour matches at Wembley where the opposition arrives, shuts up shop, and embarks on a damage limitation exercise. I scored the first of my two England goals in that game. A header from Joe Royle was handled behind the line by a defender. It came out to me and I smashed it in. The referee should have given a goal when Joe's header seemed to cross the line, but he didn't. He only awarded it after I belted it in, so it was given as my goal in the end, although Joe always insisted to me it was his.

Revie made sporadic use of me for England after that. I thought that he was very easily swayed by press opinion, and because I didn't know him well enough I was never able to raise my point of view with him. It was the polar opposite to how he had behaved at Leeds, where he'd used the press allegation of dirty tricks as a way of galvanising the team, forging a "family" atmosphere and creating a fortress mentality at Elland Road. After Arsenal bought Malcolm Macdonald from Newcastle in the summer of 1976, the London press lobbied hard for his inclusion in the national side, so when it came to the World Cup qualifier a few weeks later against Czechoslovakia, I was left on the bench and Malcolm was included. The lack of continuity and consistency infuriated me.

One of the Leeds innovations that Revie introduced to the England set-up was the dossier. Les Cocker and his other scouts prepared them, and they were done with absolutely the best intentions. One of the inherent weaknesses of English football had been that coaches taught their players to ignore the opposition and simply concentrate on their own game. There was that insular belief that if you ignored the strengths of the opposition, then you would somehow be fine. At Sunderland, Bob Stokoe rarely said anything about our opposition, and although Tony Book would sometimes give us the low-down on our opponents, the general consensus was that we should focus on our own strengths. The dossiers were all part of Don's ultra-professional approach, and his scouts had clearly done their work, but I'd heard at Leeds that the dossiers sometimes backfired on him because they made his players overly concerned about who they were facing. They induced the fear factor. It's all a question of balance, and you have to manage the situation carefully. I was given my first dossier on the night before the Czechoslovakia game, and tried to read it in bed in the hotel. It was pretty impenetrable and dense. Footballers don't really have the brains or the desire to take something like that in, and certainly not the night before a game. To be honest, your brain would have to be wired in a certain way to take on board a Revie dossier, because it wasn't visual in the slightest, and most people, footballers included, need something visual to take on board a tactical break-down of the opposition. I found it all too much to absorb, and in any case when you get out onto the pitch a great deal of that sort of detail goes out of your head. A little information about what they do at set pieces can be useful, but I always struggled to see how knowing which foot a goalkeeper kicks with is of much use to anyone. With the massive turnover of players Don had, I felt that it would have been more beneficial for him to spend time working with us as a unit, rather than getting too obsessed about the Czechs.

Over the years, the Leeds players probably became used to the dossiers very much the same as in the modern era where technology is so advanced that many managers use the Prozone system and video analysis for tactical discussions. Jose Mourinho also distributes DVDs to individual players to make them aware of opposition strengths and weaknesses. Don would have been better giving us a brief verbal run down of the strengths and weaknesses of the opposition, and making it relevant to particular players in particular positions. So I needed to know about the opposition defence, but not a great deal more. I suspect most of his dossiers ended up in hotel room bins around the globe, although I kept the ones he gave me. When I was called into the squad for the World Cup qualifier against Italy in Rome in April, this was the entry in the dossier for one Fabio Capello: "Right footed. Not a lot of pace but one that just keeps getting balls off his back players and then brings others into the game with early, simple passes. Will not go past you, but always looking to play one-twos in the middle of the field and arrive in the box. Must close his area down fast." As it turned out, Capello didn't even play. Largely, I found those Revie dossiers a waste of time. It was as if he didn't understand how footballers' minds worked. It was very difficult for him to transform the family atmosphere he painstakingly built at Leeds to the England squad when he only met the players four or five times a year. I found the whole experience disjointed and, ultimately, disappointing, particularly as I never had the chance to have a one-on-one, in-depth tactical conversation with Don. That had been one of his strengths at Leeds after all.

Revie came up against other obstacles that he never had to face at Leeds. Don's relationship with the press was edgy at times. His first priority was always the players. I remember clearly what happened before the England party flew out to Cyprus for my debut game. We all arrived at Heathrow, and Don made the journalists stand to one side while the players got on the plane first. He then allocated us seats away from the press. I noticed that this didn't go down too well, particularly with Frank McGhee from the *Mirror*, a great old-fashioned journalist, who used to wear a crumpled old suit that had never seen an iron. I could see the press hacks grumbling and griping in the background, sharpening the nibs of their pens for their next articles. Under Ramsey, McGhee had been used to mixing more freely with the players, but Revie did his best to keep many of the journalists at arm's length. They seemed suspicious of his aims to make the England set-up a more professional organisation. Some accused him of being money obsessed after he struck the deal with Admiral to sponsor our kit. Others picked up on comments by Emlyn Hughes that upping our appearance money to £250 somehow sullied the whole experience of playing for your country. I could see that at times Don pushed the professionalism a little too far, an accusation made against him while he was at Leeds but, Emlyn aside, I don't recall anyone else in the squad whinging about the extra money.

I discovered that two of Don's favourites in the press corps were

Frank Clough from *The Sun* and Jeff Powell from *The Mail*. When Ramsey was England boss, he treated all football writers with disdain, so at least they all knew where they stood, but Don was known to have the ear of some hacks but not others. That built up a jealousy amongst some writers, so they tended to pan Revie and be over-critical. One of the unwritten duties of an England boss is to manage the media effectively. It was hard for Don, especially in an age when the press was already starting to become more intrusive and savage in their comments. But he would bow to pressure, and I saw this first hand before the vital World Cup qualifier with Italy in 1977. Jeff Powell had been beating the drum for QPR's Stan Bowles to play more of a role for England, and we needed a result if we were going to qualify for the 1978 World Cup. Stan was a fantastic little player, and not only was he brought back into the squad, but he also started up front. It's no criticism of Stan to say that he was virtually anonymous during the whole match. England started quite well, and I was behind Don on the bench when he turned to Les Cocker and said, "I think I might have chosen the right team here." We lost 2–0, but over 90 minutes Italy murdered us, with the core of the team coming from Juventus, the team that had hammered us in our UEFA Cup clash a few months before. It was never going to be Stan's game, because he liked space, and the Italians stuck to you like limpets. I thought that surely, after all those games Leeds had played in Europe, Don would have known that. I certainly did, and judging by the furtive comments that were shooting around on the substitute's bench that night, so did everyone else. So for the second time in the 1970s, England missed out on the greatest show on earth, and I couldn't help but wonder whether, if Revie had stuck to his instincts and developed a more settled side, the outcome might have been different.

In the summer of 1977 I was invited to join the England tour of South America. If the game away against Juventus in Italy had been intimidating at times travelling to Argentina felt downright dangerous. After we arrived at Ezeiza airport, we were met by an armed guard to escort us to our hotel. At that time, the military junta controlled Argentina, and grim-faced soldiers waving guns around shepherded us onto the coach, and lined the route on the way into Buenos Aires. If any motorists strayed into the path of the motorcade, they had the side of their cars kicked by the motor-cycle outriders. Inside our city hotel it was very similar, as armed guards patrolled the corridors. At the time, the Junta was trying to crush the activities of Marxist guerrillas and, with the World Cup only a year away, I'd imagine that they didn't want any unpleasant incidents involving high-profile teams who were expected to qualify.

I was a non-playing substitute during our matches against Uruguay and Argentina. From my vantage point on the bench, I was able to pick up fairly heavy hints that the home fans weren't too fond of the England team. They hadn't forgotten or forgiven the English for the manner of their defeat in the 1966 World Cup finals, nor Alf Ramsey's claim that they were "animals". Now, they turned the tables on England, yelling "Animals, Animals" at us whenever they could.

I later heard that the fans also shouted "Pirates, pirates" in Spanish. It was a reference to the fact that Britain controlled the Falkland Islands, which Argentina believed were rightfully theirs. This was four years before the war with Argentina, and to be honest I'd not even heard of the Falklands at that time, but this was a pretty clear indication that the Argentines felt very passionately about them.

Guards ringed the pitch at La Bombonera stadium when we faced Argentina, who were short of their European stars like Mario Kempes. Their clubs didn't release them in time for the tournament, but Argentina had a strong side nonetheless. The fans were bubbling. Fireworks were let off. Rocks were thrown. Bottles rained down pitch-side. Trevor Cherry tackled Bertoni. He went in hard but fair, and Bertoni got up and knocked Trevor's front teeth out. There was blood everywhere, and the referee sent both men off.

It was madness, and the crowd was in total uproar. Yet, even through the carnage, I could see the fundamental weakness in Revie's team. He played Mick Channon and Stuart Pearson up front, and neither were a direct threat to the Argentines. The team was quite short, as well. I felt that, quite simply, there wasn't enough of a physical presence in Revie's squad to trouble the world's best, and so it proved. Unbeknown to us, Revie, who joined the tour late, had actually been busy sorting out his future and had struck a deal with representatives from the United Arab Emirates to take over their national team if England failed to qualify for the 1978 World Cup. We didn't qualify, Revie disappeared to the Middle East, and I realised that we would not play in a World Cup tournament until I was almost 32. I didn't know it at the time, but the South American tour marked the end of my England career. It also spelled the beginning of the end of my first spell at City, and the problem was manifesting itself virtually right under my nose.

City chairman Peter Swales was part of the travelling executive group on that tour, and at the hotel we were staying at in Rio it was obvious that he was talking business with Mick Channon. Peter seemed to tap up Mick for all he was worth to get him to come to Manchester City. In fact, all of us pestered Mick about whether he'd agreed terms. Sure enough, by the start of the 1977/78 season he'd joined City. Now, we had me, Joe Royle, Brian Kidd, Peter Barnes and Mick vying for three or four places depending on Tony Book's tactics. There's nothing wrong with competition for places, but I could tell that this wasn't going to work.

When we reported back for pre-season training, Tony Book and new coach Bill Taylor met with several of the players. He told us that he wanted to change the style from a fluid 4-3-3 formation to a fixed 4-4-2, which meant that I would become a static wide man. That, I felt, was totally against my strength of drifting in and beating defenders with my free movement. I was honest with Tony when he asked for my opinion.

"Great," I said. "Loads of crosses and no goals."

There was nothing wrong with my left foot – I could control, pass and shoot with it, but not really dribble, which is what I would now have to do as a winger. I'd always played in a flexible 4-3-3/ 4-5-1 formation. At Sunderland, we'd been successful with Vic Halom, Billy Hughes and I playing off one another, and at City, we'd won the League Cup with Peter Barnes, Joe Royle and I blending well together. This was now bound to change, because Mick Channon had made his name as a free front runner at Southampton, and Tony Book was hardly likely to force his new signing to change his style of play. I knew that I would never have such a roving role again, because that freedom would now be granted to Mick. None of the front men could understand why Tony shifted things around. Not even Mick, who seemed bemused by the tactics.

Mick was a great lad, whom I'd got to know on England duty. He was always forthright, and willing to express his opinion on anything in that Hampshire brogue of his, and that strength of personality stood him in good stead when it came to playing for England. Revie liked Mick because he could talk tactics with him, and because he was a big personality. At City, when he didn't have his nose in *Sporting Life,* preparing to place his bets, he got on very well with the players, Our reservations about his signing were nothing personal against him – Mick himself admitted to me that he couldn't really understand why City had bought him. It had only been a couple of years since we had sold Rodney Marsh, another big-name player who messed up the team's tactics, and now we had Mick who, although nothing like Rodney as a person and who was far more productive on the pitch, just didn't fit.

I began the season like a house on fire, determined to prove that I was worth my place in the team. In mid-August, I scored a hat-trick away at Villa. One of the goals was yet another overhead kick, and I began to think that maybe the new tactics might work out okay. Perhaps I would be able to adjust, and it wasn't as if I had been unsuccessful for City. But my goals came from central striking positions. Although I generally did as I was told and stayed wide, I would cut in if the opposition defence gave me space, and I could sense that goals were there for the taking. Tony was never going to tick me off after scoring a hat-trick, and before New Year I scored two more against Chelsea, and Newcastle on Boxing Day.

But already my injury problems had begun. Against Chesterfield in the League Cup in late August, I pulled my hamstring, missed a few games and missed an England call-up. When I was fit again, I didn't immediately win back my place in the first team, and I would never be selected for the England squad again. When I came back into the side, I produced the goods, but I was being left on the bench rather too often for my liking.

I never fell out with Tony Book, but in the November I told him bluntly, "If you don't want me at City, I need to go." I was 28, I knew I had the best years ahead of me, and was in no mood to sit around warming the bench. I was in a pretty foul mood about the whole thing, and I went back to Tony in November and had a chat with him which lasted about three minutes – two to ask him for a transfer, and one for him to agree.

By now, Joe Royle was also being left out of the team. It was all very strange. The previous season, Joe, Kiddo and I had grabbed over 50 goals between us, but by Christmas Kiddo was playing on the left-hand side of the midfield and Joe and I were on the transfer list – all to fit in Mick Channon. City's league form was fluctuating between the great and the downright awful. It was all so frustrating. That was now twice in a decade where, with the team seemingly destined to become a massive force, they'd failed to buy the right players at the right time, tinkered with a system which worked, and blown it. It would be another 30 years before they were anywhere near the running to win the league again.

I had just signed a new contract, and I suppose I could have stuck it out at City and seen how it went. But then I could also have done the same at Sunderland four years earlier, and I would have regretted it. I had known when the time was right to leave Roker Park, and now it felt right to leave Maine Road, too. Joan and I were very happy in Manchester, but at that time we didn't have children, so we could be flexible about where we lived. But I had absolutely no inkling about how far afield my football career was about to take me.

After my transfer request had been accepted, Ken Adam, an agent, contacted me to say that the New York Cosmos were interested in buying me, but also that they didn't need me until February. Pele, Franz Beckenbauer and Carlos Alberto were all there, and the profile of football in the USA was on the rise. The quality of the NASL had improved dramatically over the previous couple of years, and a number of top English players, such as Trevor Francis and Charlie George, were going over there in the summer to play during our off-season.

Football Focus were doing regular features on football Stateside, and my interest was certainly piqued. The prospect of experiencing life in New York was a major draw, too. This was the era before cheap transatlantic travel, and weekend city breaks, and the thought of playing in this famous city I'd only ever seen in films and on television struck me as being a real adventure. My mind was awhirl, and I thought of little else other than playing for the Cosmos alongside some icons of the world game, but I couldn't say anything because they didn't need me until their pre-season.

Peter Swales still did everything he could to persuade me to stay at City, and even asked me if I would consider playing over there in the summer and coming back for the English season. But I always knew if I was going to do anything I would have to give it 100 per cent. Peter had agreed to tell me about any other definite approach that was made. Despite the interest from Cosmos, conventional wisdom and practice suggested that I would stay in England. No other First Division player had yet opted to ply his trade full-time in the States, and I still thought that the whole Cosmos thing might end up pie in the sky.

Just before Christmas, City agreed terms of £250,000 with Manchester United, meaning I had permission to go and talk to Dave Sexton, their manager at the time. I met Dave and the United secretary, Les Olive, at Tony Book's house in Sale to discuss a transfer. Dave told me I'd replace Gordon Hill and said he was looking to buy Gerry Francis from QPR. I ended up saying I'd think about it and get back to him the next day. I was really in a quandary – Joan and I would not have had to move home, but moving to United from City would be a massive and controversial decision.

That evening I was playing in a pro-celebrity squash match at Carriages in Droylsden. I was standing in for John Cleese, who'd pulled a calf muscle, and I was up against Leonard Rossiter. I'd originally just been going to watch with Bill Taylor, my good friend and City's head coach, who obviously knew where I'd been. When I met him at the squash centre he asked how it had gone, and I told him I was thinking it over. Bill asked me to answer two questions:

"Do they have a better team than us?"

"No, but they are looking to rebuild.

"Are they offering more money?"

"Yes, they are, but only a little."

Money wasn't the issue anyway. There was the added appeal of staying in Manchester, but Bill, very sensibly, questioned what I was gaining by moving there. I had to agree with his verdict: not a lot.

I called Dave Sexton from the reception of the sports centre and called the deal off. As I put the receiver down, I suddenly thought,

'What if the Cosmos don't come in for me after all?' I felt a bit panicky. Then Rossiter absolutely hammered me on the squash court. He lured me into his trap. He kept giving me those world-weary looks associated with his characters in *Rising Damp* and *The Fall And Rise Of Reginald Perrin* and had me in stitches. But he was a squash fanatic and knew when to mess around, and when to focus. That night, perhaps understandably after events that day, I lost my focus. So I got slaughtered at squash by Rigsby, the tightest landlord in Britain.

To confuse me further, I got a phone call from a journalist friend, Vince Wilson, from the *Sunday Mirror*, who asked me if I'd take a phone call from a friend of his – Brian Clough. In fact, it was Clough's assistant Peter Taylor who called the following evening and he asked if I might fancy a move to recently-promoted Nottingham Forest, who had made a barnstorming start to life in the top flight, and how much money I wanted. The plan was that I would replace Martin O'Neill in the Forest midfield. I told Peter that I'd consider Forest, but asked if I could have time to think as I had already had a contact from the Cosmos. He was very under-standing and promised me that he would call back the following evening.

I'd also heard that Eintracht Frankfurt, Anderlecht and Juventus were interested, and there were rumours about Aston Villa, managed by the man who bought me for City, Ron Saunders, coming in for me. That 24 hours was really difficult, but the American option was the one that still appealed to me the most.

When Peter Taylor phoned I told him the Cosmos move really excited me as it was a completely new challenge. I do occasionally think that if I'd joined Forest I might have won a League Championship medal and possibly even a European Cup under Clough and Taylor. It would definitely have been an experience.

As Cosmos representatives began to firm up the offer and thrashed out a £235,000 deal, I saw out my time at City and reflected on the last few years at Maine Road. Tony Book had done much to rebuild the team, but I firmly believed that if he'd signed a midfielder in the Graeme Souness mould instead of Mick Channon a few months earlier, City could have been genuine title contenders. It's decisions like those that can alter a club's destiny, and City tailed off in fourth place in 1978, 12 points behind champions Nottingham Forest. I still think it was a massive opportunity wasted. It would be 33 years before City equalled that achievement, and those fans who cheered me from the Kippax every week later endured some serious heartache. As my sons were growing up they were given some grief at school in Hale on account of who their dad was, and the fact they were City fans. It wasn't always pleasant for me to hear, but all I ever said to them was that it was character building. Life isn't always easy, and supporting City over the years, with all the ups, downs and false dawns, certainly hasn't always been straightforward.

My last goal for City came at Elland Road on January 7, 1978, against Leeds United in the third round of the FA Cup. The game was played out in a raucous atmosphere, in front of 38,000 screaming fans. I scored with a looping header, and Leeds defender Gordon McQueen punched his own goalkeeper, David Harvey, in the face after they argued about which of them should have dealt with the corner, and the referee had to take both sets of players off for a few minutes when Leeds fans invaded the pitch in a bid to get the game called off. This was the English game at its most raw and, in some respects, its least palatable. Eventually we trooped back on, and we won 2–1. After that City agreed to leave me out of games so I would stay fully fit in the lead-up to the impending Cosmos move. The biting cold, grey British winter would soon be a world away.

CHAPTER 9

REACHING FOR THE STARS

The Cosmos move gathered pace throughout January 1978. The football side of things at the club was run by two Turkish brothers, Ahmet and Nesuhi Ertegun. If ever I needed some evidence that playing in New York would be a bewilderingly new experience, I got the first inkling when Joan and I were invited down to the Erteguns' palatial London residence, a huge Victorian house, with various rooms off the main hallway. Joan and I were shown into one of the rooms to wait for Ahmet. We were then invited to meet him and as we moved into the hallway, members of a pop group passed by.

The New York-based brothers, who were the sons of a well-known Turkish diplomat, were serious big hitters in the music industry. Ahmet had been President of Atlantic Records, and during the 1960s he had worked with top acts like Otis Redding and Aretha Franklin. A few years previously, he'd discovered Led Zeppelin, and he was friends with Mick Jagger. In 1967, the Erteguns sold Atlantic Records to Warner Brothers for $17 million, and a few years later, with Steve Ross of Warner Communications, they co-founded their "dream team", the New York Cosmos.

I knew this was a whole different ball game. Here was a seriously big international media mogul, who had been prepared to invest astronomical sums to build a club up from scratch and lure the very best to play for the Cosmos. It was a complete contrast to what I was used to at City, where local boy made good, Peter

Swales, ran the show. It was on a different scale altogether, and I was buzzing with nervous energy as I went in to meet Ahmet.

As expected, he was a very positive and driven character. He hammered away at me about my ambition, "What do you expect from your move to the Cosmos?" "What can you offer the team?" "What can you bring to us?"

It turned into quite a grilling, but that didn't put me off because I wanted to know that the Cosmos was a professional outfit, and not just obsessed with showbiz and glitz.

"I'm 28, in the England squad, and at the peak of my career," I responded.

I thought my omission from the England squad due to injury was temporary, but nagging away at the back of my mind was the thought that moving to the States could leave me out on a limb. Out of sight, out of mind, in effect, and I needed some reassurance that this was the right move for me. So I turned the tables: "Well how ambitious are you? Where do *you* see the Cosmos going over the next few years?"

I'm not sure he quite expected me to fire queries back at him, but I needed to know. I was to be the first current international from any of the major football nations who was going to play full-time in the USA, so I had to be totally sure. He told me that he wanted to keep the Cosmos at the pinnacle of the game in America, and continue to attract the best talent to the States. Ahmet won me over, and we shook hands on a three-year deal which was worth around £1,500 a week. The same logic applied to leaving City as it had to leaving Sunderland. Even though money is always an important issue for a footballer, the whole adventure was becoming increasingly more exciting, and that was what attracted me. The Cosmos agreed a fee with City for £235,000, which the City board was more than happy with, but Peter Swales continued to try and persuade me not to go. He was convinced that soccer in the US was doomed to failure. 'There's no culture, no football heritage out there,' he told me. "Until NASL clubs nurture their own talent, rather than importing expensive, ageing foreign imports, they won't get it right."

Time has shown that Peter certainly had a point, but after my meeting with Ahmet my mind was made up.

A few days later Ahmet's other brother, Nesuhi, and the Cosmos representatives came to my advisors' offices in Deansgate to finalise my personal terms. They were formidable guys: big and brash, bandying around all sorts of American jargon about "optimum targets" and "positive vibes". We sat on opposite sides of the table, and it felt like sitting in the White House facing the President and his senators.

The Americans met with my great friend and adviser Reuben Kay, who'd also acted as a mentor for Bobby Charlton. Reuben was paralysed down one side – during the war he fought at the famous battle at Monte Cassino and was later shot in the head and wounded at Lake Trasimeno, Italy, in 1944. He was a really driven person who never let his condition affect his professionalism and had a fantastic track record in advising footballers over contracts in an era when most players wouldn't even have considered using an advisor to help them in such matters. He was ahead of his time, and had been involved in starting up the footballers' pension scheme, when he was approached by the PFA secretary, Cliff Lloyd, who knew that he was the accountant to many of the Manchester United players. I'd been introduced to Reuben by his son, Howard, some years before. To add further weight to the negotiations, Reuben brought along a former tax inspector turned lawyer from Leeds called Leslie Morris.

It really was a culture clash in there. Both Leslie and Reuben were softly-spoken, pin-stripe-suited English gentlemen, who you might have presumed would be sand blasted by the Cosmos crew. But they did a fantastic job on my side of the table and we finally agreed the three-year deal.

In advance of the talks, I'd tried to gather as much knowledge as I could from players who had experience of the US game. Willie Morgan, who'd played for United in the Seventies, had also turned out for Minnesota Kicks for a while. He advised me that one thing I should try for was a "no cut" deal. Over there, clubs could farm you out to another team whether you agreed or not. I didn't like the sound of that, and pushed hard for that "no cut" clause, but I never got it. It made me aware, even before I went out to the States, that players were effectively slabs of meat, there to be marketed and traded if necessary.

Once the deal was done, I had to go through the process of applying for a visa. To comply with US tax requirements, I had to sell all my UK assets, which meant selling the share of my magnolia-walled house in Gosforth, which I'd bought with Sunderland team-mates Dave Young and Derek Foster in the early Seventies for £4,500 and rented out ever since. To qualify for the visa, I had to convince the US authorities that I had the status of a star player in the UK, and that I had skills which were 'different from what they already had.' These days, with football such a global game, all clubs have to do would be to contact the relevant TV companies, or even go on YouTube for the evidence, but I had to be a bit more creative. It was lucky that I had kept my scrapbook, as Alan Brown had recommended at Sunderland, and I was able to send them press cuttings, including ones from the game when we beat Aston Villa 4–1 and I'd scored a hat-trick back in the August. One of the headlines in those cuttings was 'Dennis The Midlands Menace'. Some of the New York press would later latch onto the nickname, and it stuck.

The officials at the US Embassy were happy with what they saw, and I eventually got my visa. I was officially a non-resident alien.

Once everything had been agreed I went back to Maine Road to say my goodbyes. All the lads wished me well. Big Joe Corrigan even asked if there was room for him in my luggage. I went to the famous Manchester City social club to say my goodbyes to Roy and Kath Clarke who had looked after me on many occasions, whether it was for a lunch after training, City club social events or the fantastic monthly Junior Blues meetings with all the young City fans. I had even dressed up as Santa Claus for the players' children's Christmas Party. I have to admit that after leaving the social club for the last time there were tears in my eyes.

After all the formalities were finished in Manchester, I had to travel to New York to sign the deal and be introduced to the press. During the negotiations in England, I'd never even seen or spoken to the Cosmos coach, Eddie Firmani. All I knew about him was that he'd been born in South Africa and played for Charlton and Italy. It seemed bizarre to me. At that time in England, the manager was the frontman of the club, who usually took the lead on transfer negotiations himself. The US model was different in many ways, as I would soon see for myself.

I also had to go for a medical on Harley Street in London – another sign of the Cosmos's absolute professionalism – and the night before we flew out to New York, Joan and I stayed at the Dorchester, thanks to Reuben and Leslie. The decor and the ambience of the famous hotel took my breath away. Opulent wasn't the word. Reuben knew the chef, and I remember him preparing his favourite pudding, crème brûlée. Coming from the East End of Newcastle, I couldn't even have spelt crème brûlée, let alone have the faintest idea what it tasted like.

Flying on Concorde the next day was something else, especially when the horizon turned purple and I saw MAC2 click up on the screen to indicate that we had flown through the sound barrier. It was all over in just three hours and 18 minutes. Barely enough time for me to enjoy my meal on those fine white-boned china plates. It was all paid for by the Cosmos.

It turned out that we were lucky to have taken off at all, because there was the mother of all snowstorms at JFK Airport. It was only when we landed that I realised just how severe winters can be in New York. As we taxied into the terminal, the snow was piled high on either side of the runway, like the parting of the Red Sea.

The first night Joan and I were there, we decided to go for a walk through Manhattan. It was everything we had dreamed of, and more. We ended up with cricks in our necks from trying to look at the top of the skyscrapers, and the bright lights of Times Square just took my breath away. The snow was heaped on the sidewalks, and steam was billowing up from the subway, just like you see in the movies.

I knew that there was no indigenous football culture in the USA, but with the likes of Pele and Beckenbauer in New York, I assumed there must be some interest. As we were walking, a yellow cab sidled up alongside us, the driver rolled down his window and yelled at me in his New York drawl, "Hey, Tueart, are you signing for the Cosmos?" It was quite surreal, and suggested that the media circus had already swung into action.

That night, Reuben, who had also flown over, along with Leslie, had booked a table at the famous 21 Club where Pele had first been introduced on signing for Cosmos. The following morning, we all went to the Cosmos's offices at the Warner Brothers Building in the Rockefeller Plaza. Reuben and Leslie had a meeting to sort out the legal and financial arrangements. They set me up with an account in the Chemical Bank, based in Guernsey, where all my salary was to be paid. My wages, as with all the foreign players, were to be paid by Warner Communications and not the Cosmos organisation. As the company was a worldwide operation, I was asked in which currency I wanted my salary to be paid. Obviously, I chose pounds.

While these details were discussed, Joan and I sat in a room nearby watching a tape of Cosmos action highlights from previous years, including clips featuring Pele, Franz Beckenbauer, and Carlos Alberto. They were all World Cup winners; towering icons of the game. That's when it dawned on me that I would be replacing Pele in the Cosmos team. I would even be inheriting the great man's number 10 shirt. But I wasn't fazed by this, I just considered it the next challenge of my career.

It seemed almost unreal that I was poised to play in the Big Apple. But I felt excited, and ready for the challenge. Before going in to meet the media, I went to the toilet, and I bumped into Eddie Firmani for the first time. It was a bit embarrassing, because he had to introduce himself. I got the impression that he was delighted with the transfer and looking forward to an exciting season ahead, though.

I'd been expecting just a small press conference, but it turned out to be rather more than that. We went down to the third floor, and I waited in a small ante room, through the door of which I could see Ahmet and Eddie speaking to the throng. Then I was introduced.

"Ladies and gentleman, please give a warm welcome to the New York Cosmos's newest soccer star… DENNIS TUEART."

As I walked through the door I realised that the press conference was actually being held in a viewing theatre usually used for previews of Warner Brothers films. There were around 40 or 50 journalists there. Although soccer wasn't in the top five group of US sports, large communities of Italians, Greeks, Spaniards and Brazilians lived in the suburbs, and loved their football, so the Cosmos, both on the playing side and from a fans' angle, was a truly multicultural set-up. The journalists who were in the Rockefeller Plaza that day represented various different ethnic groups, and it suggested to me that if the club could nurture those community roots, then the Cosmos might be able to flourish in the long term.

I was asked to say a few words about my first impressions of the USA. I could draw upon my experience on my honeymoon five years earlier, when I'd been to watch a Miami Toros game, so I was at least able to speak about that and the stadium, which was far smarter and more modernised than any English ground I'd seen. I was also able to express my excitement at being involved in the next stage of soccer development in the America.

The vast majority of questions were run of the mill: "Are you excited about the move?" "Do you like New York?" That kind of thing. But there is always someone who wants to throw a curve ball in your direction. It came from Alex Yannis, a *New York Times* journalist who was quite knowledgeable about European and English football. He'd contacted a few of his buddies in the English media and, while he was very complimentary about my record at Sunderland and City, he mentioned there was one element which he believed was my weakness.

"Dennis," he said. "I understand that for an attacker, you can be inconsistent."

Unfortunately for Alex, just before leaving City I'd been on that terrific run of form, scoring three hat-tricks in the first half of that season. I pointed out that for a guy who wasn't an out-and-out striker, my goalscoring record was actually pretty good.

"Alex," I said. "Just how inconsistent would you like me to be?"

There were hoots of laughter from the assembled pressmen, and after that they could sense I was quite confident and able to stand my ground, which in New York is essential.

The press conference helped to resolve some issues in my mind. I'd had a nagging doubt that perhaps the Cosmos was purely showbiz, like a footballing version of the Harlem Globetrotters. But I could tell that the Cosmos expected a return on their investment. That went for both the club and the media. I liked that kind of expectation. It fired me up.

I wanted to embrace the New York lifestyle fully. Joan and I found a beautiful new development on the banks of the Hudson on the New Jersey side, a two-bedroom, two-bathroom apartment on the 36th floor of the Galaxy Building complex with views of the Manhattan skyline, from the Empire State Building and the World Trade Centre down to Verrazano Bridge. The recent Hudson River plane drama would have seen the plane gliding past my bedroom window. The complex had indoor and outdoor swimming pools, a private gym, a cinema, a shopping complex, outdoor tennis courts and underground parking. Five years before, when I was still living with my parents in a two-bedroom council flat, I had been sharing a three-quarter size bed with my brother. It made me think back to when I was 15 and rejected by Newcastle United, and I'd learned that hard work and a single-minded focus can bring success.

Then I had to sort out my car. This became a bit of an issue because the Cosmos had just agreed a sponsorship deal with Toyota. I went to see Ahmet at his office in the Warner Building on Rockefeller Plaza and explained to him that my contract stipulated a company car, but that I fancied going native. He offered me a BMW or a Mercedes, but I still fancied something American, so he sent me to see Ernie at Warner Transport. He took Joan and I to a huge Cadillac dealership on the corner of 52nd Street and Central Park, led me into the showroom and asked which one I wanted. I was trying to be a bit blasé about it, so I said I'd like a look around. After sitting in several so big you could have had a game of 5-a-side in them, I chose one of the newer models, a Seville. I could have whatever specifications I wanted, so of course I had it in sky blue (City was still in my blood) and got all the electrical add-ons.

So I had a big car and a plush apartment. Now it was time to get to work.

CHAPTER TEN

SIR AUGUST OF NEW YORK

There was concern in England about the exodus of players abroad. Rodney Marsh and George Best were plying their trade in the US, and Kevin Keegan had gone to Hamburg, so there was a real fear that the best talent was draining away from English football. Only Kevin and myself were actually at the peak of our careers, but our departures were seen as the tip of the iceberg.

Shortly after I went to the Cosmos, the BBC produced a documentary called *A Whole New Ball Game*. What was interesting about the documentary was that it began by showing the generally rundown state of English grounds, and managers like Lawrie McMenemy and Bobby Robson acknowledged that fact. The grounds were dilapidated, the facilities were terrible, and the pitches were often mudheaps. Word was filtering back from English players who'd returned that the facilities were so much better out in the States, where clubs invested money to ensure that spectators sat in comfort and had decent food and toilets.

In time, playing for the Cosmos would also open up my eyes to the lack of business acumen in the English game at the time. The Cosmos brand pulled in money left, right and centre, through franchising, marketing and local TV deals. It really was a whole new ball game, and it was 20 years ahead of England, where agents and TV deals only came into the game during the Sky era. Derek Wallis wrote in the *Mirror*, "Tueart Exit a Warning", and went on to add that the money on offer to players in England was "peanuts compared to the riches in America".

I discovered that the Cosmos was the first truly global, cosmopolitan, mercenary football club. In one way, they tried to get it right, and attracted players who were still at their peak. I was only 28, and they also signed the captain of Red Star Belgrade, Vladislav Bogicevic, who was only 27. In 1979, they signed Dutch stars Wim Risjbergen and Johan Neeskens, who were both in their mid-twenties and had played for Holland at the World Cup. Where it often went wrong was that other franchises in the NASL were signing players who were way past their best, or paying a premium to third- or fourth-rate players who were out to make a quick buck. Rather than develop and cultivate youth systems, they tried to buy in success, but it didn't work – not in the short term and certainly not in the long term.

My former City colleagues were curious about my move to the Cosmos, especially when they finally got the finer points of the deal out of me. Over the next few years, several of them tried their luck in the States. Asa and Kiddo went to Fort Lauderdale, and Joe Corrigan played in Seattle. Other familiar faces also tried their luck out West. Keith Weller, who'd been at Chelsea and Leicester, played for the Boston Teamen and Garry Stanley, who had played for Villa and Chelsea, played for Fort Lauderdale. They dabbled a bit during the summer, but I remained the only England international to play out there full time. Visa regulations meant that we could only stay in America for six months of the year. The NASL season lasted six months, and I quickly learned that for much of the rest of the year we'd be touring here, there and everywhere to spread the Cosmos brand.

The weather was so bad in New York in the period after I joined that we trained in Bermuda during February in order to prepare for the season which began in March. One day, on the way to training, I was sitting on the coach next to Franz Beckenbauer and we passed a school where the students were playing cricket. Franz was very inquisitive about the rules of the game. I then spent the rest of the journey trying to explain the rules to him, as he had been following baseball since his time in New York. I failed badly.

He asked questions like, "Why are there two hitters?"; "Why do they run and change ends?"; "Why does the pitcher only throw six pitches?"; "Why is there a new pitcher at the other end?"; and, finally, "Why, if you have 11 players playing, are you all out when 10 people are dismissed?".

I was punch-drunk in the end and gave up!

After that first training camp in Bermuda, it was back to New York to get in the zone for the new season. It was something else. I'd been used to running around Wythenshaw Park with City, and freezing to death on Roker Beach at Sunderland, but at the Cosmos we trained inside the New York Giants Stadium. A couple of times, Pele, who'd just retired, joined us. Just being in proximity to him made the hairs on the back of my neck stand on end.

I've often been asked, "How did it feel to replace an icon of the game?" The truth is, it never daunted me. I didn't have any sleepless nights about it. The fact that Cosmos signed me to replace him was an honour. What set Pele apart from the rest, even in his mid-thirties, was his fantastic balance and vision. The very best in the world can dominate the entire pitch, and read the game. Even in those training sessions, Pele could see two or three moves ahead, and his anticipation was unlike anything I'd seen.

Later on in my Cosmos career, there was an exhibition game between the former Cosmos and the current Cosmos. To whip up the crowd, Pele played a half each for both sides. I was up front with him, and I was playing in a very English manner – with my back to goal, holding up the ball as much as possible and laying it off to colleagues like Roberto Rivelino (who was also a guest player) who were getting up front to support me. Pele was having none of it. The Brazilian way was that a striker would get the ball, turn, and set off towards goal. He let me know what he thought of my approach by shouting, "Tueart, turn. TUEART! TURN!". Every time I received a pass in the danger zone, I got a bollocking from Pele and, even though I'm a feisty kind of fella, I wasn't going to argue. In a weird sense, it was a badge of honour.

But Pele was, and is, unbelievably humble. For a guy who's achieved as much as he has, and with all the razzamatazz which has surrounded him, I've always found him to have his feet planted firmly on the ground. Over the years, whenever we've been asked to sign Cosmos shirts to raise money for charity, he's gone out of his way to be as accommodating as possible. With the Cosmos brand now relaunched, Pele is a roving ambassador, and in July

2011 I had dinner with him in Manchester the night before Manchester United took on the Cosmos in Paul Scholes' testimonial. There's no airs and graces about Pele. "Dennis, how are you? How is your family?" are the first questions he usually asks me.

The truly great players generally have that humble side to them. I'd discovered that years before when I met George Best at Slack Alice, the nightclub he owned in Manchester. When I was at City in the Seventies, it was an iconic place, a must-go venue where sports stars, TV personalities and journalists mixed freely. Others referred to it simply as "Bestie's", because more often than not you'd find him there talking to customers.

One night he came across and introduced himself to me – as if he needed to – and unburdened himself. He talked openly about the problems he had at United, and the vacuum created by Matt Busby's departure, and freely admitted to me that alcohol was his way of trying to cope with the stress and the sense of isolation he felt, despite his fame. I just listened, and was a bit taken aback because I didn't know George socially at all, and there he was offloading to me, a virtual stranger. But I was totally enthralled and fascinated by him as a person.

Out in the States, after the Cosmos played Fort Lauderdale, who George played for, there was a post-match party. By this time George was married to Angie Best. At the party, there were the likes of Georgio Chinaglia and Johann Neeskens – some of the world's best players – yet George came across as a playful lad who wasn't egotistical at all. Bestie told me that he thoroughly enjoyed his time out in the States because he was able to go about his business without much hassle.

Bestie's problems would emerge later, and that's when his Jekyll and Hyde personality really kicked in. I saw that for myself many years later at a Football Writers' Dinner at the Portland Hotel in Manchester when he was guest speaker. He came on late in the evening, and by that time he'd downed several glasses of wine – everyone always wanted to buy George a drink – he wasn't at his best while delivering it. He should have been put on first.

Shortly before the start of my first NASL season, we played a friendly match against Chicago in the Giants Stadium. Eddie Firmani had sent us out to do a spot of loosening up, and as I was doing my twists and turns I felt my hamstring go. After all the hype, I was forced to limp back into the dressing room, with my head down. I put the injury down to the artificial surface. These days specialists are developing fourth-generation Astroturf, but back then it was barely fit for purpose. At the Giants Stadium, it was like running on concrete, which was a real challenge to European players who'd spent their entire career playing on lush grass. Beckenbauer struggled with a knee injury, Risjbergen injured his Achilles tendon, Portugese international Seninho damaged his knee, and Johan Neeskens had shoulder problems.

I needed to get myself fit again for the start of the season. For the first ten days after the injury I spent many lonely hours in a gym on a bike, and then it was back in with the rest of the team in a bid to sharpen up. I finally made my debut in a league game against Dallas Tornado in front of over 50,000 at the Giants Stadium. The scoreboard showed exactly 55 minutes and 55 seconds when I scored my first goal with a diving header, and we went on to win 3–1.

Straight away, I realised how difficult it was going to be playing on the Giants Stadium pitch. The bounce of the ball was entirely unpredictable, and for a good few weeks I struggled with that element of the game. The accuracy of the pass became all the more important as the ball would zip across the Astroturf surface. Then there were the friction burns – whether you slid in for a tackle, or were sent flying, you'd pick one of those up. Red and raw, I'd be in agony for days, and when anything touched the burn I'd practically hit the ceiling. Within a few weeks, I had considerably less skin on both legs than I'd had at Manchester City. There was a real variety in the size of the pitches we played on, too. For instance, Memphis's was 50 yards wide because it was an American Football pitch.

The other thing I needed to get used to was the heat. The summer season ran from April to September, right through the summer. In the early part of the season, home games would kick-off at 2.30pm on a Sunday, but they gradually got later as the humidity became more intense. Sometimes, they'd even start as late as 9pm because the Giants Stadium was on a shared site with the Meadowlands race track, and we had to slot in around them. On

Astroturf, we'd wear pimpled rubber soles, and the heat of the pitch would regularly melt the sole. At half-time we'd often had to be given tubs of iced water to put our feet in as they were so hot – not a problem I'd encountered at Roker Park or Maine Road…

In the first season, our results went well, and we averaged attendances of around 50,000 a game. It did take me a while to get used to the sense of scale in the States. At Sunderland, I was used to travelling long distances by coach to get to away games, but at Cosmos we flew everywhere apart from Philadelphia because the teams were so far apart. Playing away at Washington and Tampa felt like the equivalent of a local derby. You'd sometimes have a five-day, two-game trip, or three games in ten days, which could get disorientating and tedious. It was a case of staying in a hotel, training hard and playing the game. I would never claim to have "seen America" during my time with Cosmos – I've still never been to the Grand Canyon or Las Vegas, two places I've always fancied visiting since I was a kid – but I was being paid to play football, not indulge myself in some Bill Bryson-style road trip around the States.

The amount of travel was tough on Joan, too. Once when I was away with the Cosmos, Joan smelt smoke up in our 36th-floor apartment, and the smell gradually grew stronger. She rang the intercom system and tried to speak to the concierge, but nobody was there. We didn't know our neighbours at all, and when she did manage to speak to one of them, a Frenchman, he gesticulated that they should get into the lift and go down to the foyer. Joan did that, but was aware that it could be an extremely risky thing to do. When they got down to the foyer, Joan saw other residents congregating, wondering exactly what was causing the smell. They found out that there had a been a minor fire in a garbage chute. The experience was alarming for both of us, particularly Joan, and what made it worse was that *The Towering Inferno* was the block-buster movie at the time.

My experiences out in the US opened my eyes up to new opportunities, and new ways of doing things. The way that the NASL, and the Cosmos in particular, did their business began to have a ripple effect throughout the world. It wasn't just in the area of signing players, but also in bringing a different commercial approach, with agents and various deals. American sportsmen in baseball and American Football were used to it. It had long been part of their culture. I'd never come across anything like this before, and I know that many of the other foreign players who played out in the States, and not just the English lads, were taken aback by what was going on. England players like Kevin Keegan had a boot deal, but most of us only got paid if we wore specific boots for one-off games. My only experience of sponsorship had been in the 1973 FA Cup final. Sunderland did a deal with Stylo for the players to wear their boots. I made sure that I wore mine for a couple of weeks beforehand to break them in, but some of the others only wore them in training the week before the match, and were in agony as the boots rubbed against their feet and gave them blisters. They ended up going to our trainer, Billy Elliott, to paint the Stylo logo on their old boots, so they didn't miss out on the deal. We garnered £2,750 from Stylo in total, and each member of the team made a princely £1,318.60 from the final players' pool, when all the other deals were thrown in. When I joined the Cosmos I got a $4,000-per-season deal with Nike, which probably only Kevin Keegan, of all the English players at that time, could have equalled.

The NASL kick started the football mercenary culture. I would imagine that virtually every player out there in the late Seventies was there for one thing – money. When David Beckham signed for LA Galaxy in 2007, he talked about his mission to popularise football in the States, and expressed a wish that one day it would be ranked alongside the more established sports, suggesting that he had other motives for going to the US besides the lure of the dollar, but I'm not so sure.

Financially rewarding it may have been, but the expectation at Cosmos was that in return for being handsomely paid, you needed to deliver success. We had players of 13 different nationalities at the club, and I think I ended up being able to swear in five languages. It made communication difficult at times, and sometimes I felt that the team wasn't as united as it should have been when things weren't going so well. There were agents and publicists circling all the time – the franchise situation made that inevitable. If the club is part of the community and you've grown up with the fans, there is an emotional connection. But this wasn't the case with the Cosmos in the late Seventies.

I never felt permanent or rooted in New York, and all the time I was playing I knew that I could be moved on at any stage because of the "cut" clause in my contract. Inevitably, it meant that everything was slightly superficial, and there was no deep connection with the club. It's a similar situation in the Premier League now, with the influx of foreign stars, there is much bigger turnover of players and very few of them stay at the same club for more than two or three years, because that deep-rooted link to the club or the city simply isn't there.

The most important development for the Cosmos in my first season was that they landed a deal with the ABC television network. Thrashing out a TV deal would always be problematic for the club, because we heard that many big TV executives also happened to be major shareholders in other American sport franchises. That meant that soccer was regarded as a threat to the status quo. But the Ehrteguns and Steve Ross, director of Warner Communications and passionate follower of the Cosmos, pushed the deal through. That was crucial, because in American sports if you don't have a TV deal, you're sunk. The ABC deal was a coast-to-coast deal, which took in five regular-season games, the play-offs, and the final.

First of all we played against other teams from our conference. There were two conferences – the National and the American – with three divisions within each conference: Eastern, Central and Western. In the play-offs we would only play against teams from our conference, and then the two conference winners would play one another in the NASL Soccer Bowl championship game. In the regular season games it was six points for a win, with an extra point for each goal up to three. If a game was level after 90 minutes, we'd then play 15 minutes of sudden death over-time, and then, if it was still required, we'd have a shootout from the 35-yard line. When the referee blew his whistle, you had five seconds to run at the goal, get your shot off and try to beat the 'keeper.

I thought the 35-yard line shootout, introduced in the US game in 1975, was a fantastic innovation, because it gave attacking players the chance to parade their skills in front of the crowds. Dribbling the ball in and trying to beat the 'keeper was a much better test of skill than a penalty, and American audiences demanded to be entertained all the time, so some tweaks to the traditional model were needed.

I also quickly discovered that, whereas with the European game both sides would squeeze up and suppress the creative element, here there was space. As a roving forward, I loved it. Franz Beckenbauer and Johann Neeskens had more room to create because they weren't being suffocated by opponents. There was more time to play that killer pass.

And beyond all the gimmicks – the cheerleaders and the gigantic screens in the grounds which ran adverts most of the game and replayed key incidents – there was no substitute for true class. Franz Beckenbauer, who was still only 32 when he joined the Cosmos from Bayern Munich, remains the best player I ever played with. His mantra was simple. You had to hold onto the ball. I found it remarkable that on occasion the Cosmos crowd grew restless when Franz pushed and probed in midfield. It showed that American crowds, however passionate, didn't fully understand the game. They got very excited when the ball was in either penalty area, but they got restless when the ball was played around in the middle of the pitch. It didn't mean that Franz changed his approach in any way. He absolutely loathed it when a team-mate gave away possession cheaply, and Franz never, ever gave it away. He used to play several innocuous short passes and receive the ball back, then all of a sudden he would release a terrific, penetrating longer pass. As a forward player, this was brilliant for me as he was always looking at the big picture and waiting for the perfect opportunity to play the important pass. This is very similar to the passing movements of the modern Barcelona team, who play the short pass to move the opposition around and create the space behind them.

When Franz came to the Cosmos, he was probably already well-off financially, and he'd won all there was to win with Bayern and with West Germany, but he never lost that desire and that will to win. Off the pitch, he was laid back and good company, but once he crossed that white line, he'd do absolutely anything to win. His vision was unbelievable and, with the slower pace of the game in the States, he flourished once again. He was imperious on the pitch, but like all great players he knew how to look after himself too.

There was a game we played in Tokyo on a Cosmos tour when they had a hulking defender who went man to man on Franz and kept flying in on him to prove his point. You'd get journeymen defenders who would treat it as a badge of honour if they could take out the great Beckenbauer. I could see that Franz was none too pleased, and then he got the ball and started to dribble, tempting the defender to make a tackle. Finally, the guy took the bait and lunged in, and Franz went right over the top on him with his studs high. As the guy rolled around in agony on the floor, Franz towered over him, drew a ball with his hands in the air and walked away.

On one of our lucrative, but draining post-season tours, Franz and I clashed. It was the end of our season, so we were all knackered, and we were schlepping all over the world and had stopped off in West Germany for two exhibition games against Bayern Munich and Stuttgart. The European teams were just at the start of their season and fresh and ready for us. After suffering the two defeats in Germany we had a game in Italy against Brescia. Before kick-off Eddie Firmani read out a letter from Steve Ross absolutely slaughtering us and demanding better performances, which really fired us up.

In the first half, we got a free-kick on the edge of the box. We'd worked on a move in training whereby Franz stood over the ball, I'd run down the side and Franz would slide it through to me. As Brescia formed their wall, the ball was on, but Franz wasn't looking, so I shouted at him. He passed it to me, but by then there were defenders on me, and he gave me a look as if to ask "Who are you to be shouting at me?" At half-time we were one-down, under pressure, and as we walked off we began bawling at one another. Franz and I squared up and had to be separated by Eddie Firmani and some other players.

Just after half-time Franz knocked a through ball to me. Perfectly weighted. To die for. I finished it off, and he just smiled at me and gave me a little wave. That's why he was a top player: he wasn't upset by confrontation.

In most successful sides there needs to be that element of confrontation and aggression. It shows a desire to win. I remember that when I was at Sunderland, we played Manchester City the year Sunderland were relegated to the Second Division. For the whole game, their captain, Tony Book, and Mike Summerbee didn't stop effin' and jeffin' at each other. Top-quality, fully-committed players don't suffer fools gladly.

At the Cosmos, I played alongside Giorgio Chinaglia, who'd played for Lazio and Italy. The thing you had to accept with Giorgio was that he had a big ego. Gargantuan, in fact. He had to be top boss and couldn't resist mouthing-off in his curious half-Welsh half-Italian lilt about all and sundry. From watching the DVD which charts the history of the Cosmos, *Once In A Lifetime*, I know that many who were involved with the club haven't got a good word to say about him, and allege that he was trying to meddle in team selection and was having private words with the directors about the business angle the club was taking.

Giorgio enjoyed the high life in New York and, although I didn't hang out with him, I always got on fine with him because I wasn't interested in the club politics, either on the pitch or off it. He loved to challenge authority, and would argue with anyone about anything. During a team meeting on one of our tours, Giorgio ended up punching a Cosmos executive after disagreeing about the players' expenses payments. He had to dominate, and in heated discussions had a tendency to stand up and say "I am Chinaglia" in a grandiose manner, which he believed gave him the divine right to win any debate.

After scoring a goal, Georgio often ran towards Steve Ross up in the special Warner seats. Giorgio was Steve's big favourite, and that didn't always go down too well with the other players. Steve Ross was a really excitable supporter, and we heard that it had been suggested he should wear a seat belt to stop him falling from the stand.

Georgio was only 31 when he joined from Lazio and, like Franz, his passion for the game was beyond reproach. Giorgio and I played well together, and his finishing ability was exceptional, as was his level of desire on the pitch. He was a driven individual, and all he wanted to do was score goals and win games. My kind of maverick.

My first season at the Cosmos went really well, and I think the way I played the game went down a storm with the American crowd, who demanded effort, hard running, physicality and total commitment for the full 90 minutes. Inevitably, the season really warmed-up during the end-of-season play-offs and I really came alive. In the Conference semi-final we played Minnesota on a pitch laid out over a baseball diamond. One minute you were running on grass and the next on the sand which ran between the bases. It was off-putting, but this was no excuse for what happened during the game. There were over 40,000 there for the away game, and it all seemed set-up for a great night, but after 12 minutes I chased a through-ball and collided with the goalkeeper. I damaged my shinbone and had to go off. We went on to lose 9–2. Our skipper Werner Roth scored two own-goals, and once we had conceded three goals our heads just went. The team trooped off at the end looking dazed and bewildered.

The result sent shockwaves through US football, and the Warner executives weren't happy. The second game was back in New York a few days later (aggregate scores didn't count in the NASL, luckily, and it was just down to games won), but I was really struggling to get fit. I talked it over with the coach, and for the first time, on the afternoon before the game, I allowed the medical people to give me an injection to play. I've no idea what they pumped into me, which shows the pressure I was under to get fit.

We had no training scheduled on the day of the game, but our assistant coach, Ray Klivecka, gave me a brief warm-up. He took me to the stadium so I could have a go at crossing and shooting and see how the leg felt. The New York Giants were in pre-season training and they were doing some warm-ups, so Ray got their punter, Steve Jennings, to go in goal, while I took shots at him. His hand-eye co-ordination was amazing – and it was a real eye-opener to the skills involved in other sports.

I got through the session okay, and afterwards I went back to have lunch with the rest of the players. Firmani told us to stay in the dining room after we'd finished. We were surprised by that, but then Steve Ross arrived in a big limo with the senior execs. His job would have involved motivating people from all parts of the huge Warner business community, and he certainly motivated us. I think it's the best 15-minute speech I've ever heard.

He opened it by saying that he'd been at a conference on the West Coast with 750 Warner delegates discussing their latest project, the new Superman film, when the news of the 9–2 hammering broke. "Those delegates were more interested in talking about the Cosmos defeat than about the project," he said. "I felt embarrassed, and I don't like to be embarrassed."

Then he spent the next ten minutes telling us they wanted the best, they paid top dollar for the best and that we were the best, and that they expected a return: "If any of you don't want to be a part of that, you should speak to the coach and he'll deal with it". In England, plucky losers may be tolerated, but not in New York, where winning is everything. After Steve's pep talk we were all raring for the challenge, ready to prove our point.

The return leg was the longest game I'd ever played in. There were 60,199 inside the stadium. I scored twice and we won 4–0. As there was no goals aggregate we had won one game each. What happened after that was incredible. First there was a mini-game, classified as the third game, which decided who would win the tie. It was 15 minutes each way, but that finished 0–0, so it went to a shootout – no penalties but these five runs on goal from the halfway line I mentioned earlier. Each team had five attempts, and the winner of the shootout would decide the winner of the third game and ultimately the tie. Minnesota scored with their first effort, but then their 'keeper saved four of ours in a row, including mine. I'd tried to go round the 'keeper but he'd clawed the ball away from me at the last minute. That was the first and last time I took part in a shoot-out. After the Minnesota 'keeper had saved our fourth attempt he held up four fingers to the crowd to signify that they were leading 1–0, as our 'keeper had also saved four of theirs. So it came down to Carlos Alberto to save us.

He had to score, and the pressure on him was enormous. But he was as calm as you like, totally focused. Like Franz, Carlos was a hugely experienced player who knew all about pressure, having captained Brazil to their World Cup win in 1970. He put the ball down, then flicked it up in front of him, and kept knocking it up with his knee as he advanced on goal, almost like he was show boating in a training session. It was incredible, and probably only someone of Carlos's experience would have had the nerve, never mind the outrageous skill, to do that. Then, casual as anything, he lifted it over the 'keeper: 1–1. The crowd went ballistic.

So the shootout went to sudden death as well. Our 'keeper saved their sixth, which meant that if Franz Beckenbauer scored we had won.

Of course he did – he was Beckenbauer – and the whole stadium erupted in celebration. Even Franz, normally the epitome of Teutonic cool, showed his delight by running around punching the air. Joan told me afterwards that she felt totally drained from watching it. It had been a hot, humid evening, typical of midsummer over there, and she said I looked practically skeletal by the end. Ninety minutes plus half an hour and then a shootout, as well as the sheer tension...

By the time it came to the Conference final against Portland Timbers, I felt I'd really adapted to the American game, and I scored another goal in our first-leg win at the Oregon Stadium. The Warner execs wanted us to get back as fresh as possible for the second leg on August 23 four days later, so directly after the game they put us on the Warner jet. It was only a 16-seater, so there were the 11 first-teamers and management – $7–8 million of talent on a private plane. Today's Manchester City stars enjoy the same treatment with the club's sky blue Etihad jet, but back then this kind of luxury was unheard of.

There were 65,287 at the Giants Stadium to cheer us on in the second game and we easily beat Portland, scoring three late goals to win 5–0. I got a goal and two assists. For the goal I played a one-two with Vito Dimitrijevic, cut in from the left and lifted it over the goalkeeper into the net for our second goal. In front of such huge crowds, the feeling of scoring a goal was every bit as fulfilling as it had ever been at Sunderland or Manchester City.

The NASL final against Tampa Bay was scheduled for the Giants Stadium. The anticipation surrounding the game was huge in New York, and the players knew that it would be a full stadium with 75,000 supporters, along with the traditional tailgating parties and barbeques before the match. There was a huge amount of publicity about the final because the star turn for Tampa Bay was none other than Rodney Marsh.

Ah, Rodney, Rodney. He had gained himself a great deal of publicity in the States when after Pele had suggested Rodney was a "white Pele", Rodney suggested that Pele might actually be a "black Rodney Marsh". I cringed when I heard him say that. Rodney was attention-seeking again.

The former Liverpool hard man, Tommy Smith, played with Rodney at Tampa and later described him as "a cross between Freud and Donald Duck". Another playing colleague, Marc Lindsay, said, "Rodney would always go out looking for the newspaper article and the TV camera".

Journalists from across the Atlantic flew in to see who might succeed in the clash between Tueart and Marsh. But the face-off never happened, because for some mysterious reason Rodney didn't play. It was rumoured that he wanted more money, and then I heard he had a shin infection, but Tampa's medical team had passed him fit to play. Whatever the reasons, Rodney withdrew from the game. Tampa's coach, Gordon Jago, suggested that Rodney didn't have the heart for it and that he'd really let him down. Perhaps it was because the European press were going to be there, and Rodney didn't want to look a fool in front of them. I'll never know for sure.

The ABC contract meant that the game was shown live coast to coast, on a Sunday afternoon, so it was a great opportunity for soccer in the US. I played really well, and scored twice as we won 3–1. I was voted the NASL Offensive Player of the Game and won the NASL Most Valuable Player of the play-offs.

My first goal opened the scoring, which followed a great left-wing cross from Steve Hunt, who'd signed as a youngster from Aston Villa and had a great season. I was able to volley the ball in with my right foot, which gave me great satisfaction after all the hours of practising that technique. My Offensive Player of the Game award was a huge trophy which I took to the Manhattan restaurant Mamma Leoni's, after the game. Later on all the team were presented with a silver and diamond championship ring which is traditional in all American sports. Several days later, I received my MVP trophy, which was a pure silver replica of the famous Cutty Sark ship, from the former president of FIFA, Sir Stanley Rous. There was a special presentation lunch in Manhattan with invited guests from the press, Cutty Sark Corporation and the Cosmos.

I felt my decision to move to New York had been justified, but there would be precious little time to enjoy the triumph because, in order to make money for Warner Brothers, we were due to embark on a world tour in 1978. Eddie Firmani gave me a couple of weeks off before the tour to go back to England, before ordering me to meet up with the rest of the squad in Argentina.

I flew from Newcastle to Buenos Aires International via Gatwick, then took a taxi ride across to the domestic terminal for an internal flight to Tucaman where we had a game against the Argentinian junior side. I arrived just in time to watch the game and got my first viewing of an unknown 17-year-old player called Diego Maradona. He was captain of the youth team, and he was out of this world. The pitch was rock hard, but the ball never seemed to leave his control. His balance was extraordinary, too. They beat us 2–1, with Maradona scoring one and making one.

After that South American trip, we then set-off on a European tour. We lost 7–1 to Bayern Munich and 6–1 to Stuttgart. Then we got beaten 6–4 by Red Star in Belgrade. There were a lot of defeats on that tour because we were at the end of a long season. I could feel the crowds mocking us, and the opposition players were getting pumped up for the games, as the Cosmos had had so much publicity and we were supposed to be the flagship of the NASL.

Our last game was at Chelsea in front of a capacity crowd, and Johan Cruyff guested for us. That game was one of only two that Cruyff and Beckenbaur played together. I scored and we drew 1–1, which restored a bit of pride. It's ironic in a way, because that Cosmos side was the first step towards what teams like Chelsea and Manchester City are now – a team of superstars of various nationalities.

All the criticism that Chelsea and Manchester City receive these days, we got at the Cosmos. We had a great stadium, the best players and unlimited finances because we were funded by a company that wasn't reliant on gate revenues. We were called greedy, we bought players at will, and clubs were always delighted to sell to us, because they knew that Warner Brothers would pay top dollar. Just like Real Madrid a few years back, we had to get two or three 'Galacticos' a year. Cosmos bought Carlos Alberto, Franz and Pele the year before me, then they got me, Eskandarian from Iran's World Cup team of 1978 and Bogicevic, and next it was Mourinho, the blond full-back from Brazil, Seninho from Porto, and Neeskens and Rijsbergen, who were both in that great Dutch 'total football' team of the 1970s. Warner Brothers had to keep the momentum and interest going by buying top-quality imports.

The last game before Chelsea at Stamford Bridge was against Freiburg, which we lost 2–0. I was asked to go on Brian Moore's ITV football programme on the Saturday before the game the following day, so I flew in a day earlier than the rest of the team. ITV sent a blue limo to pick me up at the hotel, and as we went across London we were held up by a socialist march. We were held up for about 10 minutes, with me sitting there in the back and the marchers streaming down either side chanting. It reminded me that, outside the Cosmos bubble, life went on as normal.

But the Cosmos road show had become quite high profile, and the A-listers began to swarm around us. I remember once after training, the Cosmos executives had booked out a suite on the top floor of Madison Square Garden so we could watch the 1978 World Cup games. On one occasion Mick Jagger and Jerry Hall walked in. Mick was just like one of the lads, and he came to many of our games when he was in New York. We exchanged a bit of banter and football chit-chat, but Mick just wanted to watch the World Cup. He and Jerry sat down cross-legged on the floor and watched the games with us. Every so often they'd pop off to the loo together. Who knows what was going on there?

And we had all sorts of famous people attending the games. There was a rule which gave us eight minutes after the game finished before the locker room doors were opened for all the press and guests to enter. Henry Kissinger was a regular visitor, and he loved his soccer. Mick Jagger often came in there, and I had a good chat with Bjorn Borg once too. Bjorn was quite shy, but also funny in a quirky way. We talked about the razzmatazz that surrounded the Cosmos, and he was very sanguine about what "being famous" really meant. I got the impression that Bjorn was never entirely comfortable with the media circus which now attached itself to him wherever he went, and that all he really wanted to do was focus on his tennis. A couple of years later, he walked away from the sport at just 24. It always fascinated me that true legends in their fields recognise that the media hype is all phoney. It's real

I played six games for England and scored two goals, but I never felt that I got a decent run in the side.

One of my most memorable games was against Scotland at Wembley in 1977. The Scots won 2-1 and their fans invaded the pitch and stole the goalposts after the game.

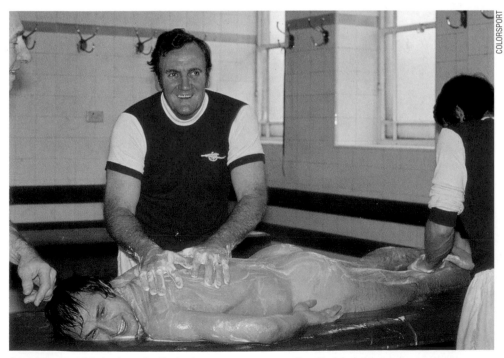

One of the best things about the England set-up was manager Don Revie's famous soap massages… they were amazing! This one was at Highbury, hence Revie wearing an Arsenal shirt.

Joan and I at the press conference announcing my arrival at the New York Cosmos. It was here that it dawned upon me that I would be replacing Pelé, arguably the greatest player of all time.

The facilities in the Giants Stadium were fantastic, and I was in pretty good company too!

I think this picture of me scoring v Rochester shows the passion of the NASL and the Cosmos at this time.

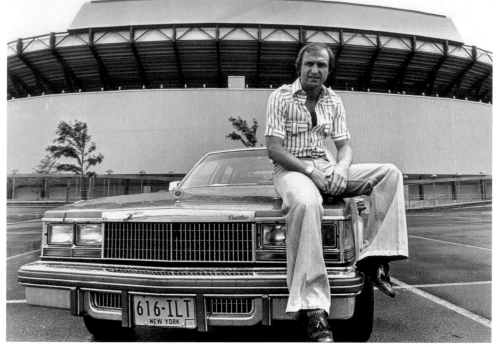

Me outside the Giants Stadium with my sky-blue Cadillac.

After games, all sorts of celebrities of sport and entertainment would pop into the locker room for a chat. This is me with Bjorn Borg at a time when he was at the height of his powers.

It was a glamorous life off the pitch at the Cosmos, as shown by this picture of Franz Beckenbauer and I on the golf course during a pre-season training tour to Bermuda.

And life wasn't bad on the pitch either. This game was actually against Chelsea at Stamford Bridge as part of a European tour, with the great Johan Cruyff (back row, second from right) guesting for us.

I scored twice in the 1978 NASL final in front of 75,000 at Giants Stadium. This was my second and our third in a 3-1 win over the Tampa Bay Rowdies.

As well as winning the NASL trophy, pictured here, I won the award for the Most Valuable Player of the play-offs.

It was great to have my brother, Kevin, there to celebrate with me.

After a season with the Cosmos I re-signed for Manchester City, now managed by Malcolm Allison (centre) with Tony Book (right) as his assistant.

It felt great to be back in the sky blue of Manchester City.

I first met Mick Jagger when I was playing for the Cosmos, and we watched several 1978 World Cup games together. This picture was taken at Giants Stadium after we'd played my former team in an end-of-season tournament in New York.

Celebrating scoring the winner v West Brom at Maine Road in August 1981.

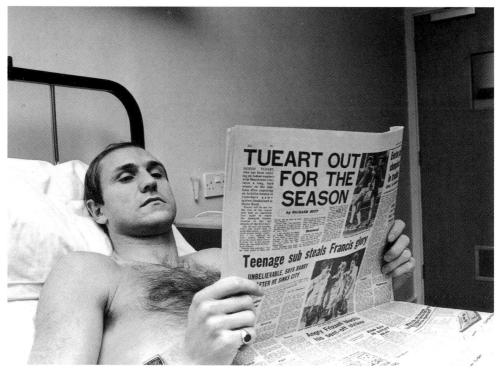

Reading the bad news about my Achilles injury in hospital in November 1981.

Playing in City's famous black-and-red-striped away strip in 1982.

And back in the famous sky blue against Forest at the City Ground in the same year.

LANCASHIRE TELEGRAPH

Signing for Stoke City in 1983 was a mistake.
I think you can see from my eyes that I'm not sure
quite what I have done.

I had a pretty good spell at Burnley, scoring five
goals in ten league games, but my Achilles injury
never fully healed and I didn't want to play if I
couldn't give it everything.

I started playing for Derry City in
1985 as a favour, but I was soon
swept along by the infectious
enthusiasm of the club and its
supporters.

In training for the 1987 Piccadilly marathon, with my support team – my eldest sons Mark (left) and Leigh (right).

Joan and I at home with the family in the late Eighties. From top to bottom, the boys are Mark, Leigh and John.

Francis Lee welcomes me onto the City board at Maine Road in 1997. Sadly, his attitude towards me changed over the course of my time in the boardroom.

Celebrating our promotion back to the Premier League with Mark Kennedy on that incredible afternoon at Blackburn in May 2000.

Although the bust of Joe Mercer serves as a reminder of past glories, Tueart is more interested in laying foundations for a brighter future

Candid Tueart means business

Mark Hodkinson treads carefully as Manchester City's no-nonsense director sets out his stall

The tea lady got the message. So did the photographer and the giddy supporter reckless enough to laugh out of turn. Dennis Tueart does not suffer fools. Not one bit.

First, the indiscreet fan. Tueart had just given one of his typically direct responses while on the panel at a supporters' club meeting. Someone sniggered. "What are you laughing for?" he snapped, his eyes ice-cold and piercing. "Have I said something funny?" "No," came the response. "Well don't laugh then."

Our photographer had asked Tueart to pose in front of City's trophy cabinet. He liked the light reflecting off the glass. "You're not going to take the piss about it being empty are you?" Tueart asked. He was also reticent about being pictured near the bust of Joe Mercer. "We've had enough of all that past-glory stuff," he grumbled. The tea lady arrived. She had been over-generous with the milk. Tueart pointed to his cup. "I can't drink that, love." Polite, but firm. Within seconds, another was placed before him. "Thanks, love."

It has been a bad couple of weeks in the life of Manchester City. Their form in the league has remained disappointing; they recorded an all-time low home attendance against Mansfield Town in the Auto Windscreens Shield; and a replay and extra-time were required to see off Darlington in the FA Cup.

"We've had a few uppercuts lately," he said. "You obviously feel frustrated by it, but you have got to play the percentages game. We try and do the right things at the right time and put in the commitment. If we do that, on the field and off it, we'll give ourselves the best possible chance of succeeding."

Tueart played 259 games for City in two separate spells in the Seventies and early Eighties. He is best remembered for the stunning overhead kick that earned City victory in the 1976 League Cup final against Newcastle United, his home-town club. When he left City for the first time, in 1977, he joined New York Cosmos, to play alongside the likes of Franz Beckenbauer and Carlos Alberto. Off the field, the company he kept was also stately. "You were more likely

to find me in the sponsors' lounge after the game than the players'. I was very interested in the corporate side of the game, the way sport dovetailed into business."

Back in the United Kingdom, he worked for a company specialising in launching products, usually against a sports backdrop. He would hire suites at football grounds to stage conferences and, rightly, he saw football clubs as a natural focus for media interest. In 1988, he bought out a partner and launched Premier Events. He also has interests in a travel agency and a property company. Clearly, he is just as at ease in a suit as he was a football kit.

His father was a fitter in the shipyards of the North East and Tueart has the flinty edge of a working-class boy made good. He has been quick to learn, shrewd and single-minded. He tells a story of a conversation that he had with a fellow apprentice professional while he was with Sunderland in the late Sixties. Tueart asked him whether he would go easy on a challenge if the ball fell between them. It took some time before his friend responded. "I wouldn't even have had to think about it . . ." Tueart said.

His vocabulary is peppered with business-speak. He rarely says "me" or "I", but talks of "Dennis Tueart" — what is good for Dennis Tueart, what Dennis Tueart believes. He has a brusque charisma. One could imagine him at a business seminar, drawing out the unbelievers, inspiring the indifferent.

He is at the point where evangelism meets consumerism. He joined the board at City last December. His company had held an executive box at Maine Road and he maintained a keen interest in the club's fortunes. He was asked to provide expertise in his specialist field of corporate hospitality and also to form a link between Joe Royle, the manager, whom he played alongside at City, and the board.

"I am not here through ego," he said. "I've come to City because I want to be part of a good spirit and an ongoing development of the club. We've had a lot to sort out behind the scenes, but we are building foundations that will serve us well. I can understand that the fans are getting frustrated and edgy, but we are doing everything we can to progress."

Though he is now 49, he works out in the gym every day. His mobile phone rings, so does another phone in the room. It's for him, obviously. He is quick to his feet, still energetic and nimble. He seems to be a man heading somewhere and others will gladly travel with him. This busy-busy aura is infectious, many will want to please him, to secure his approval. Before the interview, he had twice asked: "What's your angle?"

It is hard not to feel sorry for the off-field personnel at City and, of course, the supporters. They are the epitome of dedication and enterprise, yet the players on the pitch continue to play like 11 young men who met for the first time an hour before kick-off. The few spoil it for the many and a certain malcontent is inevitable.

Some gossip-mongers have implied that Tueart is a potential club chairman, a natural leader. They suggest that, after the tenure of the equable David Bernstein, City might require a more bullish approach, fronted by someone who has spent both foggy mornings on training pitches and long evenings in the boardrooms of multinational companies. Tueart denies the claim and laughs for the first time. The message is, for once, implied, but we get it all the same.

A newspaper cutting from *The Times* in which I outlined my vision for the future of the City.

Announcing the arrival of Kevin Keegan as manager of Manchester City on May 24, 2001, with David Bernstein on Kevin's left.

In 2007 Carlos Alberto and Jairzinho popped into the training ground at Carrington and I gave them a guided tour.

The *MEN* cutting after our lucky escape on the way back from Southampton in January 2004, when one of our plane engines failed.

It was great to meet up with Pelé again when the New York Cosmos were re-launched in New York in June 2010.

Myself, Pelé and Carlos Alberto at the official Cosmos re-launch, which was attended by the Mayor of New York, Michael Bloomberg and also the president of the United States Soccer Confederation, Sunil Gulati.

I am donating my royalties for this book to the teenage and young adult cancer centre at The Christie in Manchester.

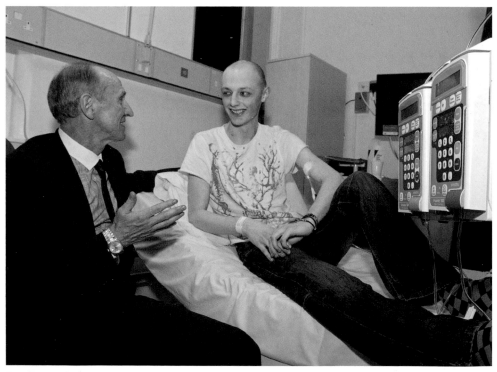

The Christie fulfils a magnificent service, and whenever I visit I am blown away by the work that the unit does, and the inspirational young people they look after.

achievement and success in their respective fields that matters. I got the same feeling when I spoke to Mick. He was passionate about music and football. There were no other airs and graces about him. To me, he was just Mick, who came to watch us play football.

In England I had been used to winding down at my own pace in the dressing room, having a cup of tea and a soak in the bath. In our locker room at Cosmos we had a fridge full of beers and fizzy soda drinks. There were no baths, only showers. I insisted on having some Perrier water to allow me to rehydrate and moaned about the lack of a bath. As the Cosmos players got what Cosmos players wanted, I got my Perrier water in the fridge and the physio installed a freestanding whirlpool bath in his room for the team's use.

The Cosmos players were big stars in New York, and after a mid-season exhibition game against Bayern Munich on July 4, American Independence Day, we were taken to the Windows on the World restaurant 107 floors up at the top of the World Trade Centre. Our friends, David Davies, the broadcast journalist and future Chief Executive of the FA, and his lovely wife, Sue, were staying with Joan and I for a short holiday and joined us. Pele was also there and we watched a magnificent fireworks display which was being set off from a ship on the Hudson River while enjoying a superb buffet meal. After dinner, everyone was then invited to Zenon, one of the "in" clubs in New York, to round off the evening. (The Cosmos regularly had tables reserved at the major clubs in town, one of which was the famous Studio 54).

Having Madison Square Garden on the doorstep was also amazing. I saw David Bowie in concert there and we were often invited to the Budweiser Box to watch the New York Rangers ice-hockey team. Rod Stewart was also on the Warner label – I went to see him in concert in New York and spent the entire night standing on my seat, craning my neck to see him, turning down numerous offers of dubiously scented cigarettes.

Joan and I knew that my Cosmos move would always be a fairly short-term option, and although we had plans to raise a family at some point in the future, we would never have chosen to in New York. Some of the players found living in the Big Apple difficult, especially if they had families. I became friends with Wim Rijsbergen, and he told me that his young son Bobby struggled to cope with the constriction of living in a high-rise flat, compared with their rural existence in Holland. Sometimes Joan popped around to give Wim's wife some moral support.

It could be tricky for some of the non-English-speaking players to adapt as well. For instance, when Cosmos signed Andranik Eskandarian, the Iran defender, he struggled to cope. Joan and I also tried to help him as much as possible. Because of the language barrier, he didn't know where he needed to go to furnish his flat, so I drove him to one of New York's massive out-of-town shopping malls, where we helped him buy a mattress for his bed. Outside in the parking lot, we tied the mattress to the top of my Cadillac and drew some curious glances from other motorists as we drove back down the freeway to Manhattan.

Although things had gone well on the pitch in my first year, there were often rumblings off it, which revealed some of the underlying problems with developing soccer in the US, and hinted at the reasons for the demise of the NASL a few years later. We had a situation when the players' union, which represented most of the US soccer players, tried to call a strike. There was a rule that there always had to be at least two North American citizens on the pitch for each team, which effectively meant that teams had to have two on the bench as well in case of injury. The union wanted to increase that number to three. They knew that if the strike was to have any chance of success they had to get the Cosmos on board, and so we were called to a meeting to try to persuade us not to play. The meeting went on so long that we missed a flight to Atlanta for an away game.

The mood among the Cosmos players, perhaps understandably given the diversity of everyone's backgrounds, was mixed. Gary Etherington, who had been born in England but emigrated to the USA at an early age, was very keen on the strike. I remember having a discussion with him, and saying that there were already 144 North American players involved. The new proposal would take that to 216, and if you had that many, it would inevitably dilute the quality of the product.

Like me, Franz Beckenbauer was very vocal against the strike, because, as he said, Europe had a history of football, and it had developed over the previous century or so. In the US, the journey was just beginning. For instance, we'd just signed a young full-back called Greg Ryan from Chicago. I remember one away trip seeing him reading a football coaching book. He was studying techniques for controlling the ball and passing – skills he should have developed growing up – and he was 22. That was the fundamental problem; there was no tradition.

The unions in other sports were very powerful, and the soccer union was trying to replicate that, but the situation wasn't the same. We got a later flight to Atlanta, and at half-time the phone in the dressing room rang – it was another team seeing if we'd started playing before they took a decision on whether to play or not. Once they knew that the Cosmos had played, there was no sense in holding out for a strike, so the season continued.

There were always doubts in my mind as to whether soccer would ever truly catch on in the States in the long term, but Joan and I made sure we lived life to the full during our time in New York. I was always very proactive with the supporters, and a couple of days each week I'd go to the Cosmos office on the 19th floor of the Warner building in Rockefeller Plaza and spend a couple of hours answering letters, sending autographs, photos, posters and memorabilia. We had friends and family coming over the whole time too. They all wanted to see the sights, and I think sorting out itineraries and selecting restaurants for them stood me in good stead for when my career was over.

In the two years I was in New York, I went to the Statue of Liberty six times. When the ferry went across there from Battery Park, I knew the ideal place to stand to get the best photographs. Everybody always made the mistake of rushing to one side, but then the ferry doubled back on itself, so I'd tell my group to stay on the far side of the boat while everybody else was jostling for position.

I didn't really experience the seamier side of New York, although one night when I was about to drive Joan, her sister and my brother through the Lincoln Tunnel, I slowed down at some lights and was approached by some ladies of the night. I think they thought I was touting for business. After I said "Thanks, but no thanks" and began to drive off, they lifted up their skirts in annoyance.

I got into the habit of driving everywhere, which was an experience in itself. Even the chequer-board road pattern was exciting. When I was driving around I used to try to time it to get through as many traffic lights in one go as I could. If I got it right, I could belt through about ten. The problem was the rush-hour traffic and the pollution on a summer's day which was unbelievable. When the roads were first built most people were using horse and carts – they would go at about 8–10 mph, which was slightly faster than the average speed of cars in the city in the late 1970s.

You had to be an aggressive driver too. On one occasion I remember slowing down to turn off, trying to work out the one-way system, and a cab pulled up alongside me. It was a lady driver and she gave me a load of abuse, "If you can't drive, don't fucking drive in Manhattan".

There were always plenty of social occasions going on, and leading up to Carlos Alberto's birthday we were all invited to his Manhattan apartment for a party. The party was to be held around his apartment's rooftop pool and terrace, and his wife suggested that there might be a chance people would end up in the pool. I went prepared with my swimming trunks underneath my trousers, as did several other players.

It was a beautiful summer's evening and the boys were in a boisterous mood, as Carlos always enjoyed a good party. Pele arrived wearing a pristine white suit and some of the boys quickly grabbed him by the arms and legs ready to throw him in the pool. Pele was laughing, but he insisted that the boys remove his gold watch beforehand. Pele never made it into the pool, but a few of the lads and myself did, and we ended up drying off in the poolside sauna.

Speaking to Carlos a little later, while thanking him for a great party, I discussed with him the fact that he loved a good social occasion but was still committed to being a winner on the field. He said something to me which I always remember – "Dennis, you must never forget when the whistle blows". I knew exactly what he meant, that there is a time and place for everything and the commitment to football has to be paramount. It was a great lesson from a world-class player.

I fully embraced the American sporting scene and regularly watched baseball on TV, with the New York Yankees being my big favourite team. Baseball takes a little bit of getting used to, and when my good friend Corny O'Donnell, his wife Betty and his son Patrick came to stay I got some tickets for one of the big games of the year at Yankee Stadium. This was called "Old Timers Day", when all the former players were invited as special guests to the game. Our tickets were just behind home plate. The game, unusually, was a 0–0 draw after nine innings and halfway through I looked along at Corny and he had nodded off. Baseball is something of an acquired taste.

Of course, we shared Giants stadium with the New York Giants American Football team, and they did some pre-season trials which coincided with the end of our season. I was amazed to see the size of some of these professional athletes and became utterly absorbed by how they had brought so much technology and analysis into their training programme. I am still a great follower of American Football on Sky TV, and the Giants remain my favourite team.

In 1978, I played 20 league games and scored 10 goals, with 12 assists. The following year, I played 27 games, and grabbed 16 goals, with 16 assists. My record in the regular 1978 season, after my early-season injury, was very pleasing, giving me a total of 32 points – as the Americans loved statistics you were given two points for a goal and one point for an assist. Pretty good. My record in the 1978 play-offs was better though: played six, scored six, assists five. They nicknamed me 'Sir August', a reference to Reggie Jackson, a hitter for the New York Yankees who was known as 'Mr October', because we both came alive at play-off time.

I got my first hat-trick in the 1979 season against San Jose, and things went well, but then towards the end of the campaign things started to go wrong.

The biggest issue for me that year was the departure of Eddie Firmani. Why he went I'm still not quite sure, but there was always a lot of politicking behind the scenes at the Cosmos, with various cliques jostling for position and trying to influence team selection, something I would experience in the future during my time on the board at Manchester City.

Eddie was replaced by Professor Julio Mazzei, Pele's advisor, who took over as interim coach. Mazzei was inclined to a South American style of football, and I got the sense that he preferred the forward,

Seninho, to me. We had one confrontation about it when he suggested that I might need a rest, but I discussed the situation with him and he eventually played me, and I justified my selection by scoring a goal. Mazzei also changed the system slightly to a 4-4-2 formation. Previously, I'd played up front alongside Chinaglia, but I knew that Mazzei would want to play Seninho. I felt that, while I was doing the business on the pitch, Mazzei couldn't complain and had to keep playing me.

Before the end of the season I was talking to the executives about a contract extension. I was on a three-year deal, but I was looking at a two-year extension that would have taken me through until I was 32. I had a meeting set with Steve Ross, and with the help of my friend, Greg Russell, a New Jersey businessman, we put together a strategy to talk to Steve about a new contract. We met Steve in his office on the top floor of the Warner Building in Rockefeller Plaza. His office was huge, with wood panelling all the way round, and he sat behind an executive desk with several gigantic computers surrounding him. He even slid open a couple of the wood-panelled units to reveal to us a bank of video tapes. His tapes featured footage of players from around the world, sent in from agents and other clubs. This was a confirmation of how seriously the Cosmos were viewed within the football world, and also that their turnover of players was likely to be high.

Despite my reservations about Mazzei, I was still happy to discuss an extended contract. We had an excellent conversation and Steve even offered me a $25,000 bonus for the previous season. I had every reason to believe that everything was fine.

The end to that season was frustrating, though. We won our division, but I pulled a hamstring during the Conference final against Vancouver. They iced me up and I played in the mini-game decider, which we eventually lost in a shootout. That was a failure by the Cosmos's standards, but I still wasn't prepared for what happened in the following couple of months.

We went on a tour of South East Asia and Australia, which was effectively another glorified roadshow. The footballing Harlem Globetrotters had to go schlepping and line Warner Brothers' coffers again. We played 13 games in six weeks in seven countries – Hong Kong, South Korea, Indonesia, Singapore, Japan, Malaysia and

Australia. I'd wake up in the morning, and sometimes I'd struggle to remember what country I was in. As we globe-trotted around Asia we always seemed to be connecting our flights through Singapore Airport, and soon I was almost on nodding terms with all the Customs and Immigration personnel there. My passport was rammed with stamps from around the globe, but it wasn't as if I was sampling a range of cultures at all.

I remember being injured for a game in Sydney and sitting behind John Newcombe, the famous Australian tennis player, at the SCG wondering what I was doing there. There was nothing to be won, and it was just a drag around airports, hotels, training pitches and stadiums. We were handled by Warner's PR company called Dentsu, who treated us like a rock band. In every city there was a press conference with a player relevant to that market. Carlos Alberto, Franz Beckenbauer and I did a press conference in Sydney, and when we'd finished all the press were invited into the next room to attend a press conference for the upcoming Sammy Davis Junior concert.

The Cosmos were getting paid $50,000 a game, but the money situation actually made the whole thing more stressful at times, and took the joy and spontaneity out of playing football. For example, in Trinidad we were kicking around the hotel in our flip-flops, with boots in our hands, waiting to go to the stadium for the match. The kick-off time was getting closer, and it was only when the execs appeared and confirmed that the money was in the bank that we received the go-ahead to play.

That wasn't the ideal way to prepare for a game at all. We were living out of suitcases, always on the move, and seemingly of no fixed abode. We were paid cash for daily expenses, which meant that everybody was carrying more and more of it around. I kept it in my case as we didn't have any access to banks when we were on the road.

I became totally fed up. It was no kind of life. At the end of the six-week tour the team was about to fly across the Pacific to Los Angeles and then New York, but I decided to go the other way and head straight back to Britain. I went to the BA desk in Sydney, got my ticket refunded, pulled a roll of dollar notes out of my pocket and paid cash for the quickest flight back to London, first class.

I couldn't wait to get back to Britain, and my homecoming was made even better when I found out that Joan was pregnant. We'd bought an apartment in Bowdon during my time at City, as we decided that Manchester was the city we would like to settle in long term, so Joan had been living there while I went on that final tour. She'd known about her pregnancy for a while, but had wanted me to be the first to know.

I was relaxing in Manchester when, with no warning, I saw a story in the *Mail*: "American Club to Sell Rebel Tueart".

I was surprised. After all, I'd discussed a contract extension with Steve Ross and there'd been no indication they wanted to transfer me. I had permission to have some time at home and I didn't necessarily want out of New York and the Cosmos – I'd loved the challenge of proving myself alongside all those stellar talents. However, the fact that I was about to become a father also meant there was no way I could keep up their touring schedule, and if you played for the Cosmos you had to buy into the whole package, or not at all. I became resigned to the fact that my New York excursion was over.

CHAPTER 11

CITY! THE SOAP OPERA

Although my jet lag faded within a couple of days of flying back from Sydney in March 1980, I continued to feel disorientated after I arrived back in the UK. My mind was in a spin. I was going to become a father within a few months and, although I officially remained a Cosmos player, I realised that I needed to sort out my future in football as quickly as possible. I'd now turned 30, but I didn't have sleepless nights worrying about reaching that particular milestone. I'd always looked after myself and been relatively lucky with injuries. I felt in very good shape when I came back to England after a two-year absence but, in the back of my mind, I was concerned about whether my time abroad may have meant that I'd become a forgotten man. There was only one way to find out; put myself out there and see which clubs were interested. I knew that my next move needed to be the right one, as it was likely to be the last defining transfer of my career.

The agent, Dennis Roach, contacted me after a couple of weeks and said the Cosmos were prepared to sell and that Derby County were very interested. Their manager, Colin Addison, had said he would give the Cosmos their £235,000 back and would pay me the same salary. I was flattered, but Derby had fallen on hard times and would end up being relegated from Division One that season. In any case, I told Dennis that we'd just settled into our apartment in Bowdon and that, with Joan pregnant, I'd only look at clubs in the North West – I'd spent enough time on the road with the Cosmos over the previous couple of years. Dennis came back to me and said that he'd spoken to Gordon Lee at Everton, who was interested, but the Toffees had no money.

I knew full well what my first choice was. Even when I was enjoying myself at the Cosmos, I knew that my heart was still with Manchester City and I kept track of their results. I also knew how excited I would be to work with Malcolm Allison, architect of City's success in the early Seventies. He was trying to develop a new young team and I felt I could bring some experience to that group. So I decided to take matters into my own hands, and rang the City chairman, Peter Swales, to see if they were interested. He said that they were, which delighted me, but I told him I needed to have a chat to the manager, Malcolm Allison, because there's nothing worse than a chairman foisting a player on a manager. Malcolm came over to our apartment in Bowdon and we sat down and talked.

In the two years since I'd left, there had been a massive change in personnel at City. From what I'd heard, this was largely down to Malcolm. That first generation of Manchester boys who I'd played alongside, headed up by Peter Barnes and Gary Owen, had been split up. There had been bad feeling too, because neither Peter nor Gary had wanted to go, but Malcolm didn't see a future for them at the club and he sold them both to West Brom. Because of his achievements at City with Joe Mercer, the crowd didn't get onto Malcolm about it too much, but there had already been mutterings among the City faithful as the club was clearly struggling. There was no Dave Watson, Asa Hartford, or Mick Channon either – they'd been bombed out too. It was all part of the Allison revolution.

I'd got the heads up from all of these lads about Malcolm. Their opinion was fairly damning: he was full of grandiose ideas and plans, but they didn't work; he couldn't mould a team. And yet there was unquestionably an aura which surrounded the man. When you met Mal, he was one of those powerful, charismatic guys who could charm, convince, and cajole you. Although I know that Malcolm was seen as having a big ego in the game, he was more sensitive and thoughtful than most people imagine. His TV persona of the cigar-chomping, champagne-swilling coach was different from the one I saw at City, where he was very conscious of the needs of the club. When Malcolm came to the house, I came straight out with what was on my mind:

"As far as I'm aware, there are two Malcolm Allisons – the one I know from Bell and Summerbee, a great thinker and tactician; but there's also the one I know from Hartford, Watson and Channon who can't handle experienced players effectively. The second one is no use to me, Mal."

I may have turned 30, but I was still ambitious, still felt I was potentially an England international and I needed to have a full understanding and relationship with the coach. I got the impression he respected me for being so direct and honest, and we more or less agreed there and then that I'd be on my way back to City. But the Cosmos needed to give their blessing.

Roach came back and said the Cosmos weren't happy with anything less than Derby had offered. So I rang Cosmos's vice-president, Rafael de la Sierra, who was handling the deal. I explained to him that, with the value of the dollar falling, if they sold me for £150,000 they would effectively be getting back what they'd paid. I felt they were trying to take advantage and that this would be a realistic offer. I then told him if they really forced the issue, I would go back over there for a year and sit out the remainder of my deal. I was nervous that I'd be stuck in limbo, but Rafael eventually agreed and asked me to get City to fax the £150,000 offer, and the deal was done.

I got some sort of closure on my spell (and was able to collect the rest of my stuff) at Cosmos when, in July 1980, Manchester City, Roma and Vancouver Whitecaps were invited to join the Cosmos and play in the Transatlantic Tournament in New York. I got a great reception from the fans, but I still felt a certain bitterness; not so much about the decision to sell me, because differences of opinion are always going to happen, but because of the manner in which the deal was done. It was all very shabby, and I found out that several of the executives were unhappy that I'd left.

I had to accept that there was a raft of different forces at work at the Cosmos, and the web of intrigue which existed between the coach Mazzei (as expected, he had brought in South American players, as well as the Belgian striker Francois van der Elst, although he didn't play much), the big bucks which poured in, and the agents who were always circling was hard to penetrate. The Cosmos were now recognised as the first global soccer club and every mercenary player, agent or coach wanted their noses in the trough.

An interesting footnote to the story of my time with the Cosmos is the re-emergence of the name since the brand was bought and re-launched in 2010 by Paul Kemsley, the former Spurs vice chairman. I was invited to New York for the official launch, announced by Pele and attended by New York Mayor Bloomberg and Sunil Gulati, President of the United States Soccer Federation, and also to Old Trafford when the team played Manchester United in a friendly for Paul Scholes's testimonial in the summer of 2011. The new owners have targeted securing an MLS franchise in the next few years, but in the meantime Kemsley has spoken of his wish to build the club up from the grassroots, and tap into the Mexican, Italian and Hispanic communities in New York, who are crazy about football. There are tens of thousands of kids playing soccer in New York and Long Island. Manchester City even have a supporters branch which assembles at the Mad Hatters Saloon and Beer Garden on Third Avenue in Manhattan, to watch Premier League games. In January 2011 the Cosmos installed Eric Cantona as Director of Soccer to help the club regain its status as the number-one team in the US and to become one of the best clubs in the world.

It will take some serious investment, but it be very interesting to see if the Cosmos can return to the glory days of the Seventies.

The big problem coming back to England was adapting to a different quality of team to the one I'd left. The Cosmos had been a team of internationals, but at Maine Road the most charitable thing you could say was that it was a team in a state of transition. Sometimes it felt like a crèche, sometimes like a refuge for over-priced footballers and sometimes both. It was barely recognisable from the club I'd left two years earlier. The best comparison I can make is that I underwent a similar experience to that of the John Simm character in *Life on Mars*, who slips into a coma and suddenly wakes up back in the Seventies, where the vibe and the attitudes and, of course, the personnel are completely different. The only difference was I was now pitched into life at 1980s City and the start of the club's problems.

As well as sweeping away the old guard, Malcolm Allison and Peter Swales had taken big, big, speculative punts in the transfer market. Mike Robinson arrived from Preston for £750,000, and Steve Mackenzie came from Crystal Palace for £250,000, making him the most expensive teenager in the country. Neither pulled up too many trees at City, although later on Robinson did well at Brighton and Mackenzie scored that stunning goal in the 1981 FA Cup final for City. By that time, City had also splashed out £1.5 million on Steve Daley from Wolves. It was absolutely crazy. I liked Steve, but he freely admitted to all of us that he wasn't even worth half that. In my early games back at City, I played alongside him in midfield, and he wasn't particularly quick, or especially biting in the tackle. Steve was neat and tidy, and that was about it. Every time he did something constructive on the park, he'd look over to Malcolm for approval, like a nervous little kid. I'd expected the most expensive midfielder in the country to take games by the scruff of the neck, but the quality simply wasn't there.

Steve was very, very honest though, and I often heard him say to Malcolm, "But I'm not sure what you're asking me to do... " He wasn't the only one who felt that way, but he *was* the only one with that ludicrous price tag hanging over him. Two years later, he was binned off to Burnley for virtually nothing. These days, I'm told that Steve does an hilarious after-dinner speech where most of the jokes are at his own expense, but he wasn't laughing 30 years ago.

I'm not sure what the Allison and Swales strategy was at that time. Maybe they felt that with some trophy signings they could once again paint Manchester sky blue. They were always looking nervously over to Old Trafford, and trying to get one over on them. But bringing in players like Steve Daley, and the likes of Colin Viljoen from Ipswich and Bobby Shinton from Wrexham wouldn't get the club anywhere.

What was in Malcolm's favour was that the next generation of City youngsters was starting to emerge. Tommy Caton, Ray Ranson, Nicky Reid and Tony Henry were showing immense promise, in the same way that Peter Barnes and Gary Owen had done five years before.

Ray Ranson was an extremely talented full-back who had cleaned my boots as a young apprentice, but he always had ambition to be a successful footballer. Luckily, he was better at playing football than cleaning boots. I was fastidious about that and on one occasion threw my boots across the dressing room floor and asked him to clean them again. Years later I joked with Ray, who is now a highly successful businessman, that I was the one who gave him a sense of discipline.

There were a lot of talented young players, but they were still learning. All the elements needed to be right at the club in order for them to succeed, and the blend was never right at City under Malcolm Allison. He often seemed to exist in his own world. He told us that the most influential book he'd ever read was *The Master Game: Pathway To Higher Consciousness*, by American author Robert Ropp. He'd talk about the "great games of life" to us, which included money games, war games and political games. Mal's higher-level thinking did little to appeal to the youngsters who, with all due respect, needed clear tactical guidance. He'd just be met with a sea of blank faces. Whenever we travelled away, he was always reading the biographies of great leaders. I remember him once reading a book about Genghis Khan, and telling me with great gusto about Khan's life. It was as though he was obsessed by leadership, always looking for the elements that made the great and powerful tick.

The fact was, though, that Malcolm had never proved himself a great manager. In the early Seventies, he'd had Joe Mercer's guiding hand behind him, and it had been Allison's decision to buy Rodney Marsh which broke up his working relationship with Mercer. Now he was struggling to get that blend again.

He was a man of many contradictions. On the one hand, he was very innovative in his training regimes. He brought in ballroom dancing champion Lenny Hepple, whom I'd worked with at Sunderland under Alan Brown, for balance training and who implemented many individual routines with particular emphasis on shoulder movements and body positioning to get into a comfortable, balanced position. Malcolm was also fantastic on a one-to-one basis with the youngsters. He'd put his arm around Tommy Caton, and talk to him in depth about his distribution, and Steve Mackenzie about his contribution to the team, but he struggled to get his grand vision across to the young players, and indeed the rest of us.

You had to have been in the game for some time to understand Mal. Often his instructions were bewildering.

There was one occasion at the training ground at Platt Lane when Malcolm tried to explain to each player precisely what our responsibility in the team was. He then sent us to set-up formation in our respective positions to begin the session. I understood what he was trying to do, but as we turned to take our positions I asked our young midfielder, Tony Henry, if he knew what Malcolm wanted. Tony looked me straight in the eye and said, "Haven't a fucking clue".

That was the problem. Malcolm needed more good players with experience, and that's why he'd been successful with City the previous time. He could deal with characters, like the Bells, the Lees and the Summerbees, but he struggled to coach and blend those youngsters who were finding their way in the game. I felt that Malcolm wanted them to run before they could walk, so to speak, and in my first season back we just about avoided relegation and finished 17th, which for a team of City's stature, and considering what I'd been used to in my first spell there, was unacceptable.

This was the most challenging period of my career, both on and off the pitch. I was starting up front with Michael Robinson, and scored my first goals on my return to Maine Road with a double against Bolton. I rarely celebrated goals as hard as I did that day, because I knew that I had something to prove after my time away. My first goal came from a Paul Power cross, and I had to backpedal before volleying in, and then I toe-poked home from a Nicky Reid cross. But gone was the buccaneering style I'd loved in the late 1970s. There was a real sense of nervousness among the players and fans at Maine Road. I found the games tight and miserable.

The bright spot was the arrival of my first born, Mark. In April I was preparing for a game away at Wolves. Joan still had a month to go until her official due date, but on the Friday night she was up several times. Then, in the early hours of Saturday morning she got up again and said she thought the baby was coming, so at 5am on the day of the game I took her off to hospital, where they said the birth was imminent. I rang Tony Book, who was still assistant manager, and let him know. The team bus was leaving at 10.30, so he said he'd come and pick me up and take me himself. He really needed me on the pitch, because City weren't safe from relegation. I wasn't that keen, but the contractions slowed down, so I rang him back. Because I was fairly confident the baby wasn't coming I agreed to play.

He whizzed me down in time for the match, and I played the first half. At half-time, though, the phone went in the dressing room, which was very unusual. Tony answered it, turned to me and said, "It's a boy." Mark had been born at 2.50pm. I went out, and scored a penalty to make it 2–1. I had to focus completely on the game, but deep down I was very proud and couldn't wait to get to the hospital and see Joan and our little boy.

All the journalists down at the game found out, and because it was in the *Manchester Pink*, a newspaper published just after the final whistle, the story was picked up by the *Newcastle Pink*. I went straight to the hospital and could only call our families then, but they'd already seen it in the paper!

The joy of becoming a dad was an indescribable feeling, but other events off the pitch, as well as the onfield troubles at City, were a reality jolt. From 1973 to 1980, I'd felt armour-plated. I'd won the FA Cup and the League Cup, played for England and starred in New York with many of the legends of world football. My star had been in the ascendancy, and I thought I was indestructible. But after I arrived back at City for my second spell, I was forced to take stock.

In 1980 my brother Kevin, who was only 24, was diagnosed with a non-Hodgkin's lymphoma, a kind of tumour, behind his nose, and we thought for a while he might not come through it. Then my uncle died of cancer at the age of 49, and my dad passed away soon after in 1981 at the age of 54, also as a result of cancer.

Three years later, our family would suffer a similar upset, when Joan had a miscarriage. We'd already had our second child, Leigh, but early on in her pregnancy she began to feel unwell, and eventually we had to go and see her specialist. The specialist gave us the sad news that the baby had died, and we had to return a couple of days later where she had to deliver the stillborn baby. Happily, we went on to have another healthy boy, John, but the emotional and psychological effects of these events in 1981 and 1984 on our previously cushioned family lifestyle were immense.

When things are going well, you're so full of yourself you think nothing can touch you. In a way, since the FA Cup win of 1973, I'd been cocooned inside a little bubble of success and, apart from not establishing myself in the England team, my football career had been on an upwards trajectory. I remember going to see my brother's specialist and asking what it would cost, saying to him that I'd pay whatever to get the treatment he needed. Money couldn't help, though. The specialist just said we had to wait and hope, and that's when I realised how powerless I was. Real issues are magnified when you play football at top level, because you are in such a privileged position, so divorced from reality that when it hits you've got that much further to come crashing to earth. Luckily, Kevin survived and is still here today. As a brother he is a source of great strength with his fantastic, optimistic view on life, even though the radiotherapy has destroyed some of his taste buds and he has regular trouble with his sinuses.

When my dad was ill, I was trying to re-establish myself back over here as a player with City, and I had a young son, so I was tearing up and down from Manchester to Newcastle, feeling that I wasn't giving enough of my attention to Joan and Mark, or Mum and Dad. I'd been up in Newcastle on a visit, and it seemed that Dad was pulling round, so I came back to Manchester. Then the next day I got a call from my mam saying he'd taken a turn for the worse and it didn't look like he was going to make it. I rang Malcolm Allison and he told me to go up. When I got there, my dad was dying. I remember looking at him lying there in intensive care, with the oxygen mask, the heart-rate monitor and all the various tubes he was hooked up to, and just thinking how quickly you can fall from a position of strength to total helplessness. All I could do was watch, and try to remember him the way he'd been. He'd always been a very opinionated man and the eldest in a family of one brother and five sisters, and it saddens me that he never got to know any of his grandchildren, of whom he'd have been immensely proud.

City began the 1980/81 season poorly, and we failed to win any of our first 12 games. We lost 2–1 to Stoke at home that September, and I scored but damaged my wrist in a collision with their goal-keeper. I was in plaster and out for four weeks, and by the time I was fit Malcolm Allison had been sacked. I felt a little sorry for him, but he seemed to struggle when he was left to manage on his own. His obvious talents were as a coach on the training pitch with talented players and his charisma was undeniable, but his management of the youngsters was found wanting.

Malcolm's replacement was John Bond from Norwich. He'd been very successful there, and was good in front of the cameras, but the question was whether he could handle a big club. Just because John had been good with limited resources at a certain level, it didn't necessarily mean that he would be able to make the step upwards. His teams had always been very attacking – at Norwich he had Phil Boyer and Ted McDougall up-front, with Martin Peters ghosting in late at the back post. Allison had signed Kevin Reeves for £1 million from Norwich that summer, and Bond was always going to look to bring in his own men. Sure enough, Tommy Hutchison, Gerry Gow and Bobby McDonald arrived – some wise old Scottish heads who knew when to get stuck in, and City needed that robustness. The whole changeover between Allison and Bond was lent a soap opera feel by the fact that Granada TV cameras were filming a documentary about life at the club called *City!* It wasn't an especially flattering portrayal. Much of the time the players seemed to be sitting around listening to Peter Swales announcing some more news about managerial changes. It took me back to my first experience of the players' lounge in 1974, and the coup which marked the end of Ron Saunders' reign. I still felt I could offer John Bond's City a great deal. I'd just turned 31, and I wanted to convince him that I was ambitious, not just a disposable member of the old guard. I'd been playing just off Michael Robinson, but he felt I wasn't effective playing up front like that. John wanted his front man to play with his back to goal, whereas my strength was getting the ball in front of me, and running on to it.

I scored four in a 5–1 League Cup win over Notts County when his new signings were cup-tied, playing with a strapping on my wrist. I hoped that would send a message to John that I was still capable, but he kept on leaving me out of the team as he tried to balance grit with flair, and I felt I was increasingly becoming just a bit-part player.

We struggled to get the balance right in the league, but we managed to make it to the FA Cup final. I didn't play in a 6–0 win over Norwich in the fourth round, so I was never going to be selected for the fifth round, which made my position even more uncertain. I didn't even travel for the semi-final against Ipswich at Villa Park, which shows how far out in the cold I was. I had a huge affinity for City, but I had to consider that my career at Maine Road might be over.

John pulled me back in the squad for the final against Spurs at Wembley, because he wanted players with big-game experience. During our stay at the Selsdon Park Hotel in the build-up to the match, I got closer to him. We chatted about my career in football, particularly at City during my first spell, and I felt that he began to understand me and my passion for the game better. Initially, John had kept his distance from the players, probably wary of the fact that many of the youngsters were Allison's pet projects, but he was extremely adept at getting his message across to both youngsters and experienced professionals.

I sat behind him on the bench during the final, shouting encouragement, but it's impossible on those occasions not to feel a little isolated when you are left out of the side, especially when I recalled the intense feelings I'd had at Wembley back in 1973 and 1976.

The game finished 1–1, and I was again named the substitute for the replay. It was a fantastic game, and if Ricky Villa hadn't scored his magnificent winner, Steve Mackenzie's stunning volley from outside the area, which made it 1–1, would probably have been replayed endlessly to this day. Spurs had just equalised at 2–2 when Bond told me I was going on, as he said that the opposition seemed to be tiring and he wanted to up the tempo and give us a more attacking option. I was just warming up when Ricky Villa scored to make it 3–2. I had two decent half-chances – a right-foot volley that the 'keeper saved, and a left-foot volley that skimmed the outside of the post – but I was left wondering what might have happened if I'd started or come on a little earlier.

At the end of the game I remember congratulating the Spurs players and, as a senior member of the squad, trying to pick up the rest of the players. Guys like Tommy Caton, Ray Ranson and Steve Mackenzie were devastated. They were slouched with their arms crossed and their heads bowed as we stood back and Steve Perryman led his team up the steps to collect the FA Cup. There were 100,000 people there, but I felt absolutely alone on the pitch, pretty much convinced that that would be my last game for City. I was getting on for 32, and I was realistic enough to realise that when it hasn't quite worked out for a manager his first thought is to prepare for the future, and that probably wasn't going to involve me.

I wasn't prepared to duck out without a fight though. I had one year left on my contract, so I decided over the summer that, as I'd more likely than not be looking for a new club, I had to get myself as fit as possible. Malcolm Allison's innovative approach to training had included taking us to the Salford University Human Laboratory for physical tests, and I'd got friendly with one of the professors there, Bruce Davies. Bruce maintained that it was pointless foot-ballers doing runs for longer than two miles in training, and that what we should be doing was completing shuttle runs within that distance, and building up both our aerobic and our anaerobic fitness. So during the summer of 1981 I put myself through a programme of physical preparation for the start of the season, based around his training suggestions. And when it came to our usual pre-season sessions at Manchester University's training fields, I was in the top half-dozen in the running tests.

John Bond told me that Arthur Cox, whom I knew from Sunderland, was interested in taking me to Newcastle. No fee had been agreed but, unbeknown to City, I met Cox for a clandestine meeting in the car park at Newcastle Airport. Newcastle were in the Second Division at the time, but with them being my boyhood team I was obviously keen to join. When I went back to City on the eve of the new season, I kept asking John about the move, but he eventually said he'd changed his mind about letting me go. He said he'd looked at my goals-to-games ratio and realised that it would cost him too much to replace me.

Remarkably, I was now back in favour and John started using me in an attacking central midfield role, which I found really suited me. I played there in a pre-season friendly against AC Milan in the San Siro, then scored from there in another pre-season game against

PSV Eindhoven. John brought Asa Hartford back from Everton and Phil Boyer to play up front. He also briefly brought back Trevor Francis, although he was soon sold to Sampdoria. That was the first clear sign to me that City's financial problems were mounting up. Along with Wolves, we were the biggest "names" in English football to really suffer with money trouble.

Trevor had a huge amount of natural talent; Asa and I used to call him 'The Happy Amateur', because while we were warming up and stretching and getting mentally prepared for a game, he'd just wander in to the dressing room, get dressed and play.

City started that 1981/82 season really well, and I scored 11 goals in 17 games. But it all went horribly wrong in November in a game against Sunderland at Maine Road. Two minutes before half-time, I made a forward run, and suddenly felt a pain as though something had cracked me across the back of my left ankle. I went down, and when Roy Bailey, the physio, came on to treat me the first thing I asked was who'd kicked me. He told me there'd been nobody anywhere near me. Both Roy and I were squash players and we both knew then that it was a classic squash injury – an Achilles tear, which was later confirmed as a complete rupture.

Thinking about it now, I realise that I'd had a lot of pain in the lower part of the Achilles for the previous few weeks, and the first 10–15 minutes of training had felt like running on broken glass until it got warmed up. After training I was having to put ice on the area. The club doctor had also given me an injection directly into the Achilles after an unsuccessful course of anti–inflammatory tablets. I feel now that it was an injury that wasn't properly treated, and that I'd clearly been carrying it for some time before it finally ruptured. There had been a game against Northampton in the League Cup when I'd scored a right-foot volley, and as I'd pushed off on my left foot I'd gone down with a spasm of cramp, which had never previously been a problem. By carrying the injury and compensating for the weakness, I'd probably been putting extra pressure on the tendon.

Roy tracked down the club surgeon, David Markham, who'd been shopping in Manchester, and by six o'clock that evening I was in the operating theatre.

The plaster came off after six weeks, but that was just the first stage of the long, slow road to recovery. I went into the training ground every day, and did a little bit of training. The hardest thing was learning to walk again, just learning technically how to do it. I also had to be very disciplined. I watched videos, read books and tried to keep a semblance of normality. I'd be laid up on the couch, then I'd get down onto the floor and do as many sit-ups as I could. Joan served my meals on plates three-quarters the normal size to try to keep my weight under control, and every day I'd eat a big bowl of natural yoghurt with fresh fruit chopped into it.

I recalled seeing the *Panorama* programme which showed how Colin Bell tried to battle back from his knee injury. The reporter suggested that, as Bell pounded the streets around Maine Road, the documentary should probably be retitled *The Loneliness of the Long Distance Runner*. And it is indeed a lonely road back to fitness. Immediately you become detached from the club and the daily routine, and inevitably your team-mates, who are busy concentrating on their own well-being, forget about you. But I never, ever gave up. All those years before, I'd become a professional at Sunderland because I had drawn upon my resolve after Newcastle decided not to sign me. I've always been resilient, and my parents and Alan Brown drummed into me that you have to be tough in life to survive.

The boredom was terrible though. I bought myself a bike and I cycled to Maine Road every day. I couldn't go down the motorway, so I had to take the bumpy back roads. After a week I'd got so saddle sore that I had to get Joan to put some padding on the seat. I've always been considerate to cyclists ever since. Every day it was 11.5 miles there, treatment, then 11.5 miles back – 33 minutes in and 36 on the way back because it was slightly more uphill.

I used to spend hours in the weights gym. It was 20 yards long with a mirror at the end, so I'd walk up and down, checking my technique. We had a set of dips bars, so I'd hold myself up on that and practise running with my legs in mid-air. It was all about manually teaching myself how to walk and run again, keeping my shoulders square to ensure that I put equal pressure on both legs. I also spent half an hour each day sitting on the edge of the bath flexing my ankle in warm water.

I had a setback in the summer. The wound on my left ankle kept on getting infected, so I had to wander round in flip-flops. I was 32, and my adviser Reuben Kay asked me if I was really sure I wanted to go on. He suggested considering a personal injury payout, but for me it wasn't about the money; it was another challenge I wanted to overcome. I refused to wallow in self pity.

I got back into the squad for a 1982 pre-season friendly against AEK in Athens, but I scored an own-goal – the first I'd ever scored. Despite all my rehabilitation efforts, I'd lost some muscle bulk in my left calf, and consequently wasn't as explosive in short sprints, so I had to adjust to more of a holding midfield role.

I was substitute against Watford for the third game of the 1982/83 season, and I proved to myself that I could still play at the top level. I came off the sub's bench after Joe Corrigan was injured early on, and left-back Bobby McDonald went in goal. I grabbed the winner with a flying header 15 minutes from time, and that goal meant as much to me as any during my career.

By October, I gradually began to feel sharper. I scored with a back-post header in a fantastic 2–2 draw against United at Old Trafford, and then at home to Swansea cracked home a volley which still crops up now and again on repeats of *Match of The Day* from the Eighties. We were awarded an indirect free-kick on the edge of the six-yard box, but with the wall so close there's not a lot you can do with a normal shot. Asa suggested that if he flicked it up, I could volley it, as we had tried it once before during my first spell at City, and it had hit the bar, but this time it worked perfectly, and finished up in the top corner. The Football League then clamped down, and ruled that the ball had to roll on the floor before another player could strike it legally.

These were rare moments of triumph, because after Christmas we began dropping like a stone, and John Bond resigned. We suffered with injuries, and the youngsters simply didn't have the wherewithal or experience to salvage the situation. The old heads who Bond had brought in two years earlier – Gow and Hutchison – had departed, and the whole thing disintegrated around us. I don't think anybody really thought we'd be relegated at the end of it all, but football is really all about momentum and, with City's financial problems, the lack of managerial stability and the brutal realisation that the quality simply wasn't there at Maine Road anymore, we were in serious trouble. John Benson, who'd been Bond's assistant, took over, but he had no full managerial experience, and it got to the point where we couldn't win a game to save our lives. I was in the last year of my contract, and I knew that the end was nigh, but I'd spoken to Peter Swales and we had an agreement that I'd get an extra year if we avoided relegation.

The season ended with the infamous game against Luton at Maine Road. There were over 40,000 there. A draw would have been enough for us (Luton needed a win to stay up), but as the game wore on, we looked more and more tired. With the match all square at 0–0, players from both sides kept pestering the referee about how much time was left. Late on, after the ball came out to him on the edge of the box, Luton's Yugoslav striker Raddy Antic shot and scored through a crowd of City players. An almost surreal atmosphere descended on Maine Road as the terrible truth sunk in that we were poised to hurtle through the relegation trap door.

I ran and ran for the last few minutes, but could feel the whole thing slipping away. We exchanged nervous glances. We yelled at one another. The home fans screamed at us to get the ball forward, but we had nothing left. No more magic in our boots. There were no more Colin Bells or Mike Summerbees to bail us out of trouble. The crowd began to feel very distant from me, and I knew that my City career was about to end in the most desperate of circumstances.

At the final whistle Luton manager David Pleat galloped like a horse across the pitch in his beige suit, and the Luton players, in their orange and white shirts, went to their fans at the far end of the Kippax. I was in a world of my own, not knowing where to go or how to react. I thought back to all the great games I'd played in at Maine Road. The League Cup game against United in '76, when we'd trounced them 4–0, the match against champions Derby when I'd pulled the trigger at the death and won us the game. Moments that I'd never, ever forget. And it all ended like this. I was the only one of the first-team squad whose contract was expiring, and at 32 I knew I wasn't going to get another one. As I walked up the tunnel the frustration built up, and as we got to the final door before the dressing room, the Luton skipper – and, as it turned out, future City boss – Brian Horton, turned to shake my hand. My reaction wasn't big or clever, but it summed up the frustration I was feeling. I wellied Brian, and after a minor scuffle, I disappeared into the dressing room, shattered and broken-hearted, like the rest of my team-mates.

A few days later, as expected, my years of service to City were ended by a four-line letter. Peter Swales didn't even tell me himself. The letter was handed to me by the secretary, Bernard Halford. There was no phone call, no discussion, no breaking it gently. It can be a tough and unforgiving world, can football.

Desperate though the final days at City had been, I still believed I had something to offer at the top level for one last season and I didn't want to leave – partly because I had become involved in business in the Manchester area. I'd always had an eye out for what to do when my career was over, and when I came back from the USA I did a Business Studies course at St Helens College of Technology, funded by the PFA. In my last couple of years at City, I made a point of speaking with the corporate sponsors in the directors' lounge. By that stage Joan had stopped coming to matches because of the baby, and because when she was given complimentary seats in the Main Stand she sat next to a group of supporters who used to give me a mouthful for the entire game. With no one to meet up with in the players' lounge, I thought I'd use my time wisely. I was always on the lookout for opportunities and Alan Taylor, a friend of mine, had been working for Bass. He used a conference production company called In Focus to manage their new product launches, and he introduced me to them. The company also had a photographic studio that was used by advertising agencies and catalogue companies. It was an experience I was prepared to look at, and in the 1982/83 season I ended up working with the photographer in the afternoons, for no money, presenting his portfolio to potential clients. That was an eye-opener. I'd been used to ringing people up and saying, "Hi, this is Dennis Tueart, the footballer", and with my profile that automatically opened doors. As I found my way in business, I'd phone a company and say, "Hi, this is Dennis Tueart" and the voice on the end of the telephone wouldn't recognise my name. Already, I was beginning to understand that, although football might give me a good springboard into a business career, I couldn't simply rely on "being Dennis Tueart" in order to be successful.

So, I drew a radius of an hour's travel around my house and looked at a list of possible clubs. I spoke to Gordon Taylor at the PFA and told him I'd be keen to move to Sheffield, Birmingham, Lancashire or the Potteries. A few days after I spoke to Taylor, Richie Barker at Stoke offered me a two-year deal, but I told him I wasn't in it for the money. I suggested we agree a one-year deal, and then if it worked out we could discuss it further.

After I'd signed the contract at Stoke I went outside onto the pitch. That was around the time when clubs were experimenting with cutting the grass in different patterns, and I remember looking at the concentric circles and thinking what a beautiful surface it was. I was really looking forward to playing on it, and I said as much to Richie. He said we wouldn't be using the surface that much, and told me that he believed in hitting the ball forward early into Positions of Optimum Maximum Opportunity (POMO). I suppose I wasn't really paying much attention because, while I kept saying how great the pitch would be once they cut it, he repeated that they weren't going to – he wanted the grass left long so that when we hit balls over the top they would hold up.

I soon realised that Richie was a zealot, completely obsessed by POMO and the long-ball game. It was very much in vogue at the time. Graham Taylor was enjoying success with direct football at Watford – but he still utilised the prodigious skills of John Barnes. The annoying thing was that Stoke had some very good players. A young Steve Bould was at centre-back, and they could also call upon the likes of Robbie James, Sammy McIlroy, Micky Thomas and Mark Chamberlain. Mark went on to play for England and is the father of Alex Oxlade-Chamberlain, the young Arsenal star. When you also consider that we had Brendan O'Callaghan up front as well, I felt that we had the nucleus of a skilful side. But Barker was adamant that we should play the long ball. He had somebody sitting in the stands during our games drawing lines charting every pass, so that if you weren't hitting it long enough and quickly enough, you'd be given the stats afterwards to prove it.

In our first training session at Keele University after the summer, Richie had us do a cross-country run. We'd done no warm-up or stretches or anything, we just got sent out on a four-mile circuit. I'd kept myself in decent shape over the summer, and I was in the top half-dozen or so, but as we neared the finish I realised nobody was slowing down. Sure enough Richie had us go and do another lap. So our first training session back was an eight-mile run. He wasn't interested in ball work – he just wanted us fit for his POMO football. It was utterly ridiculous, and went against everything I'd learnt from Bruce Davies at Salford University about what foot-ballers needed to do to stay fit.

We then travelled to our pre-season training camp in Sweden. Richie found us a great place in a forest with a 1,000-metre track covered in bark chippings. We did a lot of work there, and to be honest, once the aches and pains from that eight-mile run at Keele had gone, physically it was one of the best pre-seasons I've had.

It was all brutally physical though, and the players were worried about possible injuries, so we pleaded with Richie to compromise a bit and let us actually play football. He was having none of it, though. He wanted direct football and that was the end of it. When we did finally see a ball, it was straight into full, 90-minute, matches. He insisted on playing a load of pre-season games, so by the time we came to the first day of the season we'd already played 17 matches, and that's not good for you at all.

I was one of the senior pros at the club, along with Sammy McIlroy and Robbie James, who pleaded with Richie not to play long ball all the time, because I felt that it failed to take into account the fact there were some really talented ball players at the Victoria Ground, but Richie was stubborn and dug his heels in. I don't know what it was about Stoke, but the club kept getting managers who wanted to grind results out and play the long ball. Alan Durban had preceded Richie, and it was at Stoke that he came out with his infamous line, "If you want entertainment you should go and watch clowns". That was when it really hit home to me how much money is wasted by clubs when players are bought who don't fit with the manager's system.

There are two attributes that mark out a good manager:

motivation and recruitment. He has to be able to get the players playing, but he also has to be able to buy the right players. By that I don't mean just having a load of money and signing the best in the world – I mean the ability to blend players and to create a whole side that works together. Richie did neither of those things and was sacked in November 1983.

Richie's assistant, Bill Asprey, took over – another POMO merchant, and he had no experience of being a first-team manager. I had only played three games for the club, but I knew I wanted out.

Around that time I got a call from John Benson, who'd followed John Bond to Burnley that summer. They had a good set-up there and some quality players, like Brian Flynn, Mike Phelan and Kevin Reeves, along with my friend Willie Donachie. It was a proper football town with a traditional ground, and the offer came at a time when I wanted out of Stoke, so I accepted the invitation to move. I knew I could rely on John to play football in the right way, and I thought it was a chance to end my career on a high, maybe winning promotion to Division One.

I played ten league games for the Clarets and scored five goals but we missed out on promotion. To be honest I was never fully happy with my form after the Achilles injury. I used to speak to Asa Hartford, who ended up playing until he was 38. 'I'll play as long as my legs let me,' he said. But Asa's game wasn't about explosive play and scoring goals. Mine was, and I wanted to be up there at the sharp end. Although on the face of it my record at Burnley was good, I knew I couldn't play at the standard I demanded of myself, so I packed it in.

When I retired there was a tiny story in the *Sunday Mirror* saying I'd hung up my boots, almost the same insignificant size as the piece which had mentioned my debut. I'd entered the football world with nothing and, in the end, I left with barely a whimper.

The two years after a footballer finishes playing can be traumatic, and I got little or no help. The PFA is excellent at organising courses for players, but when they're still playing precious few footballers take advantage. When you're living such a relaxed lifestyle it's very hard to envisage a life after football: most players either can't see it or don't want to. The PFA founded the community coaching scheme to give footballers an opportunity to have a job after they have finished playing, because most players don't want to let go of that football side. That's why so many work in the media and in hospitality: football's the only thing they know. In business, people get all glossy-eyed around footballers and give them jobs because they think their profile will generate business, but you've got to be able to actually do the job. There are no free lunches after your playing career ends.

After a decade or so of earning big wages, suddenly players had to learn how to do something. Today, many of the leading stars probably have enough money that they don't have to work, but they still need something to make them get out of bed in the morning and give them structure to their week.

Joan was very concerned about how I'd cope because I was so driven as a footballer, and always focused on my game and my fitness. I had to re-educate myself at the age of 34 into a completely new full-time occupation.

In 1984 I went full-time with In Focus with whom I'd already been working, and not long after that I set up a company called Premier Events as a part of the In Focus group. Two of the things we did were kit launches for Manchester United (the kit with the white epaulettes which they wore in the Eighties) and Liverpool (the kit they ended up wearing at Heysel). I suddenly found myself on the other side of the fence, researching the history of clubs and looking for ways to market them. What amazed me was that, while United had a club historian, Cliff Butler, who had a load of resources and records at his disposal, Liverpool had nothing. I couldn't quite believe that a club of that stature, with all that European success, would have no official records, but they didn't, and I ended up getting everything off Stan Liversedge, a journalist who lived in Sale.

While I was trying to develop Premier Events, I spoke to Asa Hartford about coming to work with me and then brought in Martin Buchan, who'd just been fired from Burnley. I knew them both well, and thought both would be an asset. Asa preferred to stay in football, and after a fortnight Martin just decided it wasn't for him, and now does a terrific job working for the PFA. We also managed the TSB flotation programme, when the shares from the

TSB Group were floated on the stock market. That was fascinating for me, as it showed me how high finance works from the inside, and I was privy to a lot of confidential facts and figures.

I hadn't been looking to do anything football-wise, but in the summer of 1984 I got a call from Eamonn McLoughlin, who'd been a trainee at Sunderland at the same time I had back in the Sixties. We'd always got on well, and when I was a teenager I'd been on holiday to stay with his family in Derry. He was now a coach at Derry City, and had called a couple of times before to ask me to go and play for Derry. They'd been banned from the Northern Irish league after their fans had attacked a bus carrying a Belfast team, but they had just been admitted to the League of Ireland. This was at the time of the Troubles, and I wasn't overly keen, but he kept ringing and was very persuasive, telling me that I could catch a flight from Manchester to Belfast on a Sunday morning, they'd then drive me to the game, and I could get a flight back that night.

Eventually I agreed, but only on a game-by-game basis. I didn't want to be tied to anything. He was also looking for a centre-forward, so I recommended Gary Jones, a friend of mine who'd just retired from Bolton. For the first game I went over a day early to do some media interviews, and also featured on their local TV show, presented by a young Eamonn Holmes. My sharpest memory is of seeing a British soldier kneeling in the street with a gun as I was driven to the stadium on the day of the game. The club secretary was with me, and he went mad when he saw it, saying that the Army had promised to stay away as the club had said that they would look after their own security. Brandywell, the ground, was between the Bogside and Cregagh neighbourhoods, so you can imagine how sensitive it was back in the 1980s. The game passed off fine, and it was a great atmosphere, with 12,000 packed in. We won 3–1, I set up all three and Gary scored twice. At the end of the game, I was given money to cover all my expenses. I'd never seen so many coloured notes in my life. It was as if I was about to play monopoly. The security problems never entered my mind as the people who came to watch the games were purely and simply in love with football and wanted passionately to support their hometown team.

I went on to play nine games for Derry in total, and really took to the place. I still look out for their results today. Unfortunately, though, they changed the flight schedules, so I had to fly from Manchester to London and then to Belfast. It could be a drag as well, having to get from Belfast down to Kilkenny and places like that for away games, and if I'd missed the last flight back I'd have been stuck there overnight. This almost happened on one occasion when I was being driven back from Derry to Belfast Airport for my flight home. The road ahead was blocked by security forces who directed us on a long diversion as a parked car up ahead was a possible bomb threat.

In the end Derry changed manager, and the new manager wanted me to commit until the end of the season, which I wasn't prepared to do. Fortunately, I had my business interests to fall back on, and the Cosmos money had paid for our house, so finance wasn't a huge concern.

In many ways, I'd been fairly unusual as a footballer, because I liked to be well organised. On away trips I'd ask for an itinerary – where we were going, how long for, which hotel we'd be staying in, that type of thing. I was disciplined, and I just wanted to know what I was doing. While football is a global game, footballers live within very narrow parameters. The knowledge of life and the world in general that footballers gain during their careers is somewhere between limited and nil. I was always conscious of wanting to be part of the bigger picture.

During the rest of the 1980s and the early 1990s, I carried on building up my businesses. In 1991, I bought out Jack Pritchard Ltd, a travel agency I'd been working with, but I also learnt some painful lessons, which showed just how cut-throat business could be. In 1987 I had a falling out with my business partner at In Focus after he went mad at me for not having got formal permission from him to go home and see Joan when she came out of hospital after having our third son, so I ended up buying him out for £35,000. In the end, Reuben Kay told me to wash my hands of him, move on and to know that it would be the best money I'd ever spend.

I recruited Frank Carrodus, who I'd known at City and who later played for Villa. He'd been in insurance, and I was delighted to have him on board because I thought he could help us break into the Birmingham area. My partner wasn't sure he was right for the business and suggested letting him go after six months, but because I'd brought him in I supported him. A few months later, though, Frank left to form his own company. That was one of my first real lessons in business – that you have to be hard. The fallout wasn't too dramatic, either for the business or our relationship – at least not in the long term – but it was an eye-opener nonetheless.

During all of this time, Manchester City never entirely disappeared off the horizon. In the early 1990s, when the Platt Lane Stand at Maine Road was rebuilt, my company bought an executive box there to develop the hospitality side of our business. Because of my strong feelings for the club, I thought the time was right for a little bit of self-indulgence.

CHAPTER TWELVE

ALL ABOARD THE TITANIC

As I started watching City at Maine Road regularly during the early 1990s, it was clear to me that there was an undercurrent of discontent. Peter Reid had done well at the club, leading them to a fifth-place First Division finish in 1991/92, but over at Old Trafford United were stirring under Alex Ferguson. During my time as a player at City, I was always acutely aware of what was going on at United and we could never escape comparison with our neighbours. The late Sixties and early-to-mid-Seventies was perhaps the one time when City could have claimed to be the dominant force in the Manchester, but by the early 1990s United were starting to take shape under Alex. I felt that, unless the club changed direction quickly, they were always going to be left trailing in United's wake, which is precisely what happened.

A great deal of the fans' grumbling was targeted at Peter Swales. It always had been, of course, because he was such a high-profile figure both locally and in the media. He made some mistakes, especially in the late Seventies with the millions he splashed out on some overpriced stars, but the man was City through and through.

By the early 1990s, Swales faced a new set of problems. It was a difficult time for football clubs everywhere, because in the wake of the Taylor Report they were having to turn their grounds into all-seater venues, which meant accessing vast sums of cash. Admittedly, with Sky's involvement in the newly formed Premier League, there was more money starting to pour in, but it was very clear to me that, with the stakes raised, the new football world would largely be about the haves and the have-nots. I feared that City would become one of the latter.

In 1993, Francis Lee began his "Forward with Frannie" campaign to take over City, and oust Swales. My relationship with Peter Swales had always been good, and I knew that in the early Nineties there was a whispering campaign against him. I didn't want to be involved in any of that, so my routine was to ask club secretary Bernard Halford for just one ticket in the directors' box, never turn up too early and leave as soon as the game had ended. I never wanted to get caught up in any of the griping by ex-professionals which always occurs at a football club when the team aren't winning. It rarely does anyone any good. I'd never felt that I needed to be one of the lads in my playing days, and I had no wish to be part of a gossipy network when I retired either.

I wasn't comfortable with the way the whole takeover process was going. Mike Summerbee had loaned the club an England cap so they could display it in the museum, and he took it back to protest against Swales. Mike asked me to do the same, but for one thing I'd never loaned a cap to the club, and for another, I told him, I wouldn't condone that kind of action. I thought it was an awful campaign against Swales. When he'd arrive at Maine Road, he'd be surrounded by a mob screaming at him, and some people went round to his elderly mother's nursing home and rang up Swales in a threatening manner, describing the wallpaper in her room.

I'm not suggesting that Francis Lee actively supported such nasty actions, but then he wasn't exactly scathingly critical of them either. I would have preferred to see a more professional campaign involving sensible and confidential meetings.

The whole Swales Out/Franny In campaign rumbled on for months, a sorry affair that split the club's support right down the middle. The Centenary Supporters Association, which backed Lee, was a splinter organisation which broke away from the Official Supporters Club – the official club condemned the action taken against Swales. The two groups didn't unite again until 2010, which shows the destructive impact of that kind of campaign.

On the one hand, I could certainly see why a Francis Lee-controlled City was an attractive proposition to many fans. In the Seventies, he'd been a magnificent player for the club, and his sheer presence and aura was one of the reasons why I joined City from Sunderland. I only played alongside him on a few occasions and he had explosive pace over short distances. He'd been hugely successful in business too, and it's rare that a footballer does well both on the pitch and away from it, so I respected Francis for that.

I'd heard a lot of rumours about the amount of money Lee was supposed to be putting in – it was never really confirmed – and as a supporter and a former player I was excited for the club. The City team certainly needed a great deal of investment if they had any thoughts of challenging for honours again, and Peter Swales's decision-making was clearly suspect. Peter Reid, who'd been a good manager for City for the previous two years, was fired by Swales on August 26, 1993, after City made a slow start to the season. It wasn't an especially popular move. City had had so many managers down the years that the team was forever in transition, and to be successful you need stability and unity, as United were showing under Ferguson.

I was in my box in the Platt Lane Stand for the game against Coventry on August 27, 1993, and we knew the name of the new manager would be revealed that night. I remember all the guests talking about who it was going to be. There was talk of Joe Jordan and of Steve Coppell, who were both exciting young managers even though they would forever be linked with the red side of the city. I felt that Steve, with his excellent track record at Crystal Palace, and Joe, who'd done a good job at Bristol City and appeared to be moving up in the managerial world, could do a good job for us. So did my guests. Then at the end of the game we found out it was going to be Brian Horton, who hadn't pulled up too many trees as boss of Oxford United. You could sense the disappointment around the place, with City fans asking "Brian who?". Even though he actually did do a good job of steadying the ship, and is still very much respected at City, Brian's appointment was an anti-climax and a major blow to the credibility of the Swales regime – if that was the best City could offer at a time when

United were winning the league, then there were real issues. When Francis Lee eventually took over, he gave Brian until May 16, 1995, and then he was eventually fired as well.

Peter Swales had got caught between the old way that football was run and the new. With the amount of money that came in after the start of the Premiership, clubs needed completely restructuring, and he was undone by that transition. I'd said to Peter earlier that he needed somebody in the higher echelons of the club who understood the football side more. I've always believed that clubs should have a more European-style system with a general manager and a head coach – like Uli Hoeness at Bayern Munich. He listened and months later brought in John Maddock as general manager to work with Peter Reid, but he disagreed with Peter over policy on transfers and the use of agents. John struggled to gain credibility within the club because he came from the media and not from the world of football, even though, as a respected football writer, he had a huge network of football contacts. The structure just wasn't right at City, and the vibes coming out of the place were awful. John eventually left the club in November 1994.

Francis finally took over at City late in 1994 after John Maddock's departure, when he became chairman and majority shareholder, and he promised a bright new era at City. I even sent him a good-luck letter.

He told fans and the press, "This will be the happiest club in the land. We'll sing ourselves hoarse and drink champagne as we win trophy after trophy."

If ever a statement could backfire on you, then Francis had just uttered it. Even more oddly, he then told Sky Sports that, if things hadn't turned around at the club within three years, then he'd walk away. Behind all of that bluster, I detected more than a hint of self-doubt.

After Brian Horton was sacked, Francis appointed his former England team-mate, Alan Ball, as manager, but Ball couldn't arrest the slide. I'll never forget the last game of the 1995/96 season, when City were staring relegation straight in the face. They were drawing 2–2 with Liverpool, and a message from the bench instructed City's Steve Lomas to keep the ball in the corner and waste time, because results elsewhere were apparently going City's way. From the Teletext scores in my box, I knew that information was incorrect, and I was screaming my head off, telling Lomas to get the ball into Liverpool's box. It became a crescendo as other supporters, who'd got to hear what was going on in the other games and realised that Lomas was acting under misinformation. City went down that day, and for me, as a crestfallen fan watching from the stands, that incident involving Lomas summed up a great deal about the club and its lack of professionalism.

A business venture of mine started up a drawn-out chain of events which led to me going back into the Manchester City set-up. In 1996, I organised a dinner to celebrate the 20th anniversary of City's League Cup win, and that was when I met John Wardle, as his company, JD Sports, sponsored the video sequence for the dinner. A little later, Geoff Durbin, who was City's commercial manager, asked me to lunch at the Platt Lane training centre with David Makin, who was John's partner in JD Sports (John/David Sports) and a big supporter of the club. Francis Lee had persuaded David and John to invest £5 million in City between them, and Steven Boler from Kitchens Direct, to put in another £5 million. The investment should have been enough to get City back into the Premiership, but at that stage the team was floundering around mid-table in the Championship. I had absolutely no inkling about what would happen as a result of my meeting with David, but we had a really good, in-depth discussion.

"This club has such huge support, it's a scandal that the team is doing so abysmally," I told him. "When a club has such a high turnover of personnel, it suggests that there are massive underlying issues beneath the surface."

All I really did was speak from the heart, like a fan. I don't think I blinded David with advanced business strategy; I just spoke common sense. I went away from the lunch feeling that at least I'd got a few things off my chest, but nothing more than that.

Coincidence played its part in nudging me back into City's arms. I handled a lot of the promotional activity for Umbro, who made the England kit, and before the home qualifiers for the 1998 World Cup I used to do all the pre-match hospitality. For one of those games, David Bernstein − a big City fan and a non-executive director of French Connection – was there as a guest of Umbro, and shortly afterwards he was invested onto the board. When I first met him I was very impressed. He seemed very professional and straight talking, and not long after he'd joined the board he rang me and asked if I wanted to have lunch with him. When we met in London, I recounted a story which I felt summed up the "corner shop mentality" that was blighting City.

A year earlier, I'd been trying to promote a concept for the beer company, Bass, with Manchester City – I'd done something similar with United. United had rebuilt the North Stand at Old Trafford, so capacity had been down to 30-odd thousand during the 1992/93 season. These being the days before *Football First* on Sky, I realised there would be thousands of fans who wouldn't have seen the games live, who would be desperate to see the action, particularly with United doing so well. As soon as a game was finished, I would have the video of the game couriered into a production studio, have some Bass promotional stuff edited onto the front of it, and the complete tape would then be delivered to the Bass pubs who'd bought into the scheme, and they could show it on Saturday night or Sunday morning. It had proved to be really successful with United and their fans, and I felt the same concept could be applied to City matches. So I set up a meeting between the promotions director of Bass, John Unwin, who was a big City fan and a season-ticket holder, and Colin Barlow, who was City's chief executive. John travelled up from the Midlands for the meeting held in City's temporary offices in Princes Parkway, which they were using in 1995 while the Kippax Stand was being redeveloped.

In all my years in business, this was the most embarrassing meeting I've ever attended. I felt Barlow was disrespectful to John, which didn't make sense at a time when all clubs needed to be developing as many revenue streams as they could. He didn't seem to have any vision or be at all interested in the commercial possibilities of developing a relationship with Bass and providing an additional service to City supporters. In the end I felt uncomfortable that I'd dragged John up from the Midlands for the meeting. On one occasion, as John was speaking, Colin saw somebody out the window of his office, picked up the phone, and asked his secretary who it was, completely ignoring what John was saying. As soon as John got back to his office, he rang me to say that, as much as he loved City, he thought Barlow had been utterly unprofessional and he had no interest in taking things any further.

David closed his eyes and shook his head. He told me that in just a few weeks of serving on the board, he'd already discovered that my experience in Colin Barlow's office was symptomatic of problems throughout the club.

I shared with David the stories I'd heard over the last few years about Francis meddling in team affairs. During Alan Ball's tenure the team was staying in London, and assistant boss Tony Book and Ball filled out the team-sheet for the referee during the pre-match meal. Francis Lee joined them and a heated discussion ensued. On the coach afterwards, Ball pulled Book to one side and told him to change the team. There was another time at a home game when Asa Hartford was interim manager. This time Tony Book was presented with a piece of paper from the directors' box "strongly advising" a substitution. Dave Bassett had been approached by Francis to become manager. Initially, Bassett accepted the post, but the next day he backed out because he had reservations that he would not be allowed to manage the team himself.

David listened, took in what I was saying, and nodded. I was most impressed with him, and matters were now moving on swiftly behind the scenes.

On November 22, 1997, during a game between City and Bradford, I got a call to go and see John Wardle in his box. John said David had been impressed by how candid I'd been at our lunch, and that he too was concerned about the direction the club was taking after he'd been persuaded to invest. While John and David were both major shareholders, they weren't directors. John had been invited in to observe a board meeting, and he'd been dismayed by the way Lee dominated the other board members and at how no one seemed to be allowed to comment about the football side of things or to question the manager (who was Frank Clark at the time). John and David both felt I could make a positive contribution to City as a director and wanted me to be their nominee on the board and attend meetings on their behalf. (I discovered later that David Bernstein had been in contact with them following our meeting in London and agreed with my nomination.)

Initially, I was dumbfounded, but I told John I'd think about it and get back to him and the two Davids. I discussed it with Joan, and then I took advice from Reuben Kay and Michael Hall, a personal friend and the main director of HSBC insurance brokers. As usual, Joan was very supportive because she knew my love for football and for Manchester City in particular. "If you want to do it, then do it," she said. Both Reuben and Michael thought I should definitely take the position.

The only person who was concerned was me. I was running three successful businesses – Premier Events Ltd, ably assisted on the production side by Dave McGeoch, who is still an invaluable friend and work colleague, MLJ Properties (named after the initials of my three sons) and the travel agency I'd bought from my great friend and big City supporter, Jack Pritchard. My major worry was that John and David just wanted me to attend monthly board meetings, but my experience of working in different areas of a football club told me that in practice it would be more full on than that. My main company, Premier Events, was at a position where I was going to have to make a decision on running it at the size it was or to develop it by bringing more employees into the business. Accepting the City offer would mean sacrificing that development. Also I had a family – Mark was 17, Leigh 15, John 10 – and the impact on Joan and the children was my greatest consideration of all. But Manchester City was part of me, and for all my reservations, I was hugely excited by the prospect.

I had another meeting with John Wardle, for further discussions on the implications of becoming a director. I didn't want to go about it in a half-hearted manner. When I make up my mind to do something, I want to go at it full tilt, and in the end I couldn't resist the challenge. In life, you get certain opportunities, and I'd rather have a go than later regret not even trying. Finally, I told John I would accept.

There was an extraordinary amount of secrecy about it. Within my family I only discussed it with Joan. The boys were upstairs studying when they heard the news of my appointment on the radio in December 1997. They have since told me that they looked at one another in complete astonishment. My appointment, described by Rodney Marsh on Sky as "cosmetic" (surprise, surprise), was pretty well received by the supporters.

I met with Francis Lee and David Bernstein just to talk generally about me joining the board. John Wardle and the two Davids were most concerned about the ridiculously high turnover of managers and players. Francis did most of the talking about player signings, and I listened with interest. Then I asked for a meeting with Francis on his own. I felt it was important that he understood my ambition for the club, and I wanted to make clear to him how I liked to operate in business.

It took a few attempts to sort out a time and date, which surprised me because issues at the club needed resolving quickly. The response from Francis was that the club was busy trying to sign a new Georgian player, and he was tied up with that. The delay gave me an uneasy feeling that perhaps he might not be 100 per cent happy with the whole idea of having me on board.

Before the meeting, I prepared a full list of our squad of players, their ages and contract status for discussion. I phoned Francis to ask what he was intending to do on new contract offers. He said he had provisionally arranged to offer a new contract to Martyn Margetson, who was the back-up goalkeeper to Tommy Wright. I pointed out that we had just signed an exciting young goalkeeper called Nicky Weaver from Mansfield, and if we were to going to give him a chance to develop, would he not be worthy of the back-up place the following season? I suggested to Francis that he ask Alex Stepney, our goalkeeping coach, for his view about whether or not Nicky could fulfil that position. Alex, when asked, confirmed that he would be certainly capable of that position as part of his development. The proposed one-year contract offer to Margetson was withdrawn, and before the end of the season Nicky had made his first-team debut in a friendly game and then went on to be a great servant to Manchester City. It was my first positive act as a City director.

Before my appointment was confirmed we eventually met at Francis's house and I was completely upfront with him, as I had been with Malcolm Allison all those years ago.

"I know of two different Francis Lees," I told him. "One is the famous international, the outstanding footballer with Manchester City and England, and the successful businessman who has made his millions in the toilet roll industry. The other one is the Francis Lee that Colin Bell has been dealing with."

Colin, who'd worked at the youth academy at City, had been sacked during Francis's reign as chairman, and taken the club to court for unfair dismissal. Colin won his case and because of the way the club handled it during Francis' chairmanship, has hardly spoken to Francis since.

"The second Francis Lee is no good to me if I am going to have a working relationship with him," I said.

I've always been a believer in taking people as I find them. I'm never influenced by others' opinions or rumours. Everyone, in my view, is given one chance. I'd been given no specific remit from John and David, apart from using my knowledge and keeping them up to date with what was going on in the boardroom. Effectively, I was a conduit between the boardroom, the dressing room, John and David – an observer of events. That suited me down to the ground.

I said to Francis that I was going to give the opportunity my best shot. We shook hands, but I just got the feeling that he wasn't entirely happy with me being involved.

It was December 1997, and there was more unrest. Shortly after my appointment, Colin Barlow, David Holt and John Dunkley all left as part of a boardroom reshuffle. I'd imagined myself as a knight in shining armour coming in to sort the problems out, but I quickly realised how naive that attitude was, because the problems at City were everywhere – in the boardroom, the commercial and catering departments, the scouting network, the youth development area and, most importantly, on the pitch.

I spent some time with the then chief executive, Mike Turner, looking at the budget, the financial statements and the salaries. It was scary stuff. Many of the players were still being paid Premier League salaries, with the expectation that the team were headed for a quick return to the top flight – in fact they were headed in the opposite direction. Added to the fact that the parachute payments were about to expire, City faced an uncertain future.

Players like Lee Bradbury, who had cost £3 million, Nigel Clough £1.5 million and Ged Brannan £750,000 were being extremely well paid for the division we were in, but were not producing on the field.

I wasn't afraid to ask awkward questions. I noticed that we were paying a monthly retainer to the agent Jerome Anderson, which club secretary Bernard Halford explained were fees for signing players as we had had many in the previous years. This was discussed at a later board meeting, and the payments ceased as the board agreed that we did not need to be associated with one single agent.

I made a point of meeting up with Jim Cassell, the youth development officer, and he expressed huge concerns about the structure we had for nurturing young talent. That frightened me, as I have always been passionate about grassroots football. City had once been famous for bringing through local lads. I'd seen that during my two spells at City. But in the last few years, the reservoir had basically run dry, which didn't reflect well on the club's scouting networks. I asked Jim to explain why we had good quality 13-, 14- and 15-year-old boys in our academy who graduated to our full-time system between the ages of 16–18, and yet only a minute percentage made the first team and the rest seemed to disappear into obscurity. Jim and I agreed that we needed to look at the reasons, whether they were physiological, psychological or hormonal. Jim said that if he was allowed to implement his views on the development of players, we would produce them good enough to play for the first team, but first he had to change the current structure into a more modern approach within the FA Academy guidelines. I was most impressed with Jim's views, which were in alignment to my own, and I made it my mission to assist him where I could in discussing financial support with the board where possible.

As soon as I became a director, I went to see the manager, Frank Clark. A couple of years previously, when Frank was being successful with Forest, he had been touted as a rising managerial star, and was even linked with the Arsenal job in some sectors before Bruce Rioch was appointed. But Frank was now struggling hugely at City. I'd known him for 30 years, from the time he was a player at

Newcastle while I was at Sunderland. We'd met socially, and once when I'd been doing promotions with guests at Nottingham Forest when he was manager there, I'd been called into his office before the game and had a good chat with him.

I liked Frank, and I was looking forward to supporting him. When I went to see him, though, he was quite off with me and I could sense that, because of the team's results, he was becoming concerned about his position. Looking back, I can understand Frank's suspicion, because there were elements within the club pulling in different directions. Frank said to me that he felt there was a "fifth column" inside the club.

The club was heading in the wrong direction in every sense. A management report produced in January 1998 by KPMG was highly critical of the club's operation and structure. Football organisations are massive, and I soon realised that I did not have the skills for every aspect of the business. I decided then that I would ask the manager football questions and give football opinions, and ask other experts if I was unsure about something. I had my doubts about whether Frank and his deputy, Alan Hill, were the pair who could turn things around, but it was now down to them.

With City sinking towards the relegation zone in the Championship, the media was always looking for an angle. Like vultures circling around a dying animal. Shortly before Christmas, I agreed to a Sky interview, and I stated my view that I wanted Frank to be a success at Maine Road. But they edited the interview, making it sound like I'd suggested that Frank was under huge pressure. They asked me if Frank would be accountable for the team's performances, which I thought was a strange question because obviously managers are responsible for the team's results. So I said "yes," and Sky focused only on that question and comment.

Immediately after it was shown, we had a club Christmas lunch, and when I walked in I could feel everyone looking at me oddly. I tried to explain to Frank that the interview had been twisted, but I don't think he was totally convinced. I'd always considered myself quite media-savvy, but I was now operating in the era of the soundbite, and knew that I'd have to more circumspect in future.

To counter what happened with Sky, I did an interview with

the *Mail on Sunday* writer, Joe Melling. He was a friend of Frank's so I knew it would be a balanced piece.

However, soon after, the *Daily Mail* ran another article claiming there had been a "crisis board meeting" at Maine Road and that I had personally approached Joe Royle about replacing Frank, which was completely false. Again, I had to go to Frank and assure him there was no truth in the story, and there never had been crisis meeting at all. But I knew, and Frank knew, that unless the team began winning some games, the rumour mill would just keep turning.

I quickly realised the enormity of the job at City. My first home game as director was against Nottingham Forest on December 28, 1997. We were 3–0 down at half-time and never really in the game, although we got two back in the second half. The team was poor, the performance was poor, and there was a real sense that any sparkle the team had had was long gone. Francis Lee would always take a Christmas holiday in Barbados, so Bernard Halford asked me if I would ring Franny to tell him about the game. After the game Bernard took me into a small office and gave me the direct dial number in Barbados. I was absolutely shocked that after several rings the phone went to voicemail, so I left a message regarding the game. If I had been on holiday, I would have been sitting by the phone waiting for the call.

That Forest game shook me. It was difficult to adjust, and difficult to get my head around sitting in the front row of the main stand – the view was lousy because it was too low. But I could clearly see the squad members sitting in the seats behind the dugout, and I calculated that there was approximately £12,000 a week going out to players who were not contributing to the team and were not likely to contribute in the future. I made it my business from then on to try and urge the City board to incorporate a perfor-mance-based element in players' salaries.

I felt like somebody boarding the *Titanic*. The fans were begin-ning to simmer that day because Frank Clark had replaced Michael Brown, one of their favourites, with Tony Scully, another winger. Brown was tipped for great things back in 1997, but never really fulfilled his potential. At that time, however, he was one of the few creative players at City who could do something a bit different.

Watching as both a fan and a director is difficult. Like any other supporter, you have your favourites, those players who can make you jump up out of your seat, but you have to balance that with whether or not they are producing on the pitch or not. Too often, Brown didn't produce. The same could be said of City's other fitful star, Georgi Kinkladze.

There was a cult that surrounded Georgi at City. The fans loved him, because he could produce the unexpected. When he worked up a head of steam, he could drive forward and terrorise defences at will. His close control was superb, and he was probably the one City player at the time who could lift fans off their seats. At the time, Oasis had released the song *Wonderwall*, and the fans adapted it at matches to pay homage to Georgi. I felt for Frank in his dealings with Georgi, though, because Frank and I both knew that he was coasting. And you can't have that in a team at the best of times, let alone when you are struggling to stay up.

Georgi was being paid three times what his team-mates were getting, and he wasn't producing. Frank occasionally omitted him from the team in a bid to gee him up. He'd usually come back in and play superbly, as was the case when we beat Portsmouth early in the New Year of 1998, but then disappear again for several games.

He got away with things in the fans' eyes because he was 'Kinki', but he didn't ever prove that he had the discipline to prosper in the long term at City. After he signed a new contract in January 1999, he bought himself a brand new red Ferrari. Within a few days, he'd crashed it and sustained a cut to his back, requiring 50 stitches in the process. Georgi was out of control, but he was treated with kid gloves by Francis Lee. Although you couldn't lay City's problems at Georgi's feet, his lack of application did the club and his team-mates no favours. The situation was never properly addressed, and just carried on rumbling for the remainder of the campaign.

Given City's current status as a major player on the world stage, it's remarkable to think that at this time the perception was that the club might be permanently stuck as a second-string outfit. Early in the New Year of 1998, I got a call from Raymond Donn – a solicitor in Manchester who was a big City fan and a friend of Peter Swales – saying he was interested in a meeting to discuss investing in the club. He had connections with Juventus and was interested in a tie-up with them by which City would effectively become a feeder club. He also suggested that Brian Kidd, Alex Ferguson's assistant at United, would be interested in managing the club.

I spoke to John Wardle about it, then we went to see Raymond. The way he talked about the situation, it was evident he wanted to be chairman and to take control. I wasn't convinced by his ideas. I didn't want City to be a feeder club, or in a subservient position to anyone. I believed we were big enough to stand up for ourselves and that, with hard work and unity, we could eventually move forward. After discussions with John we decided the best thing to do was to try to get Frank Clark through to the end of the season, so we, as a board, had time to choose who the new manager would be for the following season, if it came to it.

I was very conscious of Frank's lingering suspicion of me. I didn't want to be a man who was perceived to have been brought in just to make changes. There needed to be more planning, because City's issues were so deep rooted. However, events at the club meant that change arrived more quickly than any of us would have liked.

On Valentine's Day we played Bury at home, but I had to go up to Newcastle for my sister-in-law's 40th birthday straight afterwards, so I'd arranged to leave a quarter of an hour from the end. We were 1–0 down at that stage, and when I headed for the exit security tried to stop me. They'd ringed the front entrance with barriers and they were concerned about letting me go because they were expecting protests. The local derby match wasn't against Manchester United anymore, it was against Bury. It rammed home the situation in which City now found themselves. I shared the fans' anger and embarrassment, but I was very much of the opinion that we would have to stick together if we were to pull ourselves out of the mire. Eventually I got away, and listened to the last couple of minutes on the radio; we did lose 1–0, and the fans protested vocally. David Bernstein rang me later to tell me that David Makin had done a post-match radio interview slaughtering Francis Lee and criticising various aspects of his management of the club.

On the Sunday we were at my sister-in-law Dorothy's for lunch, but I spent most of the day upstairs in the bedroom on the phone. Bernstein had said the board was considering a statement. He read it over the phone to me. I wasn't happy. I felt the whole thing was poor – saying that the board had nothing to do with the manager and effectively cutting Frank Clark adrift. I still don't really understand the logic of it, but I realised that, because the other board members were in favour of putting it out, I couldn't stop the statement, so I insisted on having it rewritten. I rang Brian Clark, a big City fan who worked for the Manchester Piccadilly Radio, and we composed a new draft. When that was done, we sent it to Bryan Bodek, our legal adviser. It took three hours until we were all convinced that the statement was both professional and fair.

A couple of weeks earlier, just after Raymond Donn had made his initial contact, Joe Royle had rung me asking what the situation was with Frank Clark. Joe had had a chance of both the Northern Ireland and West Brom jobs, but he didn't want to take either if the City job was about to become available. I said to him that ideally we'd get Frank through to the end of the season.

I sensed that Frank was struggling, though. After another City defeat, he was interviewed and said, "I just don't know what's wrong, I can't put my finger on it." That is the last thing you want to hear from your manager.

By now, City were mired in the relegation zone. I wasn't clear on what Frank's fate might be at that time, but sensed that the board was thinking a change might be for the better. On the other hand, the last thing I wanted was for Joe to get the job and then be forced out after only two or three months. On the Monday he called again, and said he was prepared to take the job until the end of the season. I told him that I'd take his comment back to the board, but that there were no guarantees.

I rang John Wardle and said we had an opportunity with Joe Royle, and then I got in touch with David Bernstein and Francis Lee, and gave them the heads up on the situation with Joe. By now, the board was unanimous that Frank's time was up. John and I went to see Joe, but obviously we didn't want it to be public knowledge, so we arranged to meet him privately. Francis Lee said he'd call Frank to give him the bad news, but Frank was on his way up to Sunderland to watch a game and Francis couldn't get hold of him by phone. Consequently, Frank heard on the radio that we'd been speaking to Joe and that he was about to be replaced. I was devastated about that, and I know that Frank was appalled at the way he heard about his dismissal. After he departed City in March 1998, he has never managed a club again.

Joe came in and he had 15 games to get us safe. He was a naturally bubbly and lively character, who'd done a fantastic job with Oldham in seeing them promoted into the old Division One. I felt that Joe would know his way around the division, and that if the unthinkable happened and we were relegated to the third tier, he would know the type of players who could get us moving onwards and upwards again.

Before Joe had a chance to get his teeth into the job, however, Francis Lee dropped a bombshell. In February, at the end of a board meeting, Francis asked for an endorsement of his position. He said his children were getting aggro at school, and he became a little emotional. I couldn't quite believe I was hearing him say that, when I knew what Peter Swales had gone through as an albeit indirect result of his campaign.

He went out of the room while the board discussed his position. The board were unanimous that it was time for him to go. John Wardle had asked me earlier if I was prepared to take a bigger role as the football link between boardroom and dressing room. Rather than observing events and reporting back to the board, John wanted me to influence change more readily around the club. I'd turned him down. I had my businesses to run, a family at home and I was comfortable with what I had.

Nothing happened immediately after that board meeting, but there were discussions about David Bernstein becoming chairman, and again he asked me to become the football representative on the board. I had a long think, and eventually David said that he couldn't become chairman unless I took on greater responsibility. I finally agreed, as I was conscious of the importance of retaining some stability in the boardroom. I would remain a non-executive member of the board, though, because I was still, in the loosest sense of the term, part time.

We played Port Vale on March 14, and it was decided that director Ashley Lewis and David Bernstein would meet with Francis Lee at his home on the Saturday morning before the game and tell him the board's view. David Bernstein called a meeting with John Wardle and myself to discuss Francis's resignation. David's idea was that, because of his image and his contribution as a player, he'd be given the opportunity to resign, and leave with dignity. I fully endorsed this view.

Francis Lee stood down as chairman, but remained as a shareholder so he still kept a presence, albeit on the back benches. I remember John muttering that Francis would come back to haunt us, and he wasn't wrong.

The challenge was to save ourselves from relegation, but things got worse. For me, the nadir arrived when we lost away at Port Vale. It was a horrible day – really windy with lashing rain – and it was made worse by the fact that they were extending one of the stands at Vale Park, so the rain was gusting through the gap left by the building work. That was the day that Joe fell out of love with Georgi Kinkladze (although I don't think Joe had ever really been under the Georgian's spell). It was a game for players to get stuck in and fight for their lives. All season, other clubs had been gunning for City because they were the big-name club to be shot at, and too often our players had been unable to rise to the challenge. Georgi was the biggest culprit of all. He was a magnificently talented player, but that day he was a disgrace. Vale put a man marker on him, and Georgi just didn't seem interested in running at him, or trying to muscle him out of it. He was on about £12,000 a week, but his contribution that day was nil.

Joe came into the boardroom after the game raging about "that cheating Georgian bastard". From then on Kinkladze's days at the club were numbered, and Joe left him out of the team. He never achieved anywhere near what he should have in the game. At the end of the season, we sold him to Ajax, where he was unable to establish himself. A year or so later, he ended up back in England at Derby, where he flattered to deceive for a couple of seasons. A dreadful waste of talent.

Like me, Joe didn't feel either Georgi or Michael Brown were part of the team unit he was trying to develop, yet Georgi had a powerful backer at the club who still believed that he could be City's saviour.

On April 15, Francis Lee sent a fax to David Bernstein: "I implore you to ask the director of football to ask the manager to bring 'Gio' into the squad or I fear the director of football could be directing us into the second division."

Now, director of football is a full-time position, and entails over-seeing the scouting, transfer policy and Academy structure, which certainly wasn't my remit, but it was pretty obvious Francis was referring to me. I was absolutely shocked: we'd allowed him to go with dignity, and yet he, the person who assured me when I became a director that he ran a strict non-interference policy, was still trying to meddle in team affairs.

From then on, whenever I saw Francis around the place, I was curt, to the point, and moved on. I'd made a commitment to do what I could to help Manchester City, and that was my total focus. Nowadays, if I ever see Francis at City functions, I don't even bother to speak to him.

I don't know what it was that made him turn on me like that. Maybe he was bitter that things hadn't worked out with his regime at City. Friends have said that maybe he had a vendetta against me because he feared that I might be successful at the club where he had singularly failed to make an impact. I still can't really put my finger on it, partly because Francis did it from afar, by fax and letter. I'd have been more than happy if he'd come to me and talked things through – if he'd looked me in the eye and said, "Dennis, why isn't Joe selecting Georgi?", I'd have been more than happy to argue Joe's case for as long as it took. I'd have been happy if we'd agreed to disagree.

I'd never had any issue with Francis apart from his relationship with Mike Summerbee. I always found it strange, on club social events when Mike was in the company of Francis Lee, that he seemed to be in awe of him. At the 80th birthday celebrations of former *It's A Knockout* presenter, and massive City fan, Stuart Hall, at Manchester City last year, Mike and Francis were there with their wives, and I was a guest of Stuart's son Danny. Mike never came across to speak to me, for which he apologised when I met him shortly afterwards at the City at offices. I said to him, "Mike, you know you never speak to me when Francis is in the room, but don't worry, I understand and it has never affected my relationship with you." I was surprised that Tina, his wife, who was always very supportive of him, seemed comfortable with the situation.

I have huge respect for Mike as he took me under his wing when I first signed for City and was living in a hotel. He invited me many times to his shirt shop in Manchester for an afternoon coffee, to talk about Manchester as a football city. I'll never forget his kindness, and I'm delighted that he now has an ambassadorial role at the club, in which he seems to flourish. Francis's and Mike's friendship does not affect me – they had been pals for many years, long before I joined the club – but Francis is now someone I refuse to have anything to do with.

Anyway, David faxed Francis back, saying firstly that the club had no director of football, and that he was happy with the level of football representation on the board.

I remember the club's honorary president, Keith Pinner, who has always been, along with his family, a great supporter of the club, saying when I was first appointed that I must try and work with Francis. "Remember one thing though," he warned. "Whenever you are in the company of Francis Lee there is only one opinion."

Francis's behaviour at that time merely reaffirmed Keith's point. At that stage of the season we had to galvanise the spirit of the club, not indulge individuals like Kinkladze.

Over the years, Francis made further attempts to undermine me. In February 1999, he wrote another letter to David Bernstein, saying "the shareholders" (he never made it clear who this group consisted of) wanted "more football representation on the plc board". In another obvious dig at me, Lee claimed that "robust football representation was lacking". David replied, insisting the board had the support of the shareholders, and asked Francis precisely which shareholders he believed were unhappy. There was no response.

Before the March 1998 transfer deadline, Joe brought in Shaun Goater from Bristol City, but even his goals – three in seven games – couldn't help us. The big problem was Kinkladze's underperformance, and our horrible habit of shooting ourselves in the foot too often. I guess the most infamous example of that came in a home game against QPR, when Jamie Pollock, who'd dispossessed their attacker, inexplicably headed the ball over our goalkeeper and scored the most ridiculous own-goal I'd ever witnessed. Jamie was a good lad, but it made me realise the huge pressure our players were under, and that when footballers panic they are capable of doing the most bizarre things.

We went to Stoke, who were a point above us, on the last day of the season, but we knew that even if we won we needed Portsmouth or Port Vale to drop points as well. We were 1–0 up at half-time, but both the other two sides were ahead as well and, although we ended up winning 5–2, Port Vale won 4–0 at Huddersfield and Portsmouth beat Bradford 3–1.

City were now in the third tier for the first time in the club's history. My heart went out for our supporters who'd suffered the ignominy of a second relegation in two years. I know that many writers at the time effectively wrote obituaries for the club, and that City was a laughing stock. But, personally, because I knew the plans that our new chairman David Bernstein had in place, I wasn't devastated. I saw that we had to take a long-term view, so there was no doom and despondency from me; just acceptance.

Immediately after relegation was confirmed, David proved his aptitude for the role. He released a chairman's statement, first of all apologising to fans, but also offering a message that restructuring in all departments was going ahead. I had great belief in him and his vision.

I was fed up at the amount of rumour and gossip coming out of the club. I wanted to ensure our fans were kept informed of what exactly was happening at the club in a professional manner. To this end, at the beginning of 1998 I had introduced Chris Bird to the board to be interviewed for the position of PR representative. Before that, anybody could have rung the club and whoever answered would have given their take on what was going on behind the scenes. David took that problem on board and nominated employees to comment on subjects in which they had specific expertise. It was a massive forward step. Leaks from the top had been City's Achilles heel for years, but from now on it would be a much tighter, more professionally run business.

In every operation the three things that are of paramount importance are stability, unity and team spirit. As a director, that was my one overriding target across all facets of the club. To move the club forward would need an awful lot of change in several departments, and I knew that, as usual, there'd be trouble in making those changes.

CHAPTER THIRTEEN

RISE AND FALL

Our local derby in the Championship had been against Bury. Now, in Division Two, local grudges would be settled against Macclesfield, not long promoted to the Football League.

It was easy for the press to suggest that Manchester City turned its nose up at the thought of playing in such outposts as Colchester, Wycombe and York, but I can honestly say that wasn't the case. There was an acceptance which ran right through the club that we were in the third tier because we deserved to be there, and that feeling sorry for ourselves would most likely end with us staying there. I liaised closely with Joe Royle to ensure that the players we had at the club were ready for the battle, because there was no doubt every team would ratchet up their performance as they took on the fallen giants.

There was also an overriding demand for cost control as our cash-flow forecast meant we needed to get promotion at the first attempt, otherwise we would have to sell many of our top-paid players. I did have an issue with some board members who wanted to cut some expense out of the coaching staff, though. They questioned whether we needed a goalkeeping coach in the Second Division and queried the salary that Asa Hartford was on as a reserve-team manager. I said that Joe needed good quality staff around him and that our young goalkeeper, Nicky Weaver, needed top-quality coaching.

I explained to the board that Alex Stepney would be very important to Weaver and that I would speak to Joe in relation to Asa's salary. Asa totally understood and, because of his commitment to the club, undertook a review of his salary. That satisfied some of the board members and allowed Joe to retain his good quality coaching staff, which was vital.

City's defending in the relegation season had been shaky, and we needed to tighten up massively. One of Joe's first signings during the early part of the 1998/99 season was Andy Morrison from Huddersfield, a real old-fashioned centre-half who knew what it took to fight and scrap in the lower leagues. At £30,000, he was an absolute bargain. We knew that Andy had a reputation as a drinker during his career at clubs like Blackpool and Blackburn Rovers, but Joe appointed him captain. This was an inspired decision because Andy had the experience and the temperament to cajole his team-mates and it showed that Joe was the perfect manager for City at this time.

In his first game for us, at home against Colchester, Andy not only scored one of our goals from a corner, but he also made a hefty tackle on his ex-Huddersfield team-mate Marcus Browning. I knew full well that we'd never get out of the division unless we could show a backbone of steel, and display the type of controlled aggression which Morrison exemplified.

Already within the squad we had Paul Dickov. Paul had never really made the grade at Arsenal, but was a similarly fiery character to Andy who could dig in and get physical with opposing defenders when the situation called for it. He never plundered huge numbers of goals, but Dickov rolled up his sleeves, and got on with the job. And that was what it was all about.

I felt that at the start of the campaign, we had cut our cloth accordingly, and we pulled together a squad who could work for us and, most importantly, for each other. That hadn't happened for years at City, and I was optimistic that with other good players in the squad like Richard Edgehill, Kevin Horlock and Ian Bishop, we could progress.

The first thing that I did was to initiate a public relations campaign with our long-suffering fans. I felt we needed everybody pulling in the same direction, and with 80-odd supporters' branches in the UK alone, the fact was that City remained a huge club. Talking to large numbers of our fans, I realised that, miraculously, their loyalty was intact. They would see it through whatever. City was in their blood.

I also saw the gallows humour which was needed if we were to pull ourselves out of the mire, and get back to the top of the game. There were so many anti-City jokes circulating, many of which were penned by United fans, I'm sure...

What do you call the new version of the Manchester City OXO cube? The Laughing Stock cube.

What happened when Joe Royle opened the City trophy cabinet? He was shocked to see Shergar gallop out. Even worse, Lord Lucan was riding him.

What's the difference between a lift and Manchester City? A lift doesn't take nine months to go down.

There were dozens of them. In a masochistic way, I thought some of them were even quite funny but, as I said to fans, the only way these jokes would ever go away would be if City were successful.

The supporters were used to massive underachievement, financial strife and relegation at City, albeit not on this scale. But the feeling I got was that fans hoped this was really as bad as it could possibly get, and that if we could have a successful season in Division Two, at least there would then be a culture of winning infused back into the club, which we hadn't had for years.

Crucially, the attendances at Maine Road stayed high – around the 30,000 mark – which gave us a huge boost, both financially and psychologically. The fans' view was that, if they stuck by the team and tried to see the darkly funny side of the whole thing, then we could all get through this. I shared their optimism, their positive outlook and, in speaking to many of them, I knew because of their love for the club they would give us time to turn things around.

I initiated the supporters' visit programme, whereby the official supporters' clubs could request a guest for Q&A sessions at their monthly meetings. Joe and the chairman thought it was a great idea, and it had a fantastic response. Mixing with fans, the lifeblood of any club, had always been important to me during my playing days with both Sunderland and City, and in the situation City found themselves, the players needed to show the fans respect, and demonstrate that we were all in it together. No them and us – unity.

I feel that the players got an awful lot out of those experiences. One of the reasons why that generation of City players have earned such respect from fans is because they gave so much back to the club and its supporters. We had people from all parts of the club – directors, players, coaching staff, medical staff, ticket office staff and commercial staff – going out to supporters' branches' monthly meetings. Even now, when I see the likes of Paul Dickov, Shaun Goater, Nicky Weaver or Kevin Horlock, they look back with pride on their strong links with the City supporters. And so they should.

The members of the board also visited the larger supporters branches to hold Q&A sessions. On one hugely successful visit to our Reddish branch, I commented that we had a unique group of people on the board: David Bernstein, an extremely capable and professional chairman; John Wardle, the vice-chairman, major share-holder and retail merchandise expert; Ashley Lewis, a highly respected accountant who represented the Stephen Bowler share-holding; Chris Bird, PR and communications expert; and last, and hopefully not least, myself, from the world of football. The board had the full backing and support of long-serving secretary, Bernard Halford, who was my rules and regulations guru. We all had that extra special element which was that we got on together as a group and were all Manchester City fans.

As part of our efforts to keep costs under control, we looked closely at the players' bonuses. With the quality of our squad, I felt that we should never be out of the top six of the table. Joe agreed with me, and so I proposed to the players' committee the sugges-tion that bonuses would be paid monthly, and only if the team were in the top six. The players knew that they were all on contracts far in excess of anyone else in the Second Division and many in the First Division, as contracts had been awarded by the previous regime, to get us back into the Premiership.

To their great credit, the players voted to accept the idea. I was delighted, not simply because it made financial sense – in fact, it was a necessity – but because I felt that we were getting a semblance of unity among the players which we'd need over the next nine months. They also accepted the clause in their contracts that they would attend a minimum of eight club functions a season to assist with the PR campaign. I felt that was a huge step forward too.

RISE AND FALL

We also invited Colin Bell back into the fold, as he'd not been a part of the club since his court case three years earlier. We gave him an ambassadorial role, the first time this role had been brought into football. Mike Summerbee was working with the sales department as well, so it meant players, both current and former, were out there, facing the public.

I also wanted to develop a player liaison department, as there were a lot of foreign players moving into English football, and I wanted to try and make their transition into the club as smooth as possible. This was prompted from my own business experiences when I would visit a hotel or conference venue and I would be given a comprehensive welcome pack. I spoke to Chris Bird, and through the design part of his PR agency he mocked up a welcome pack which would include information about the club, the various departments, executive contacts, along with recommended estate agencies, furniture stores and general information on schooling, banks and utilities. David Bernstein liked the idea, but felt we didn't have the budget or the demand in the club at this stage. Today, most clubs in the top two divisions in England have an in-house professional player liaison department.

I felt it was important to support Joe Royle in every way possible and to ensure that there was a more transparent manager's presence at board meetings. What prompted this had been an occasion when Kevin Keegan, who was manager of Fulham at the time, had done some corporate work for me, and delivered a speech at the Copthorne Hotel in Newcastle. He'd just been speaking to Arthur Cox, who'd been chatting with Frank Clark, our manager at City at the time. Frank had told Arthur that he'd listen to any offers for any of his first-teamers. When Kevin told me the gist of the conversation, I just shrugged, and Kevin joked that he thought I was supposed to know everything on the football side of the club.

I realised that Kevin was right, so I made a point of having regular discussions with Joe and noting all the things that happened on the football side to present to the board at the monthly board meetings. This created a better sense of understanding in the boardroom of the manager's approach and strategy, and I would act as a conduit if the board had any questions for Joe. When the team was successful, there weren't too many searching questions, but this arrangement would become quite testing when form on the pitch slipped.

Whatever comments the press cared to make about the "Shame of Manchester City" at the start of the 1998/99 campaign I felt the whole club had the right feeling about it. I missed the first game at home against Blackpool because I was in holiday in Barbados, but I was so nervous I spent the days before the game ringing Joe and Chris Bird to find out what was going on. I ran up a phone bill of almost £150 during that holiday. We won 2–0, but just as important was that fact that 30,000 fans turned up at Maine Road.

"I don't like the idea of front-running," I said to Joe facetiously. "Moving into the top six in February would be about right!"

But things didn't go smoothly at all during those early months. By October, we were only 12th, every game was a battle, and the players were feeling the added pressure. The fans were getting restless. I was forever going to supporters' meetings back in those days and having to defend Shaun Goater to the fans. He was ungainly. He could look clumsy and miss sitters. When we played at Wycombe, I bumped into Joe Jordan who'd managed Shaun at Bristol City.

"You need to understand three things about Shaun," he told me. "Firstly, he'll always work his socks off. Secondly, he'll frustrate the hell out of you. Thirdly, he'll always get you 15–20 goals a season."

Shaun was true to that statement and ended up scoring a large number of goals for City in three different divisions. He never let his head drop if he missed the target, a quality all good strikers need, and never gave up the chase.

It took time for supporters to warm to him, but it helped that Shaun is a real diamond of a person. Whenever supporters wanted autographs Shaun would sign every single one of them, whatever the weather, or whether or not he was in a hurry to get somewhere. When he retired, the Academy was delighted to support his grass-roots soccer festival in Bermuda, where he was instrumental in setting-up coaching clinics. This was typical of Shaun, trying to give something back to his home country.

In his last few months at City, Shaun and I developed a bit of friendly rivalry because he was closing in on my mark of 107 goals for the club. He just failed to beat it, but he was still a great player for the club.

The game that I feel summed up what that season was all about, and the fight we faced, was an away fixture at Lincoln in late October. It was a midweek game, and Joe was still finding out what the team was all about. Sincil Bank was one of those grounds we'd never played at before. It was a trip into the unknown for pretty much of all of us apart from Andy Morrison. Our supporters outnumbered the home fans and sang themselves hoarse for the entire game about the wind, the rain, and playing in the third tier. "What are things coming to, with Man City in Division Two?" and "Joe Royle's Sky Blue Army" pumped out for almost the entire game. One of the abiding memories of that year is how our fans would virtually annexe some away grounds, and usually out-sing the home supporters.

They didn't always have it easy on the road, though, and that match at Lincoln typified the third-tier experience. It had been absolutely bucketing it down all day, and we stopped halfway up the A1 to check that the game was still on. You could barely see through the windscreen. We'd just got to the ground and got settled when there was a fire alarm and we all had to leave again and stand outside in the rain until the all-clear was sounded. When the game finally started, we were losing within five minutes. We were battering them for the rest of the game, and when they got a corner with about five minutes to go they only had one man in the box and kept everybody else back to defend. Lincoln had grabbed their goal, and were determined to beat the once-mighty City, whatever it took. They did just that. A week later we lost at home to Reading, and we were stuck in mid-table. This was going to be a very different season, and it was all about perseverance.

One incident can change the mood within a club, though, and maybe even the course of its history. This happened to us on December 28, 1998, when we played Stoke at home. The place was packed, but we were 1–0 down at half-time. The crowd wasn't happy, and were conveying their feelings to the players in no uncertain terms. Andy Morrison was misplacing passes, our winger Terry Cooke couldn't find the killer ball and Shaun Goater was having one of those afternoons. It just wasn't happening, and I shared the fans' growing frustration. I realised that being stuck in mid-table at the turn of the New Year would leave us with a colossal amount of work to do. There needed to be a spark from someone, but as a director I was helpless when the players crossed the white line.

In the second half, Stoke seemed unsure whether to sit on their lead, or go in for the kill. They started to become indecisive and dawdle around on the ball. Just after half-time the ball was played across to the Stoke full-back and Paul Dickov, with fire and passion in his belly, ran 30 yards to make a crunching tackle. The stadium erupted in support of his attitude. At that moment, I could feel the mood change. Suddenly, the crowd were with us, the players were up and at them, closing them down, but at the same time creating chances of our own.

We came back to win 2–1 and only lost once more in the league, finishing third behind Fulham and Walsall to clinch a play-off place.

In the play-off semi-final, we played Wigan, who'd finished six points behind us. I was nervous because part of the lottery of the play-offs is that you can be knocked out by a team that finished below you in the league. These nerves weren't eased a few minutes into the first leg when a defensive mix-up between goalkeeper Nicky Weaver and central defender Gerard Wiekens let Wigan in for the opener. But it was early in the game, and Paul Dickov managed to grab a late equaliser.

We hadn't played well, and we didn't play well in the return leg at Maine Road, either, when Shaun Goater scored a goal which bobbed in off the top of his left chest. A Goater special (earlier that season he even scored a goal away against Leicester off the back of his head when he wasn't looking at the goal). It wasn't pretty by any means, but now we were through to Wembley to face Gillingham in the final.

It proved to be arguably the most dramatic game I've ever been involved in, as player or director. As you'd expect of a team managed by Tony Pulis, Gillingham were well organised and tough to break down. Our support was loud and vociferous and colourful. I fully expected us to win, but as the game wore on without a goal, our supporters grew more and more nervous, and I spent most of the time shifting uneasily in my seat, as did my fellow directors. Then bang, bang – Gillingham scored twice in the 81st and 86th minute, through Carl Asaba and Bob Taylor.

Two-nil down with four minutes to go. This was surely game over. The City fans went deathly quiet, and in the directors' box we just sat there, stunned. We were ashen-faced, heads down, beaten. Churning through my mind were thoughts about how hard we had all worked that season – players, directors and fans – only to be shot down like this. I was already thinking about how could we possibly pick up the players' morale during the close season after such a shattering blow. Even when Kevin Horlock prodded home after a defensive mix-up in the 90th minute, I never thought that it would be any more than a consolation, with the Gills fans baying for the final whistle.

But then the referee's assistant signified that five minutes' injury time would be played, and suddenly it was like a bolt of electricity surged through all of us. Paul Dickov had missed several sitters for City that season and Joe had had words with him about not lashing at the ball, so when the ball rebounded to him with 93 minutes gone, after a scramble in the Gills' box, I just hoped for the best. He smacked the ball home. In the directors' box, we hugged each other in sheer relief, and the vast City contingent emitted an unbelievable guttural roar, the like of which I hadn't before heard at a football match.

I really thought that we would beat Gillingham, who were crestfallen after Dickov's goal, in extra-time, but Pulis's side were made of stern stuff and held out for a penalty shootout. So it was that Nicky Weaver, the young goalkeeper who Joe had pitched in at the deep end that season, was able to make himself a hero after saving the fifth of Gilingham's spot kicks. I loved Nicky's daft, headless chicken celebration after he'd kept out the penalty, because it was all about pure joy and spontaneity. He tore around the pitch, inviting our players to catch him, and then ended up with half the team on top of him when he ran out of breath.

A lot of City fans have since told me that in all the seasons they have supported the club, that was their favourite. That team spirit and unity was an unforgettable mix, even though we weren't in the top flight. A fantastic celebration continued at Wembley before I finally got onto the M40 to drive home. After a couple of hours, we stopped at Warwick Services, and it seemed that most other City fans had also decided to stop there too, because there was a huge line of them doing a conga around the place. It was brilliant. I'll never forget the look of joy on those fans' faces.

Some say that if City had lost to Gillingham that day, the club would have become terminally ill. I don't know about that because our fan base was huge. But it would certainly have been difficult to sell our supporters the vision that what we were doing was right, if we had been mired for another season in Division Two.

Three days later, Manchester United beat Bayern Munich in the Champions League final to complete an historic Treble. It showed how far we still had to go but, to our supporters, those City players who beat Gillingham that day are heroes, and will always remain so. I still hear of campaigns by City fans to have statues made of Weaver and Dickov. These guys remain as revered as Bell, Summerbee or Lee. Rightly so, because that afternoon Manchester City recovered some of its pride and self-worth. The culture of winning and achievement was back at Maine Road and, crucially, the club, which had been in free fall in the last few years, had forward momentum.

We kept the celebrations quite low key once we got back to Manchester. There was no civil reception, although I'm sure that our fans would have turned out in their droves. We still had a huge amount of work to do if we were to make it back to the top.

Joe was at his very best during this time – confident, ebullient, and looking forward to the challenge of getting City back into the Premiership. Kinkladze was sold to Ajax for £5 million, but Joe didn't splash out on players during summer, he just brought in a defender, Spencer Prior, and winger, Mark Kennedy. Joe's eye for bargain players who could do a job for us at this level was crucial. The previous season, he'd brought in Richard Jobson, who'd served him so well at Oldham and, even at 36, Jobson did a superb job for us in Division One.

Back in Division One, and firing on all cylinders, a five-game winning run in late August and September pushed us among the leading pack. We stayed there until our final game, at Blackburn Rovers when we required at least a draw to guarantee promotion. Our fans virtually invaded Blackburn for the day and I'll never forget the last half-mile drive to Ewood Park where it was virtually wall-to-wall sky-blue and white. Thousands of our supporters who couldn't get tickets climbed up the hills surrounding the ground, trying to grab a view of what they hoped would be a second successive promotion.

It was another classic Manchester City experience. Joe had a fever on the day and was sweating buckets. Our performance in the first half didn't help him either: Blackburn were all over us, taking the lead through Matt Jansen, and hitting our woodwork on no fewer than four occasions. Joe brought on Ian Bishop and Paul Dickov, which changed the balance of the team and the match. Shaun Goater grabbed his 29th goal of the season, a Christian Dailly own goal put us ahead, and then Mark Kennedy scored a third, tearing off down the touchline into Joe's arms. Brilliant. A further goal by Paul Dickov put the result beyond all doubt. We were up, back in the Premiership.

It was what we'd planned of course, but the actual realisation that we were back in the promised land was indescribable. I'd spoken to David Bernstein the previous week asking if he wanted to consider what celebration we were going to have if we were promoted. He couldn't bear the thought of tempting fate by arranging anything, so wouldn't discuss it. I was sitting next to him at Ewood Park, and after our third goal I nudged him and said, "Can we talk about our celebration evening now?" He immediately rang Layashi, our player liaison contact, who arranged for the Midland Hotel in Manchester to reserve a private room for that evening.

It was a fantastic evening, with our fans driving round the city beeping horns and others congregating outside the hotel. There were blue-and-white colours all over the city, and the players went out onto the hotel balcony to acknowledge the supporters.

While I was delighted, I tried not to get too carried away with the wave of joy which was engulfing City. I was already thinking about how Joe could move the club ahead. His transfer budget wasn't huge by spiralling Premiership standards, but if Joe could get value for money, there was no reason why we couldn't aim to consolidate in the top flight. In this situation, it often comes down to a manager's skill set, which was an issue I'd first encountered with Bob Stokoe at Sunderland, who'd managed in the lower leagues all his career, and after the 1973 FA Cup win had been unwilling, or unable, to invest in that better class of player. Immediately after promotion, much as it pains me to say it, I began to have similar reservations about Joe.

At Oldham, Joe had blended the kind of team he had at City during the two promotion campaigns, and did a fantastic job of getting them into the top flight. He'd won the FA Cup with Everton, but that masked the fact that their performances tailed off during Joe's final months there. Others within the game had mentioned to me that they felt Joe lacked the abilities to be successful at the top level in the long term, and that he'd struggle to manage a higher quality of player, and blend them into the team.

These doubts came to the surface within days. After the season finished, Joe went with some of his mates from within the game for a boys' holiday in Mallorca, and immediately after that he went to Vancouver with his family. I know all bosses need a breather, and there is no question that Joe had worked hard over the last couple of years, but I was also aware that City needed to make a positive statement in the transfer market, and not end up scrabbling around for possible signings with the season moving ever closer to kicking off.

John Wardle asked me which players Joe was looking to bring to City. Joe had said nothing to me about possible targets at that stage, but I covered for him, saying that it was important for Joe to have a break and refresh his mind before starting the new challenge. I'm not sure I convinced John, or indeed myself. Football management, and looking out for and signing new players, is a relentless business.

Eventually, we signed Alf-Inge Haaland and Steve Howey, solid players who did a decent job for us, but initially there was very little activity. It was too quiet for everybody's liking.

I went on holiday to Cyprus, but I kept ringing in to see how things were going. One day I spoke to Joe's secretary, and she said it had been manic because they'd just signed 34-year-old George Weah, who was a free agent, and Paolo Wanchope from West Ham. That came completely out of the blue. I had heard that George was leaving Chelsea, where he had been on loan, and Joe had jumped in when he heard he might be joining Fulham. I just felt the whole thing was opportunistic rather than planned. I also knew that with George's ageing legs it was essential we kept things tight and get the ball to him, because there was no way he was going to be able to go chasing it. George ended up as a substitute for much of his time at City, and never made anything like the kind of impact that we would have liked him to.

Another problem for us was that Andy Morrison's knees were highly unlikely to last the course of the season, and we needed to inject a sense of leadership into the club. We were negotiating hard with Ugo Ehiogu from Villa, which would have helped with that, but he ended up going to Middlesbrough. Instead, with the season underway, Joe brought in Richard Dunne from Everton. In time, Richard became a big hero with City supporters but, like Goater, it would take him time to bed in.

Joe also signed Lauren Charvet on a free transfer from Newcastle. Laurent got one of the best contracts at the club, but he never settled. When Kevin Keegan took over he said he was a liability to the squad, always seemed to be injured and took up a lot of the physio's time. As his contract had not expired, we agreed a termination, and I felt sick when I had to sign his final severance cheque for over £600,000.

We actually started the season solidly, taking 14 points from the first 10 games, which led David Bernstein to say he thought we might be alright. But then in the run-up to New Year we won only one of 11 games. From then on, we plummeted like a stone. It was then that I began to wonder if Joe was right to show such loyalty to certain players – particularly Richard Jobson, at 36, and Ian Bishop. They had both been terrific players in Division One, but they were found out in the Premiership. Even when he was in his twenties, Bishop's pace hadn't been great, and now he was in his early thirties it was virtually non-existent. I spoke to Joe about it, but he was insistent that Bishop and Jobson could do a job. I wasn't convinced and heard that Preston were interested in Bish, so as he lived in the Southport area I suggested to Joe to thank him for his efforts and let him have a free transfer. Joe retained Bish, but by February 2001 we had terminated his contract and he left for Miami Fusion in the NASL. Richard Jobson also left us in March 2001, which confirmed that Joe's opinions had been misguided.

By Christmas 2000, the board was under a lot of pressure to consider Joe's position. Nevertheless, we made a decision to support him, which I think was important. Players always deny it, but it's inevitable that when the board starts to show doubt, the insecurity somehow creeps down to the dressing room and everybody loses confidence. I felt that we had to avoid that scenario.

We came to the transfer deadline and we had about £2 million available for Joe to spend. Wolves left-back Lee Naylor was the only name Joe presented to the board as a target. John Wardle was surprised because the acquisition of a full-back was unlikely to solve the deep-seated issues within the team. The usual problem of a lack of goals was the major issue and we were drifting down the table.

"Is that all?" John asked.

Joe, in his typically bullish way, looked him straight in the eye and said, "Yes".

His team was sinking fast, and bringing in a full-back from Wolves was the extent of Joe's ambition. I thought that showed a lack of preparation and creativity, and at that moment I knew he had lost John, if not the rest of the board.

David Bernstein had also been worried about the scouting at the club. Joe had made John Hurst, his old colleague from Everton and Oldham, his chief scout. Bernstein liked to have the heads of departments come into board meetings and make presentations, as you would in any other business, and when John came in he gave a really poor presentation. Joe kept answering the board's questions, rather than John, and did most of the talking himself.

The consensus among board members was that our scouting activity tended to be too localised, centred around games in the North West and Midlands area. By 2001, clubs like Arsenal and United were using their network of scouts and contacts abroad to try and attract and nurture the best which the continent had to offer. I'd discussed this with Joe, and he brought in Jean-Luc Witzel, who was based in France, to run our scouting operation in Europe. We felt Jean-Luc wasn't really covering enough games, or even the right games, and it was evident that major issues were festering.

The Paolo Wanchope situation was also beginning to simmer. He'd cost a record £3.75 million from West Ham, and was clearly a very gifted player. The problem with Paolo was that he could be very inconsistent. In some games, he could rip teams to shreds. Early in the season, he had scored a marvellous hat-trick against Sunderland, and a few weeks later was the Man of the Match against Leeds United at Elland Road. He'd amazed us, because he'd been away on international duty with Costa Rica all week, and then a day or two later played a blinder against a team that was chasing the title. But with his lumbering gait, when he was not contributing he could look both lazy and disinterested. Maybe he was.

Paolo was a very confident player, and was convinced that he was always in the right when he asserted his views. He was totally different from guys like Morrison and Jobson, who'd played under Joe in the lower divisions. Blue-collar players like that owe the manager a debt of gratitude. When the likes of Paolo and George Weah ride into town on much higher salaries than those players who have won you promotion, it takes different managerial skills to blend the two groups, otherwise jealousy and suspicion can set in. It was difficult to judge whether the varying groups did get on, but the fact that results on the pitch were poor indicated that there might be some ill feeling in the squad.

Early in the season, Joe had taken Paolo off at half-time in an away match at West Ham, and then he did it again against Chelsea, a game we lost, which led to a huge dressing-room row, with the two men squareing up to one another. Joe felt that Paolo was winging it, and not contributing to the team. I rang Joe on the Sunday and he said he was disgusted with Wanchope, but wanted to leave things for a couple of days to see if he would apologise. I could understand his frustration, but when you have such a highly talented player, sometimes it needs a different kind of managerial approach. Alex Ferguson has shown this on many occasions, in particular his handling of Eric Cantona.

On the Monday I was going to recce a hotel in Barcelona with a conference client. I was sitting in Liverpool airport waiting for my plane when my phone rang: it was David Bernstein to say that Joe wanted to put Paolo on the transfer list. I was astonished – this was less than 24 hours since he'd told me he wanted to leave it a few days to settle down. This suggested to me that Joe was feeling the pressure and was acting impulsively as a result, but it also worried me financially. We'd given Wanchope a £400,000 signing-on fee. If we put him on the list he was entitled to the whole lot, but if the player wanted to leave, we could negotiate towards an agreement.

At the next board meeting, David asked Joe what the situation was with Wanchope. Joe's reply, which I wouldn't care to repeat, was abrupt, inflammatory and unprofessional. I was shocked. All of the board members were. We sat there for what felt like hours in silence, shifting uncomfortably in our seats, until David nervously took things on, and steered the conversation away from Wanchope. When Joe left, Ashley Lewis turned to the rest of us and said, "We're showing that man too much respect." I knew then that Joe had lost Ashley's support.

On New Year's Day, after a draw against Coventry, Joe looked awful; really tired and grey-faced. When he came into the lounge after the game he had to ask to sit down. I would never really discuss things with managers immediately after games because they tended still to be so uptight, but it was obvious there was something wrong. We were concerned for Joe's health and well-being. So concerned in fact that Bernstein went to see him at his home in Ormskirk the following day, but by then he seemed fine.

We subsequently received the bills from the hotel in the Midlands where the team had stayed, and they showed that a substantial amount of alcohol had been consumed on New Year's Eve, and a lot of the bills had Joe's name on them. He denied that he or his staff had been drinking, and insisted it must have been other people at the hotel using his name. I left David Bernstein and Alistair Mackintosh to continue the internal investigations, but the incident certainly damaged his fragile relationship with the board.

The confident and outgoing nature that Joe had displayed on the way back to the Premiership was rapidly disappearing, and he was becoming more tetchy and irritable by the day which could not have been good for team morale. Despite this, I still supported him. Ironically, it was putting into action one of his ideas which led to us falling out.

Willie Donachie, Joe's assistant, had brought in a conditioning consultant called Mark Bellamy to make an assessment of the players' fitness programme. The results suggested that our players' fitness could be improved significantly and he'd concluded that we needed a specialist. Joe invited me in to ask if I would support his request for that specialist, and I was only too delighted to agree. I told Joe that I'd speak to David Bernstein and that, as usual, we'd get a panel together to find the best man for the job. As I said to the board, we weren't in the market for £10 million or £15 million players, so what we had to do was to put the support structures in place to get the best out of what we could afford.

With Joe's approval I put a committee together consisting of Bellamy, Donachie, Rob Harris (the club physio), Paul Connolly (Joe's sports psychologist) and me. Mark placed an ad in a trade magazine, and when the applications came in he whittled them down to a shortlist. Mark assessed the shortlist but kept telling me about a conditioning coach whose name kept cropping up whenever he asked around. We interviewed the candidates, but Mark was very keen on Juan Carlos Osorio, whom he'd heard had studied sports science at John Moores University in Liverpool. He'd been born in Colombia, but at the time Mark said he was working as conditioning coach for the New York-New Jersey Metrostars. He couldn't come across for the interview, but because of Mark's recommendation we kept him in when we cut the shortlist down to three. Joe later claimed that he'd been kept in the dark about the whole thing, but board meeting minutes prove that I kept him and the board up-to-date at every stage of the process and I assumed his assistant, Willie Donachie, had been doing the same.

Near the end of the season we got those last remaining candidates – Juan Carlos, one from Loughborough and one from Durham – in for face-to-face interviews, and an outdoor and an indoor practical assessment with members of the Academy. By that stage everybody left in the process was excellent, but what set Juan Carlos apart was his football background. He managed to dress his sports science in a football language, which meant that the players trusted him. He was also utterly meticulous. He would, for instance, arrange a specific session to work on the tiny muscle at the top of the groin that's key to sidefooting the ball. The panel members voted unanimously in favour of appointing Juan Carlos. I didn't even need to vote.

I spoke to David Bernstein and Alistair Mackintosh to agree a package to offer Juan Carlos. I was assuming Willie would have told Joe; he was, after all, his assistant, so it was fair to see him as Joe's representative on the panel.

We had Ipswich away on the Monday night, the second to last match of the season, and a game we needed to win if we were going to have any chance of staying up. I met Juan Carlos at his hotel on the Saturday. Early on, when Juan Carlos had come to the training ground, I had asked Joe if he wanted to come up and meet him. He said no, which struck me as odd, but I didn't really think too much of it at the time. I agreed the contract with Juan Carlos, and as far as I was concerned that was it. On the Sunday, I went to the gym and on the way passed the Marriott Hotel, where the coach picked-up players who lived in south Manchester on the way to away games. I saw a load of them waiting, stopped, and excitedly told Willie that we'd agreed everything.

The next day, I rang Joe, assuming he'd be pleased it was all sorted. Instead, he did his nut.

"How dare you hire staff without asking me," Joe yelled.

I was standing by the window in my front room, looking outside, hardly able to speak I was so staggered. It had been his idea in the first place. He'd had his individuals on the committee, we'd gone through every process that we'd used in the past to recruit staff, he'd had access to all the details, and I'd assumed he'd been approving every step of the way.

This put me in a very awkward position. I said to Joe that the most important thing was the game that night, and then I had to ring Juan Carlos. I was desperately seeking some kind of holding position, so I told him that we were still waiting directorial approval. It may well have been down to the pressure Joe was under at the time with the team, but pressure or no pressure, I found his reaction to be disturbing and bizarre.

On the way to Ipswich that night I felt ill. Up until then I'd been fairly positive; although we'd been battling uphill, things were gradually shaping up the way I wanted. This argument with Joe had shaken me, though. We were relegated that night, which just made me feel worse.

The next morning I woke up with terrible stomach pains. I sat on the edge of the bed for five or ten minutes wondering if I should go into the office, but the pains weren't getting any better, so I went to the doctors. It was appendicitis. I was supposed to be producing two conferences the following week, so I wanted to delay the operation, but the doctor was insistent. I had to go straight into hospital that afternoon. That complicated things further, because there was a board meeting hastily arranged for the Wednesday to discuss the implications of relegation and what conditions would be discussed with Joe.

I missed that meeting, but I rang David Bernstein from hospital to see how things had gone, and he said worse than anticipated. The board had lost confidence in Joe's abilities as a manager at the top level. It was difficult for me as Joe had been a friend since my playing days, but the problems that had built up were huge, and he didn't seem to be reacting to them. Maybe he didn't know how to. The club had to come first.

David told me that Kevin Keegan's name had been mentioned in the meeting as a potential successor to Joe. So we agreed that I would ask Kevin to see if he'd be interested in taking the job. At that point that's all it was; putting out the feelers. We agreed that David would meet with Joe after the season ended to review in more detail what had gone wrong that year, so there was some possibility that Joe might save himself, but after what had happened in the New Year, I always felt that was unlikely.

I'd been good friends with Kevin Keegan in my playing days, but after he'd left the game I hadn't really spoken to him until he became manager of Newcastle United in 1993. We had a client who did sponsorship at Newcastle as part of an incentive scheme, and whenever we went to a match at St James' Park when Kevin was boss there he would come and see us beforehand. He used to wander in and meet guests at 2.15 and sit with them for 10 or 15 minutes talking about the game. Invariably, when Kevin walked into the room they fell quiet, and were slightly star-struck, but he was excellent at talking to the supporters and making them feel at ease.

Kevin's galvanising impact on Newcastle in the 1990s had been nothing short of miraculous. Once, I asked Corny O'Donnell about where the majority of Sunderland fans came from, because I knew he'd done an analysis of it back in the Seventies. He told me they hailed from various villages from Durham right up to Ashington, but that had begun to change. Keegan's mere presence at Newcastle had a magnetic effect on Sunderland's traditional supporter base. Several pubs in what should have been Mackem heartlands had gone over to Newcastle.

I felt that Kevin would be the perfect remedy to disperse the black clouds of relegation at City, if David Bernstein was adamant that there really was no way back for Joe. I also knew that I would need to have a contingency plan of manager options to present to the board if Kevin wasn't interested. From my hospital bed, I made an analysis of the current most successful young managers in the game. I came up with a lot of Ms! There was David Moyes at Preston, Gary Megson at West Brom, Alex McLeish in Scotland, and our former player Mick McCarthy with the Republic of Ireland team.

Also, from hospital, I rang Kevin to find out whether he would be interested in taking the job. Kevin insisted that he would never go anywhere near any football management position while there was a manager still in place, which I reported to David Bernstein.

That season there was the unusual situation of an FA Cup final played the week before the final games of the season, and I was laid up in hospital for the next few days and then was banned from driving for the following two weeks and had to rely on my wife and other friends to get me around. The Thursday after the final, David had a long meeting with Joe at a local curry house. I thought the discussion was to find out what changes Joe was prepared to make if he was going to keep the job. We as a board had come up with a list of elements for discussion, covering the scouting, medical, conditioning, drinking culture and particularly the Academy linkage into the first team. But Joe wasn't forthcoming, according to David, or willing to tease out what the problems had been or, more importantly, what the possible solutions were to those issues.

Joe fiercely argued that the scouting systems were indeed solid enough, which everyone within the club knew was untrue. If Joe had had some kind of strategy, some blueprint in place, then maybe the situation would have been salvageable, but David wasn't impressed. I knew that David had come around to the idea that changing manager might be the best solution all round. I was disappointed in Joe by that stage. He wasn't the same man we'd hired at all. He was overly sensitive, stubborn, and not as relaxed, which had always been one of his attributes.

We lost our final game 3–0 to Chelsea. They murdered us, if truth be told, and that was simply a confirmation for me that the team prepared by the manager was not good enough. When David rang me on the Friday, he said we'd meet Joe on the Monday after the Chelsea game to discuss the implications of relegation. I spoke to Kevin again, and told him that events were moving along fast. All the time, Kevin was insistent that he would not even consider the job if Joe was still in place. He suggested that we should make sure we had another couple of candidates because he didn't want us taking it for granted that he'd take the job.

David spoke to Kevin on Sunday, and he explained that on Monday the board would be meeting with Joe to terminate his contract. Even then Kevin wouldn't commit. David said, "If today were Tuesday, would you say yes?" Kevin still did not give the go-ahead but said he'd seriously consider it.

The following day, David met up with Bryan Bodek, John Wardle and Joe to formally terminate Joe's contract. I had asked David if I could be in on that meeting, as I wanted to be there when Joe was given the news. After some sensitive consideration, he suggested I miss that meeting as there would be enough board members there.

After the meeting, David asked Bryan and I to go up to the North East and see Kevin to finalise a contract. There had been a fans' forum meeting arranged for the Thursday, and it was decided that we would officially announce Kevin as our new manager then, but just to prove that City was still not entirely free of leaks, word got around in advance.

For me, the next four days were tinged with great sadness. I felt very sorry for Joe and his family. I'd known him since 1974, and our wives were also good friends. But in my role, I had to do what was right for City. I'd been delighted to support Joe that year, but he had struggled. From December 16 to February 10, 2001, we didn't win once in ten games, and the board had come under a lot of pressure, but we looked at the positives, backed him and did everything possible to see if he could turn it around. In the end, we were relegated by eight points, which speaks volumes.

The stark reality of our decision to fire Joe was that, financially, the football club could not afford to be out of the Premiership for more than one season. Joe and his staff had been instrumental in drawing us from the depths of Division Two to the Premiership. I felt we had done a huge amount to build the foundations that would make us part of the elite, and the failure that year came as a real kick in the teeth. The ambition of the board, I think, was seen in the fact we moved instantly to correct the situation, and I know David Makin said to me later that he couldn't believe we'd been able to get somebody of the stature of Kevin.

I phoned Joe a few weeks later to try and explain what had happened from my angle, and why we'd taken the decision we had, but he didn't want to know. I think our conversation lasted seconds rather than minutes, and we haven't spoken since. In his book, he accused me of being a busy bollocks, and of poking my nose too much into team affairs. Joe suggested that I was hanging around the training ground too much, and when he met David Bernstein at the end of the season he told him that he wanted me to stay away in future. The fact was that David was in London for large chunks of time, had concerns about what was going on training-wise, and had asked me to keep an eye on what was happening. That was my job, and I had done exactly the same thing for the previous two seasons without Joe commenting. At Oldham, Joe had been used to being chief cook and bottlewasher, but managing a big club like Manchester City in the Premiership required a totally different approach.

Joe took the club to the High Court over the terms of his dismissal. His contract stated that if he was sacked while we were in the Premiership he'd be due £750,000, but only £150,000 in the First Division. By the time he was fired, we'd been already relegated for two weeks, so morally and legally I felt sure we were in the right. Joe repeatedly made the point that he felt the lesser compensation package was 'unfair,' but he was very well renumerated in the Premiership, on an annual wage of £750,000, and he received a handsome extra bonus for leading City to the Premier League. Now he was expecting a big pay-off for failure. I was not comfortable with that. In the end, Joe received his £150,000 compensation as he lost his case in the High Court, despite strong PFA backing.

Joe and I are highly unlikely to speak again after what happened at the tail end of the 2000/01 season, but if he is really honest with himself I hope he can admit that, for all his success in his first two years at City, he struggled in that relegation year. It wasn't to do with anyone else. The board never picked a team, bought or sold a player over his head, and I supported him as much as possible. A little later, David Bernstein said that David Sheepshanks at Championship side Ipswich had asked for an endorsement of Joe's managerial abilities. I told the chairman I would have no problem in recommending Joe.

CHAPTER 14

THE KEEGAN EFFECT

I was hugely excited that we'd been able to recruit someone of Kevin Keegan's stature to Manchester City. I felt sure that he would be able to motivate the squad rapidly and get us back up to the Premiership within a single season, which was an absolute necessity. Kevin told me that City was one of the few clubs he'd have gone to, because he knew there was a huge reservoir of support behind the club.

I'd known Kevin since my days with the England squad back in the 1970s, and we'd been friends back then, but I hadn't really seen a great deal of him during the intervening years. As a player, he was all action, all go, with his bustling style, and that reflected the way he was off the pitch too. He was always wanting to be active when he was with the England party, be it playing tennis or squash, or cutting record deals and endorsing products like Brut aftershave. I was always impressed with his get-up-and-go attitude. In his eyes, anything was possible.

Kevin was a kindred spirit, in many ways. He wasn't someone to sit around and wait for something to happen to him. He would go out and grab life and the opportunities it presented by the horns.

Back in our playing days, he once told me that he'd never stay anywhere for longer than five years, and his career as both a player and a manager has borne that out. He's someone who needs change, and he recognises that trait himself. Of course, I was aware, as were the rest of the board, of the view some people had that, after Kevin's abrupt departure from both Newcastle and England, he was somehow "damaged goods", that he was a bit "flaky". I never bought into that view, though. I found him very self-aware. He'd walked away from the England job after admitting that it was too much for him. But managing an international side requires different skills from managing at club level, and he'd been successful in the lower divisions with Newcastle United and Fulham, and re-established Newcastle as a power in the Premier League. We weren't looking for the next England coach, we were looking for someone who could re-establish City as a force in the Premiership within a few years.

Kevin was one of the first footballers to have made sufficient money from the game that he could choose whether to work or not. It was Kevin's passion which made him such a positive force at Newcastle, for instance, and once that passion dimmed he walked away. He also needed to know that he was being fully supported by the board of directors, and that he could do things his own way. As we'd eventually find out, it's when Kevin doesn't get things his own way that the problems start to emerge, but back in June 2001 that was some years away.

My view, which was shared by the other City directors, was that Kevin was the right man for the City job at that time. He had a proven track record at Premier League level, and his short-term motivational abilities were second to none. I also felt that he had toughened up since his abrupt exit from Newcastle. When he took over managing England, I'd warned him that the press would eventually turn on him, like they do with almost every England boss. Kevin is a big family man, and I was concerned about the impact that any negative press reaction might have on him and his wife and children. He thought about my comment for a minute, then countered, "Dennis, I've been through so much that they can't hurt me anymore."

The day we appointed him as manager and he spoke to the press the energy and dynamism he displayed electrified the room. "With Manchester City's fan base, they will one day rival Manchester United. I am certain of that," Kevin proclaimed. I felt that, within a matter of hours, all the doom and gloom surrounding the club after the relegation and the sacking of Joe had disappeared.

I discovered very quickly that Kevin's main strength is managing quick and rapid change at a football club, and making an assessment on the suitability of players and staff for whatever level the team is playing at. When he arrived, I put him in the picture about my problem with Joe Royle over Juan Carlos's appointment, and Kevin said he was happy to take Juan Carlos on. After what had happened with Joe, I said I'd rather they met up before we settled anything, so Juan Carlos came over for a couple of days and spent time with Kevin. I also highlighted the terrific job Willie Donachie had done for the club, and Kevin said that he'd heard good things about him too. He was happy to take him on as well, although he brought in Arthur Cox as his right-hand man, which was fine by me because he'd been my coach back at Sunderland in 1973. He had a tremendous amount of experience, and was a real wise old fox. Kevin also wanted to bring in Peter Bonetti, who he'd worked with as England manager, as goalkeeping coach, so Alex Stepney left in the wake of Joe's departure. Alex didn't speak to me after that until recently. What he didn't know then is how I'd had to persuade the board to keep him when the club had been relegated to Division Two three years before.

There was a very quick transition, which was necessary if we were to bounce straight back. We had to get people in position: the manager, his assistant, a head coach and a conditioning coach. We still didn't have the resources to go after £10 million players. United were able to spend lavishly, but we had to be more frugal in the transfer market, produce young players and ensure we made the most of what we had. Kevin was fully aware of the situation, and the onus to get us back to the Premiership, but I also let him know that if we did get back at the first attempt there would then be a substantial amount for him to spend on players.

One of Kevin's first signings was the legendary England left-back Stuart Pearce, who was just the kind of leader we needed on the pitch. When I first met Stuart after he signed for City, I sensed straight away that he realised the potential of the club, and what Kevin could achieve there. Stuart's arrival was the first evidence I had of the Keegan effect. Kevin's mere presence drew players to the club like a magnet and, being honest, it's unlikely that Stuart would have come to City if anyone else had been in charge.

He was now well into his thirties, but Stuart's passion was undimmed. I told him that the club was like a volcano, and I knew that it would explode sometime. The problem was that I didn't know when, or how high, but having gained a feel for the place over so many years I knew that anything was possible. And I hoped that when the explosion did finally happen, I would be around at the club to see it.

Apart from Stuart, Kevin also persuaded the previously disaffected Paolo Wanchope to come off the transfer list, brought in Eyal Berkovic from Celtic and signed Ali Bernabia from Monaco in September. I would say getting Ali was one of the coups of Kevin's City career. Benarbia was just about to go for a trial at Sunderland when Kevin stepped in. Arthur Cox had been watching him since he saw him playing for Monaco against Newcastle, when David Batty had caught him with a forearm smash. Ali had just turned and looked at him with disdain. It had no effect on him whatsoever. That was a sign of his character, and as soon as the season started he began to pull the strings on the pitch. The Maine Road faithful adored him. He was strong and creative, and could deliver killer passes to open up the well-marshalled defences of teams determined not to let City, the big guns in the Championship, get one over on them. After a 6–2 win over Sheffield Wednesday Paolo Wanchope said, "Ali sees us before we see ourselves," which summed up his quality perfectly.

Ali and Eyal were typical Keegan signings. Quick, nippy, attack-minded and always looking for that final ball; players who could cause havoc on the pitch and put smiles back on everybody's faces. Within a matter of weeks, we'd gone from a fairly defensive side grimly trying to grab points and fight for scraps in the top flight under Joe, especially in his latter days, to a fast, incisive team which brought our fans to their feet. It was Kevin's style of play, and that was what many City fans wanted to see from their team. We needed a reinvention, a rapid makeover, and we got it.

We sailed to promotion that season, and the team scored an amazing 124 goals in all competitions. Generally, it was a very happy ship, and as early as March Kevin and I, along with the board, began to talk about which players we needed to bring in to strengthen the squad in order to push onwards. I always felt that we needed to quickly push on to the next level and plan ahead, which we hadn't done two years before under Joe. Kevin often spoke of momentum, and we needed to be prepared.

At that time, Kevin was spot on in his assessment of players. In February 2002, with promotion looking a dead cert, he suggested to the board that we sign striker Jon Macken from Preston. The fee would turn out to be £5 million, admittedly an awful lot of money for a lower-division striker, who as it turned out would never cut it really in the top flight, partly due to a succession of injuries. Yet I still felt that in this case Kevin's reasons for signing him were sound. He said that Jon would help guarantee promotion to the Premier League, and he certainly freshened things up in the attack, gave us another option, and scored a few goals on the run-in. After promotion, he would then be the third striker behind Nicolas Anelka and Robbie Fowler. His wage demands were reasonable and the transfer fee was the going rate – Clinton Morrison had left Palace for Birmingham and Peter Crouch had moved from Portsmouth to Aston Villa for roughly the same fees at the time, so it wasn't as outlandish as it might seem.

I felt that I was developing my skill at negotiating contracts, too. For instance, after we went up, Kevin Horlock, who was on about £7,000 a week, asked for a pay rise. I spoke to Keegan and Paul Elliot, Kevin Horlock's agent, and said that even though Horlock had been one of my favourite players in the lower divisions, we had to make sure that he could contribute in the Premier Division. Anxious to avoid the problems of being lumbered with and unable to shift players on huge wages which we'd had in the past, I suggested that back in the Premiership Kevin be paid £7,000 a week, but his appearance money would rise on each group of appearances, which meant that if he played or was in the squad he was rewarded with Premiership level wages. Ultimately Kevin, who was a good lower-division player, didn't really cut it, and West Ham came in for him. The fact that he was on 'only' £7,000 a week helped him in the long run, because it meant that his wage demands weren't so ridiculous that other teams wouldn't take a chance on him.

For me, some of the shine was partly taken off that season because of an ongoing financial issue that threatened to engulf me. There had been occasional mutterings about me being a director from supposedly disgruntled shareholders, who had suggested to David Bernstein and other board members that there still wasn't sufficient football expertise on the board. I had a fairly good idea who the puppeteer was that was pulling those particular strings, too. Maybe this was the "fifth column" that Frank Clark had told me about.

The board had always been very happy with my work, and had batted back any complaints from any supposedly unhappy customers. But I always sensed that someone in particular was whispering in the background, and using others to try and undermine me. It annoyed me intensely, because I felt that I was doing a good job, and had City's interests at heart, but also because in my first two years as a director I'd spent so much time working at the club that turnover in my company Premier Events and its subsidiaries had dropped by 30 per cent. I showed David Bernstein and John Wardle my accounts to prove the effect being a director was having on my business.

Then there were accusations made by a mole from within the club that I hadn't paid for my executive box at Maine Road. These accusations were then repeated in the *Manchester Evening News*. There was an internal investigation led by Bryan Bodek, a lawyer and club director, and I was cleared of any wrongdoing, but my concern was who had leaked the story and why they saw fit to do so.

There was a local businessman with corporate facilities in one suite who'd been ejected from the boardroom suite restaurant by director Chris Bird, who was simply ensuring we were operating good business practices in the corporate area. The businessman had no right to be there, and hadn't paid to be there, but seemed to think that because he'd been an ally of the previous regime at City that he had free access to wander around. He was annoyed by the way he was treated, and it appeared that he'd started a campaign, under the control of a disaffected previous employee, whipping up shareholders and getting in touch with the *Evening News*. Only someone with an inside knowledge of the workings of the club and the boardroom could have whipped up the "scandal" of my apparently not paying for the box.

I found it sad that I was sacrificing the development of my own business to do all I could to help the club go forward and I was being hampered by forces whose only apparent aim was to undermine the board's efforts. As I said in the *Evening News*, I believed the group that had attacked me was "less concerned about the progress and success of the club than about self-glorification".

Many shareholders were contacted prior to the AGM asking them to vote against me. A shareholder and friend of mine, Simon Clarke, who was a great City supporter, contacted me, showed me the letter that was being sent out, and told me how disgusted he was as he knew how hard I had been working for the club. He replied to the letter by saying, "As shareholders, we have appointed a board of directors to look after our interests and we must place our faith in that board to do the best job that they are able, rather than look for minor and insignificant issues, about which we may criticise."

I was re-elected by a large majority at the next AGM, despite a local radio station announcing I'd been fired. I have a pretty good idea who leaked that misinformation too. John Wardle demanded an apology from the station for reporting an untruth, and he got it. But it alerted me to the fact that football clubs can be destabilised by those suits with axes to grind and egos which need massaging lurking in the background. It took me back to my early days at the club, when the entire place used to buzz with gossip and was full of leaks. I thought we'd got past all that nonsense, and the issue with my corporate box really shook me.

The future of the club still looked bright, however, and a major benefit and attraction for any potential signings was that in the summer of 2003 we would be moving to a brand new stadium built for the Commonwealth Games. It was a major draw – I took Nicolas Anelka and his brother Claude on a tour of the site before he joined us in the summer of 2003. They were thoroughly impressed with what they saw. Maine Road, for all its memories and comparatively recent redevelopments, was by then a really awkward-looking shape and design, and was restrictive in terms of what it could offer us on the corporate side of things, which was beginning to become a major consideration.

Moving to the new stadium was a great opportunity to propel the club forward, and I was asked to be on the stadium design sub-committee when the plans were first presented. The two main things I considered of paramount importance were, first, a good pitch for the players and, second, (drawing on my conference business knowledge) ensuring that we had superb function rooms to make the stadium profitable on non-match days. I take great pride in seeing the stadium now, knowing that I contributed greatly to its high-quality functionality.

David Bernstein, along with other members of the board, worked extremely hard to come up with a fantastic deal for the club. The first demand was that the stadium would be a dedicated, football-only stadium, without any running track. We also involved supporters in the whole process, and in the end we had around a 95 per cent positive response to moving from Maine Road.

When Kevin Keegan is your manager, you realise quickly that he needs to "churn" footballers. He makes quick decisions as to whether a player is suitable for the club or not, and unless the board supports him in the churning process, there are problems. But if you are churning talent the whole time you are likely to be paying players off to go if they don't cut the mustard, and if Kevin was bringing in top players, and possibly deciding quickly that they weren't suitable, I knew it would cost us big money. In the back of my mind, I was worried about what could happen if things didn't work out, but certainly, at first, Kevin's transfer approach worked when we signed Anelka and Peter Schmeichel. Both were unbelievable physical specimens. I remember visiting Nicolas when he was having his medical on the day he signed, and he was stripped to the waist. As well as being tall, he was built really powerfully, and in training I could see that we'd bought a class act. At one session, I watched Nicolas turn Steve Howey inside out. I'd not seen anything like it in a long time. By the time he joined City, I felt he'd matured from his days of being labelled 'The Incredible Sulk' at Arsenal and Paris St Germain. We didn't have the kind of issues with Nicolas or his brothers that other clubs had, although towards the end of his time at City the fact he was basically a lone wolf worked against him.

Schmeichel was a colossus of a man, and in training I saw that he'd lost none of the ire he'd possessed at United, as he barked and screamed at his defence to protect him and avert the danger. Nicolas and Peter were a cut above the rest, and their influence during Kevin's first season back in the top flight was immense. I knew exactly why they'd come to City – it was because of the Keegan effect.

Although the player turnover during my time at City was constant, one thing that never changed during my ten years as director was my commitment to the Academy system. I never needed any convincing that nurturing youth players was the way forward at City, or indeed at any club. The great teams at Madrid, Ajax, Milan, Barcelona and United all had that core of homegrown talent. At Sunderland, I was one of six players who'd progressed through the youth ranks. The 1976 League Cup final-winning team at City contained seven players from the Manchester area who graduated through the club's youth teams, and when I played in the 1981 final the City team had six local lads in the side.

I only had to look across the city to Old Trafford, where the Nevilles, Butt, Beckham, Scholes and Giggs, all graduates of Fergie's youth team, were at the core of that United team. Fergie's approach was typified by his statement in the book, *The 90-Minute Manager*: "We do well with them [young players] because anybody who comes, knows that if they are good enough they will get a chance. We are patient, don't discard too easily and we prefer to let players develop."

If you have a group of youngsters who are part of the club culture, and believe in the ethos of the club, then you have every opportunity of being successful. Our Academy director, Jim Cassell, was a highly astute judge of talent. Around the time of our promotion in 2002, his work was beginning to bear fruit, as Joey Barton and Shaun Wright-Phillips had already broken into the first team. Jim strongly believed that players developed at different rates, and while some, like Shaun, were ready for the first team at 18, others, like Joey Barton, need a couple more years to mature.

The story of our goalkeeper, Nicky Weaver, at City was typical of how things often don't turn out how you'd expect, though. He'd made a real name for himself after his performance in the 1999 play-off final, but he started to go off the rails a bit, lose focus and his place in the team. In 2002, we got a letter from a supporter who was a barrister complaining about Nicky's behaviour and telling us that he'd been drunk, and subsequently been sick in a dustbin in Cheadle High Street after watching an England game in a local pub. Young players have these problems in football. They suddenly have an elevated social status, time on their hands and money in their pockets, but they lack the wherewithal to manage it. I called in to see Nicky at his home and had a good chat with him about the situation, and I always remember that he said what he really wanted was a girlfriend so that he could just sit in with her, get a pizza and watch a DVD. Because he was single, his mates would ring him up and ask if he fancied a lager. One would become two, and two would become three. I felt a lot of sympathy for him and I told him that then dedication and individual focus is critical to being successful, repeating my mantra, "To be the best, you have to be different from the rest".

Nicky then sustained a really serious knee injury, and for a while it seemed that his career could be over, but the determination he showed to fight back from it was unbelievable. At the time of writing, he's plying his trade at Sheffield Wednesday, and is performing to a high standard. Nicky is still only in his early thirties and, given that goalkeepers can now play into their forties, he could still have several years left in the game.

There was also the case of our young Irish midfielder, Willo Flood, who looked set for a great future in the game. Willo had just bought a place of his own, but one night he was held at knifepoint in his home by a masked intruder wearing a Manchester City shirt, and forced to load his stuff into the burglar's car. Willo had nightmares for months, received counselling, and was so terrified by the whole ordeal that he moved back into the club's digs. We expect so much from young, immature footballers, and forget that they are open to temptation, in Nicky's case, and horrible luck, as in Willo's case.

Jim Cassell's view was that if a player joined our club in his early teens, and learned to look after himself effectively and discipline himself, then he stood a great chance of making it in the game. David Bernstein appointed Jim as head of the Academy back in 1998, and was nothing but supportive of it throughout his tenure. We had a meeting early on in David's tenure when he inquired about the future development of the Academy, and Jim and I reassured him that we could make it work.

"Mr Chairman," Jim said. "Just trust me, I promise you we will deliver first-team players."

Jim had a fantastic staff around him. There was Barry Pointon, head of recruitment, who had that great ability of finding players, and Alex Gibson, head of youth coaching, who was extremely professional at organising the training programmes. Ex-City legend Paul Power and, in the early years, Frank Bunn, the former Oldham star, supported Alex on the training pitch. We brought in Robin Sadler, who was soon promoted to join the first-team medical staff at our Carrington training ground as our physio. They all created a great team ethic.

At the time, City didn't have a great deal of spare money, so I headed up a fundraising committee which included Jim, Academy secretary Debbie Glynn, Steve Bottomley, Tudor Thomas, Andrew Shaw, Gary Lewis and, in the early days, Gary Lee. Together we arranged four or five functions through the year. These guys were all City fans and volunteered all their time for free. In September, it was a golf day; in November, a sportsman's evening with guests such as Sir Bobby Robson and Terry Venables; in January it was a sportsman's lunch with a Q&A with the manager; at the end of the season, a gala dinner; and in early summer, a celebrity cricket match. We raised money for laptops for staff, floodlights for one of the grass training pitches, weights for the conditioning programme, Christmas gifts for the Academy boys, Academy trips abroad and, most important of all, their pre-season training camps. These introduced the players to the elements needed to be a professional footballer. In my opinion, knowing what I know about the financial situation of the club, I don't think it's any exaggeration to say that Jim's work at the Academy, along with David Bernstein's professional chairmanship and restructure of the club, plus John Wardle and David Makin's financial input, and the fantastic, patient support from the fans, prevented the club from going belly up on several occasions. As well as Joey and Shaun coming through, the Academy also produced Steven Ireland, Micah Richards, Nedum Onuaha and Michael Johnson. In total, spread across all four divisions, at the start of the 2011/12 season there were 70 footballers plying their trade in the professional game who came through Jim's system, of which 30 have made their first-team debut for Manchester City and 17 have become full internationals. City have pulled in around £50 million from the sales of many of those players, the most notable being Shaun's £21 million sale to Chelsea in 2005.

I would have to say that my involvement in the City Academy gave me my greatest pleasure and fulfilment as a director. I really felt that we were making a difference, and adding value to the club when a young player "made it". When Jim and I met the new inductees and their parents, I would emphasise that, as well as developing the player, we would also develop the person, and that even if the lad didn't make it as a professional player he would become a more rounded individual. I simply can't speak highly enough of Jim, or his staff at the Academy. The job they did, which went largely unrecognised, was incredible, and I could never spend too much time at the Academy with staff who shared my passion for grassroots football.

I am very excited about what has been happening at the club in the past few years, but the one thing that never ceases to amaze me is that Jim was never involved in the transition of the Academy. Tony Carr, Jim's counterpart at West Ham, who was probably along with Jim the best producer of young players in the country, received an MBE and a testimonial from his club, but Jim was just moved on to special projects at City. He produced players in an environment of severe financial restrictions, and I would have been very interested to see how the future strategy of the Academy that Jim and I spoke about would have turned out with the investment that is now available. Those things we discussed, such as individual player development, video analysis and sports science, are now being implemented by many clubs, but Manchester City would have been ahead of the game.

Kevin Keegan was always very supportive of the Academy, and would liaise with Jim and myself as to which young players would benefit from training with the first team, or needed to be held back for their own good. On one occasion, Kevin and I went to Goodison Park to see our youth team, which included Shaun Wright-Phillips, play against Everton who featured a young 15-year-old player called Wayne Rooney. Rooney was outstanding on the night as Everton beat us 3–1. A few minutes before the end of the game, Kevin and I got up to leave the directors' box, and he went up to the then Everton manager, Walter Smith and said, "He would be in my squad on Saturday".

Successful though the Academy was, Kevin couldn't rely on the youth system alone to push the club on, and wanted to bring in more high-profile signings. With the team progressing well during the 2002/03 season, he wanted to keep the momentum going, and pushed the board hard to back him. It was always going to be a difficult business, because the cost of turning us, a mid-table side, into one which could challenge for the Champions League would be astronomical, and we didn't have a limitless supply of cash. But, within reason, we had to aim higher, of course.

On one occasion during that season, Kevin's teambuilding efforts were hampered by tragedy. We had the Cameroon international Marc Vivien Foe on loan with us. He was a lovely man and an excellent central midfielder. Kevin was very keen to sign him on a permanent basis, and the board was actively trying to secure funds to sign him. On a June night around the same time I went to meet Pele at an exhibition of photos of him in town. Midway through the evening, my phone buzzed, and I received a message saying that Marc had collapsed during an international friendly. I managed to get hold of Kevin, and as the evening went on it transpired that Marc had suffered a heart attack and died. I was barely able to speak when I heard the news. He had been on loan and was just beginning to settle into the club and perform at a high level. The news staggered the whole club, from the dressing room to the boardroom and the supporters. We eventually retired his number in respect for him as a player and a person.

By this time, David Bernstein had stood down as chairman, over Kevin's attempts to sign Robbie Fowler from Leeds. The positive vibe at the club would never be quite the same again, in my opinion, and it proved just how difficult it is to take a club to the next level.

Kevin had wanted a top-class striking partner for Nicolas Anelka and, initially, I was quite excited by the prospect because Robbie had been a deadly finisher during his heyday at Liverpool, he was one of my favourite players and I was convinced he could link up effectively with Nicolas. Kevin also wanted to sign the Bordeaux defender David Sommeil, but together they would have cost the club around £8 million. The board was divided on the issue, and David Bernstein pointed out that buying the pair would require a level of borrowing which was 'in excess of our facility'. He pointed out that Robbie's injury record made him a risky investment, and I could see his point.

Kevin is an emotive, impulsive man, an instinctive manager, but this double deal would have flown in the face of the tight-ship mentality which we had forged, through necessity, at City. I could see where all this could go, because if Kevin felt that he wasn't getting a sufficient return on the players he had, then he'd always be banging on the door for more signings to fix the issue. But our money had largely gone. It was a very difficult situation to manage the need for exciting new talent with the need to balance the books, but on this occasion I felt that we needed to speculate to accumulate, and sign Robbie Fowler.

With David in London so often, Kevin had become very close to John Wardle and convinced John that signing Robbie would be a good move for the club. In fairness to David, and against his better judgement, he promised to look into getting the funds together for the move, and ultimately John and David Makin pulled in the money required for the deal. Signing Fowler would have huge ramifications for City. With negotiations continuing for Robbie, David expressed concern in a board meeting that the unity and togetherness which had personified City during my first years at the club was disappearing, and it was clear that he was upset when it came to the arguments over whether or not to sign Fowler.

There had also been ructions on the board because David wanted to elevate one of our joint managing directors, Alastair Mackintosh, above the other joint MD, Chris Bird. Initially, John Wardle accepted David's suggestion, but then he abruptly changed his mind for unspecified reasons. The tension in board meetings was palpable after that, as we all waited to see what would happen next. It saddened me, because, Mackintosh aside, we were all City fans, but there was clearly indecision about where the club should be headed next.

In order to try and clear the air, with David Bernstein absent, the board met at Manchester Conference Centre to try and work through the issues. Despite the differences on the board, the feeling was that David should stay, but I knew that he would only do so if Kevin backed down on trying to sign Robbie Fowler. I went round to Kevin's house to try and get him to reconsider, but in the back of my mind I knew he never would. When Kevin makes his mind up about something, he never changes it.

I rang David to tell him that Kevin was still insistent and that John Wardle was supportive of him. David resigned at the next board meeting, which saddened me greatly because he was a man who always had City's best interests at heart not something you can always say about a club chairman.

It puzzled me that my name was mentioned as a possible successor to David. I suppose it was flattering in one sense − even my friends mentioned that they felt I could do a job − but I knew that I did not have the necessary attributes for the position. In fact, the suggestion that I could do the job was quite disrespectful to the role of club chairman. Too many chairmen seem to think they can run a football club like they would a corner shop down the road. David had years of corporate experience in accounting and in business, and to be an effective chairman you need to also under-stand marketing strategy and public relations on a large scale. Although I felt that I'd done a good job at City as a director, and my own businesses had done well, you'd need to have someone with far more experience of a global brand than me at the helm. Ultimately John Wardle, who'd had a huge amount of corporate experience with JD Sports and who was very much a Keegan man, took over as chairman, and Robbie Fowler arrived in early 2003. Kevin then convinced John to sanction the signing of Robbie's former Liverpool team-mate Steve McManaman from Real Madrid. It was at this point that I felt Kevin and the club really began to lose its way.

CHAPTER 15

NO MORE CASH FOR KEVIN

While I could see the potential of signing Robbie Fowler, I was considerably less enthused when Kevin told me that he wanted to bring Steve McManaman to City. I made a point of never trying to interfere directly in the manager's role of running the team, but I would always voice my opinions on potential signings. By 2003, when Kevin told us that he wanted to bring him in, Steve had been warming the bench at Real Madrid for the best part of four seasons, and yet was one of the best-paid players in Europe because of his Bosman transfer status. He was on around £60,000 per week, more than Juventus's big star Alessandro Del Piero was earning.

I questioned Steve's desire, and whether at 30 he could really raise his game and add value to the team. In short, I was concerned that he may already be in his comfort zone. He'd been a good player at Liverpool, unquestionably, but his pace was on the wane, and his lumbering gait could give the impression that he wasn't too interested. That wouldn't be an issue if he was producing the goods, but I always had my doubts. I'd seen "brand" players before at Sunderland who'd played successfully elsewhere, but were at the tail-end of their careers. The likes of Jim Baxter and Gordon Harris didn't always have a good influence on the younger players at Roker Park, with their occasional "seen it all, done it all" attitude. Inevitably, training can become a chore as you get older, and seasoned professionals have an unfortunate habit of sounding-off in front of youngsters. I remembered Malcolm

Allison's warning to me when I arrived at City not to "listen to that lot".

The board sanctioned the signing of McManaman, and to be blunt it didn't go too well. Only a few years before, Steve and Robbie had both been part of the so-called "Spice Boy" culture at Liverpool, and although I accept it was partly a media creation, it's a fact that neither Liverpool nor Robbie and Steve achieved what they should have done. On paper, Liverpool had appeared to be the equal of Manchester United, but United always seemed to have more desire, and could perform week in week out. Liverpool's stars, including Steve and Robbie, didn't. It proved to be the same at City.

Steve is a very sharp individual – very articulate and savvy in many ways. Robbie has a razor-sharp wit. They were both from the first generation of players who were set up financially for life by their late twenties, and in those circumstances you have to be extremely determined and focused on football if you're not going to let your desire to win slip. Because they'd already earned so much from football, they were able to diversify off the pitch into areas such as property development and horse racing. They also got into one or two well-documented scrapes. I felt their passion for football had dimmed, and that they had started to coast, which wasn't much good when we were trying to take City to the next level and nurture the youngsters at the club.

They lived near each other and formed their own little clique, in training and off the pitch, of which Joey Barton became an honorary member. It wasn't good for Joey who, given his difficult family background and fiery reputation, needed really strong role models. I'd learnt from long experience that the minute there are cliques at any club, problems inevitably follow.

Because his pace had diminished, Steve was forced to change his game from being a winger who cut in from wide, to playing a more holding role in midfield. Fans can accept that age means players have to adapt their game, but he never performed. When Steve reflects on his 18 months or so at City, I think he must be incredibly disappointed with the way he played. In plenty of games, he produced next to nothing and the fans got on his case, nick-naming him 'Steve McMoneyman' because of his salary.

We played Manchester United in an FA Cup match, which United won, and Steve got involved in a daft altercation which saw Gary Neville get sent off. Afterwards, Alex Ferguson commented that the altercation with Neville was pretty much Steve's only contribution to the game. It was very hard for me not to disagree with him. Then in an away game at Norwich, Steve was having a stinker, and our supporters were making their feelings plain. He lost the plot completely and gave them the finger. He was never going to redeem himself in our fans' eyes after that. Eventually, Steve played 37 games for us, and didn't score a single goal.

I always felt that, although Robbie Fowler was unlucky with injuries, he didn't always help himself, either. When Kevin first signed him, David Bernstein had expressed concern about Robbie's fitness, and it was pretty obvious that he wasn't as slimline as he'd been when he burst to prominence in the mid-Nineties. In the 2004 close season, I suggested to Kevin that we should pay for a personal conditioning coach to work with Robbie for a couple of weeks before pre-season training. This was similar to something I heard that Ryan Giggs had used, and I felt that Robbie mainly needed to work on his sharpness – in training he was one of the most natural finishers I have ever seen, even better than Nicolas Anelka and Georgio Chinaglia in New York. Kevin had a word with Robbie who said thanks, but he was going to do his own preparation. It goes without saying that that was a bad decision, as Robbie never fully regained his fitness and didn't return to the player had been.

In the end Kevin took him out of the first-team group for a month and put him with Juan Carlos for a one-to-one conditioning programme. Although you can never compare footballers, as their physical make-ups are different, the fact that Ryan Giggs was still performing and winning medals for United in his late thirties shows that you need to be mentally tough and totally professional if you want a long and successful career in football.

The problems were beginning to surface, both in terms of Kevin's man-management of players, and at board level. In our first season back in the Premier League (2002/03), we'd finished ninth, and there were some really impressive performances. In the last-ever Maine Road derby, I felt that Nicolas Anelka and Shaun Goater dovetailed to perfection, as we beat United 3–1. Famously, Goater robbed Gary Neville on the touchline before slotting the ball past Fabien Barthez. Shaun was unplayable that day, which proved that Joe Royle, a couple of years before, had been right to stick with him, despite the grief that Shaun occasionally copped from our fans.

On occasion, Nicolas appeared to be a striker of the absolute highest quality. But by the time of the second season back in the Premier League, I could see that he was starting to become more and more remote and distant, which is what had happened at his previous clubs. His form and goalscoring became more sporadic. When he did score, he tended to net doubles or hat-tricks, but couldn't take a game by the scruff of the neck and grab us a winner when we were up against it.

The chemistry between him and Robbie Fowler fizzled away completely. They were polar opposites: Robbie – outgoing, cheerful and cheeky; Nicolas – introverted, serious and distant.

Things were not right at the club, but they almost got a whole lot worse in January 2004 when the club directors nearly didn't make it home from an away match. We'd taken off from Southampton airport after an away game at Portsmouth in a 12-seater plane. After a few minutes, I noticed sparks on the wing, and then smoke began to belch out of one engine. The whole plane went deathy silent. Being a good Catholic, club secretary Bernard Halford began to say his Hail Marys. I honestly thought that we were goners, and the whole thing just made me go numb. I don't recall my life flashing before me, but I was just gripped by this overwhelming sensation that this could be "it". After what seemed an eternity, with the plane rocking and rolling all over the place as the pilot tried to balance the single propeller, we managed to make an emergency landing at Biggin Hill. The experience really shook me up. It didn't put me off flying, but it certainly made me wary for some time.

You always know when you have a happy club when everyone at whatever level is talking to one another. The worry comes when it all goes quiet. What are people thinking? What are they hiding, or worried about? Who isn't getting on? I saw that when England played in the 2010 World Cup finals. There was no cajoling or shouting, no passion, enjoyment or laughing on the pitch. Just silence, and miserable faces. That began to happen at City, towards the tail end of the 2003/04 season, when Robbie and Nicolas simply stopped communicating. Top managers would have spotted the early signs – the cold looks and the strange glances – and intervened, rather than let the situation worsen. They'd have spoken to both individually, and then pulled the pair of them in and mediated. It would never have been an easy job, pulling two such disparate characters together, but that's what was needed in order to get the best out of both players for the team. It never happened.

Linked to this – and it's probably the case that his mood both influenced the atmosphere and was also caused by the declining on-pitch results – Kevin was becoming visibly tetchy and irritable, not his normal self. This was shown clearly when he asked me to organise the negotiations with Alistair Mackintosh for Joey Barton's new contract rather than do it himself. Kevin had grown frustrated with Joey's penchant for getting into scrapes off the field, but he knew he needed him because he was becoming an increasingly influential midfielder for City.

We'd always tried to support Kevin's teambuilding as much as possible, but the simple fact was that by the time the January 2005 transfer window opened we had to tell him that there was no more money available for new players. At a previous board meeting, I had asked what money we would have available for Kevin in January. None, I was told. I said Kevin may have a problem with that. If he can't buy and sell players, Kevin grows frustrated. But in the modern era, churning players is a costly business, and continued, rapid change rarely delivers success at any large organisation. In some ways, I felt that his insistence on churning suggested that he had "lost" some of the players.

Nicolas Anelka grew increasingly morose and was sold to Fenerbahçe in the transfer window for £7 million, and it was clear that the two ex-Liverpool players had not taken us up a notch. I wouldn't necessarily blame Kevin for not managing Nicolas properly, but I sensed that he struggled with players who don't share his raging enthusiasm for the game, and who don't automatically give 100 per cent in training and in every match. Players come with different psyches and makeups, and only the very best can motivate and man-manage all those different types of footballers.

However, I have to accept that we knew exactly what we were getting with Kevin, and things panned out pretty much as expected: a quick impact which had got us back in the top flight, a good first Premiership season, where we'd finished ninth, and then growing frustration at not being able to build on that initial success. He'd been effective at City for three years which, give or take a season, Kevin accepts is his shelf life as a manager of a football club. What happened with him disappointed me, though, because with the new stadium, our fan base, and the Academy producing a conveyor belt of talent, we should have had the potential to compete, but we were out of money. We had no more finances to give the manager, and could not fund his insistence on short-term team-building, rather than a long-term strategy.

Little problems, which previously hadn't mattered, became big issues. The thing with Kevin is that he has a very expressive face; he simply can't hide his emotions, and when he is unhappy and unsettled that vibe is transmitted to his players. During matches, he looked frustrated, and downbeat if things were going wrong. He had a habit of burying the lower half of his face in the top of his coat when things were going badly, as if he simply wanted to hide away from what was happening around him. He had also lost his right-hand man Arthur Cox after the club arranged a retirement settlement for him.

To try and find out how Kevin was feeling I spoke to Neil Rodford, his good friend and former colleague at Fulham. Neil intimated that Kevin might be prepared to look at a new contract, which really surprised me, so I thought I would speak to Kevin and find out for myself. We met up at his apartment for a cup of tea, but he wouldn't give me any real indication of his plans.

"The chairman will need to speak to me about it, Dennis," he told me.

I reported this back to John Wardle, who made arrangements to meet up with him.

In March 2005 Kevin left, with the club labouring in the bottom half of the table. I think that, disappointed though he was with things, he seemed to accept that his time was up, and I was relieved that, unlike the scenario we had with Joe Royle, Kevin left with good grace. I'd say Joan and I are still friends with Kevin, Jean and their girls – from afar, anyway. He lives just around the corner from me, but he's so involved with ESPN and other business interests that I rarely, if ever, actually see him. Sadly, football friendships go like that sometimes.

We decided to give the interim job to Stuart Pearce, who'd been Kevin's reserve-team boss at City. It was only an interim job as we were unsure of Stuart's abilities as a manager, and Kevin had also expressed his reservations to me earlier. The skills required for a reserve manager position compared to a first-team management job is totally different, and there have been many failures in the past. A manager has to be fully involved transfers, coaching and scouting, dealing with players' needs on a daily basis, dealing with the media, and of course ensuring that the team wins its matches. It's not an easy transition at all. But we only had about ten games to go, and our main priority was to ensure that the club was still in the Premiership at the end of the season, so continuity was key.

CHAPTER 16

TREADING WATER

S tuart Pearce began with tremendous energy and enthusiasm, and the team and our supporters seemed to be lifted by his approach. In the weeks after Kevin left the club in March 2005, experienced team members responded very positively to his coaching techniques and their form was excellent and we only just missed out on UEFA Cup qualification when Robbie Fowler missed a penalty against Middlesbrough in the last match of the season. Stuart really did have something to build on, and in the summer I recommended him for the full-time job.

The board hoped that Stuart could do a good job at City, because from the outset he understood the situation that faced us. He realised that with the finances being what they were, we would need to rely upon the nurturing of young players from the Academy, and that, as we began an active search for more funding, there was a need to look for good value in the transfer market. In his contract negotiations with the chairman, he surprised me by not asking for any compensation either way in the event of him leaving the club. If he left for another club we wouldn't get any compensation from that club, but if we sacked him he wouldn't receive any compensation either. I told him that I respected him for taking that decision, which is very unusual in this era of compensation culture.

I also met up with Stuart to discuss the task facing him. I told him, "In my opinion, a manager needs to get three things in order: recruitment, team management and motivation. That means buying the correct players, blending them into a team unit and then motivating them." (Watching the film *The Damned United*, I see that Brian Clough and Peter Taylor had a similar approach: "Find them, sign them and manage them.") Hardly rocket science, but these observations were garnered from 17 years in the dressing room and eight years in City's boardroom, as well as experiences in my business life.

In the 2005 close season, we received the £21 million from Chelsea for Shaun Wright-Phillips – excellent business, and a testament to Jim Cassell's work with the Academy – but it also showed that when it came to doing the business at the highest level, City were becoming a selling club. I have always been realistic, and I understood perfectly what the financial situation was, but the whole thing made me feel a bit deflated. I'd played for City at a time when the club had a host of stars in the 1970s, and then in the early Eighties when the likes of Trevor Francis and Kevin Reeves came to Maine Road, each for a million pounds. We were big players in the transfer market back then. Not anymore.

Our support base was as strong as ever, and after the fans had endured the double relegation in the late Nineties, it would have been nice to think that we could have kept the club's upward trajectory going, but I knew that without any new investment we could never hope to challenge for top honours. It was a disconcerting feeling to be treading water, and not something I'd ever wanted for City.

I always enjoyed working with Stuart, and discussing future strategy at the club. But I'm sad to say that during his two years in charge, I became increasingly disillusioned by the way in which the club's strategy was moving.

A lot of the issues which annoyed me came down to player recruitment, and because Stuart was new to the role of manager he was inexperienced in dealing with transfers. By this time, I was being left out of some football meetings, as John and Alistair were dealing directly with Stuart. This put me in an extremely difficult situation, for instance, when Andrew Cole was brought in during the summer of 2005. He was offered a bonus if we qualified for the UEFA Cup and a different bonus for the Champions League, but there was no stipulation that he had to play a certain number of games to be eligible for it. Andrew was an excellent professional, and scored nine goals in 22 starts for us, but still, to my mind, the deal we struck was crazy, and I explained that to the chairman, John Wardle. John had known that I believed strongly in rewarding players as long as they contributed and performed, and I thought that he also agreed with that policy. But it was too late; by the time I went to Alistair Mackintosh, the deal had already been agreed. In the previous eight years, there had always been a level of joined-up thinking about transfers, and separate members of the board would discuss key issues as a group, but the lines of communication, clearly, were now being cut.

That was also the case when Claudio Reyna and Antoine Sibierski were offered new deals just before Christmas 2005. Neither were regulars, both were in their thirties, yet both were offered deals on the same basic salary terms they were already on. They were both good professionals, but we didn't have money to waste on players sitting in the stand. I spoke to Peter Reid, who'd managed Claudio at Sunderland, and he stated that he just couldn't get him on the pitch enough times.

"These players start between 16 and 20 games a season," I said to John. "That's normal when players get older, and injuries affect their contribution even more, so their contracts should involve more performance-based elements."

"I'll speak to [vice-chairman] Bryan [Bodek]," he replied.

I was staggered. "Bryan's the expert when you want final confirmation on legal matters, not on football issues."

It highlighted to me what was happening in many boardrooms around the world, when highly successful businessmen were coming into football and six months later claiming to have become experts. It's like me saying to Sir Philip Green, "Philip, I'm your man to run Topshop,"

"Terrific, what do you understand about the retail trade?", he'd reply.

"Nothing, but I'm a good businessman…"

I think I would be out of the door before I could blink.

I won't say I considered resigning, but I did wonder then whether I really wanted to be part of the regime anymore, although my real concern was to make sure the Academy was still supported.

Directors weren't talking to one another, and non-football experts were making football-related decisions.

The craziest deal of all involved a player whom I had huge respect for, Paul Dickov. After his contribution to our team in the late Nineties, he was rightly regarded as a hero in the eyes of our supporters. Prior to the beginning of the 2006/07 campaign, John Wardle told me that Stuart wanted to bring back Paul, now 34, on a two-year contract. I was utterly gobsmacked. Paul was a great pro, but he'd been deemed surplus to requirements four years earlier, so I couldn't see any logic in re-signing him now. It gave me no pleasure to see Paul suffer with injuries and loss of form, and he didn't score once in his second two-year spell with us. I argued and argued my case before we signed him, but to no avail. It made me furious, because I could see exactly what would happen, and no one at the club – the manager, the chairman nor the chief executive – could see that it was the wrong move for both the player and the club.

I imagine that Stuart thought I was going out of my way to be obstructive and difficult, but I will always ask football questions, and I did that with many of the transfers at the time. It is the responsibility of directors to support their manager as much as possible, but they must ensure that the manager has paid as much attention to detail before signing players. When players are signed on long-term contracts and the manager leaves, it is left to the directors to pick up the financial waste and, ultimately, it's the ever-faithful supporters who pay for such folly.

I never felt Stuart had a full grasp of transfers and recruitment when he was in charge, and that's a big issue. An example was when he brought in Bernardo Corradi from Valencia for a large sum. The problem was that Bernardo was a six foot-plus striker who was strong in the air, but we didn't have a winger who could supply the ammunition for him. We had had Albert Riera on loan the previous season, but Stuart hadn't pursued the possibility of extending that arrangement. I said to the chairman that I'd seen footage of Corradi scoring goals from crosses and Stuart must look for a wide player. Instead, the American DaMarcus Beasley, a jinker and a dodger, was brought in but crossing wasn't really one of his skills and Corradi struggled because he never got the service that he needed. I expressed my views to John about our recruitment policy and said we had no pace up front and wouldn't score 30 goals in the season; we ended up scoring 25.

The days of us being able to sign players of the quality of Nicolas Anelka were over, and this was evident in our league form. Despite starting well in 2005/06, we lost nine of the last ten, and ended up in 15th place. That form continued into the following campaign, which ended up as my last at City.

By now, the board was actively seeking new investment, and there were press mumblings about the future not just of Stuart Pearce, but the whole board at City.

In January 2007, Trevor Brooking approached the club about the possibility of Stuart taking over the coaching of the England Under-21 team on a part-time basis. I opposed the idea. By now, City were on a horrendous run of form which saw us fail to score at home after Christmas and avoid relegation by just four points. My view was that Stuart was struggling to manage City, so I was very much against the idea of him taking on extra responsibility. I thought ahead to June, when ideally a manager should be looking at which players to buy and sell, and Stuart would be involved with the Under-21s instead. I didn't believe that this was in the best interests of the club. When this potential situation was reported in the press, we had one of the biggest negative responses from our supporters, the majority of whom agreed with my own views about Stuart and the Under-21s job.

Alistair Mackintosh and I met up with Trevor and Stuart to discuss the situation. It was explained to us how much time Stuart would be away, and I was totally against him being away during the period around Easter time when we had an intensive programme. I said to Trevor Brooking that the games over that Easter period could define our season as we were playing against some of the teams around us at the bottom of the league. I also expressed my concern that Sylvin Distin, Micah Richards and Joey Barton – arguably our three best players – were in contract discussions and they might think, "The manager is looking for his next job. Why should we stay here?"

Stuart being Stuart, seemed keen to try and ignore the speculation surrounding both him and the club. "Perception doesn't bother me," he once told me. I felt that was a slightly naive view, and told him that the point was, as directors, we had to *manage* that perception and try and downplay the rumours, rather than ignore it, because ripples of uncertainty can seriously undermine the team's performance on the pitch. We didn't want to put off any prospective buyers of the club either.

In the end, we reached a compromise with Trevor Brooking, allowing Stuart to take the England job on a part-time basis, on the condition that he would not away from the club during the Easter period.

But it was hard to disagree that, with City struggling on the pitch, matters at the club were at a low ebb, and by February 2007 discussions were in full flow about a possible takeover.

We couldn't afford a repeat of the previous season, where the team had lost nine out of the last ten games, and I spoke to John about calling a football meeting to prepare a contingency plan. We had a full board attendance and also invited non-board director David Makin to join us. There were four possibilities we discussed to ensure Premiership survival.

First, did Stuart need a more experienced adviser or, second, an experienced number two to assist him? Third, with a potential takeover in the news, did we need a complete change of manager who could get us safely to the end of the season – in other words a short-term troubleshooter? Finally, was there a coach available who would be prepared to come in on an 18-month contract, knowing that the club could have new owners by the end of the season?

We went through each section and the board members were able to put forward their opinions and views. At the end, the chairman gave me a mandate to speak to George Graham and Terry Venables about the advisory position.

I had two terrific conversations with two highly intelligent and experienced football people. I spoke to Terry about the help he had given Bryan Robson at Middlesbrough and said that we'd be delighted if he would consider helping Stuart. But he said it wasn't quite the same situation, because he knew Bryan Robson through the England set-up, and Bryan had asked him personally.

George made some good observations about the position but

then said he would like 24 hours to think about it. He rang me back and said that after analysing our run-in, he thought we would struggle to get the right results and therefore would decline the opportunity.

I reported this back to the chairman and he then asked me to move on to the next part of the agreed board strategy, which was an 18-month contract for an incoming coach. The three names who were available and fitted within our criteria were Lawrie Sanchez, Graeme Souness and Bryan Robson. I was to speak to the each of them to assess their level of interest and what sort of staff they would look to bring in. All three of them were very interested, so I handed over their contact details to Alistair, who was going to arrange one-to-one meetings.

The fixtures coming up prior to the Easter period were Newcastle and Middlesbrough away, then on Good Friday Charlton at home, followed by Fulham away on Easter Monday. Alistair told me he met up with Lawrie and had an interesting discussion. I met up with Graeme to find out a little bit more about how he would approach our situation and I reported the crux of the conversation back to the chairman. He asked me to arrange for Alistair to meet up with Graeme after the Middlesbrough game.

Surprisingly, we beat both Newcastle and Middlesbrough 1–0, and on the Sunday after the Boro game Alistair rang me to say the chairman wanted to postpone the Monday meeting. We then went on to draw with Charlton and beat Fulham. Ten points out of 12, including three away wins, was an unbelievable return and without them we would have been relegated. My prediction to Trevor Brooking about the importance of these Easter fixtures had been spot on. Stuart certainly earned his corn during this short, intense period, and arguably it wouldn't have happened if we had allowed him to be away with the England Under-21 team. I was still happy, though, that we as a board had professionally prepared a contingency plan to ensure retention of our Premiership status.

We were safely in the Premiership for another year, but by then events behind the scenes at City were moving rapidly.

CHAPTER 17

TAKEOVER AND OUT

In 2007, nine years after he'd left the position of chairman at Manchester City, Francis Lee was still a shareholder in the club. It had been rumoured that he was involved in a takeover attempt by Brian Richardson, the former Coventry City chairman, but funds didn't materialise. This hadn't deterred him.

On February 4, Francis contacted the chairman suggesting he should sign up with an American hedge fund company called Galileo. He explained that the plan was that Galileo would spend the next three months trying to find a buyer in the US, with Galileo and Lee linked up with the agent Jerome Anderson on a commission basis for any deal. Eventually, as a board, we unanimously opposed Lee's proposal.

The thought of Francis having any kind of say in the sale of City disappointed me, given his previous poor record at the club during his time as chairman. The fact that he was still a business associate of Jerome Anderson concerned me even more. When I'd first taken my place on the board I'd queried a regular monthly payment going to Anderson, who had a close relationship with Lee, because I didn't believe agents should have exclusive arrangements with clubs.

It was an eye-opener for me to see all the grey suits jockeying for position during this period, as the real football issues became secondary. It was all about profits and egos, rather than sorting out the future of the Academy or City's grassroots policy, the things that really mattered.

With all of this simmering, John Wardle rang me.

"Are you sitting down," he said.

He told me that Jocy Barton had been in a fight with Ousmane Dabo after training. This was the last thing we needed. Around the same time, I heard about the death of Alan Ball, who I'd played with for England and had been my favourite in the 1966 World Cup win. A real football man who achieved so much in his career had passed away, and here we were at City fretting about money and misbehaving rich kids.

In April, we then received an approach, via agent Seymour Pearce, from former Thai Prime Minister Thaksin Shinawatra, who'd already lodged unsuccessful bids for both Fulham and Liverpool. We were aware of the corruption charges which had been laid against him in Thailand. But I was guided by the financial experts on the board as to whether this was a good financial deal, and the British government and the Premier League had no issues with his reputation.

We also had an approach from Ray Ranson, a former player and a friend of mine who had been very successful in the insurance and financial industry. Ray spoke to me about his hopes and aspirations for the club and said, if his bid was successful, he would like me to retain my position on the board. I said I was incidental in this situation. The club was my first concern and if he could do a good deal with the chairman I would be delighted. I let Alistair and the chairman handle all the contacts and meetings with the prospective buyers.

There was a heated discussion between Francis Lee, Alistair Mackintosh and John Wardle at this time. Francis was still very keen that John sign a mandate which would give Lee the right to an agency agreement to sell the club. Both Mark Boler and Bryan Bodek vehemently objected to this request. Alistair and the chairman, backed unanimously by the board, blocked Francis and Jerome Anderson's attempt to use Galileo, turned down Ray Ranson's offer then came back with a recommendation that the Thaksin deal was best for the club.

I had a conflict of interest about Thaksin taking over. Aside from the human rights concerns, he'd already tried to take over Liverpool and Fulham, so it did bother me that he might not have City's best interests at heart. As for the fit and proper person aspect, I was aware of what was being rumoured about his actions in Thailand. I wouldn't say that I felt especially comfortable about it. Not really. But sometimes you have to be guided on these things. The Premier League and the British Government deemed him a fit and proper person. My financial colleagues on the board also believed the takeover would be good for the club. I'm not bigger than any of those, and I went with the decision, in the interests of City. It was difficult, but I made a business decision.

It was alarming, then, to discover that Thaksin's football adviser was Jerome Anderson. With this decision, Anderson was now a central part of the bid, and that didn't sit comfortably with me at all. But the club needed investment, and that was the most important issue. The team ethic that we had in my early years on the board was falling apart. We'd always said that we were custodians of the club, but now I feared it was turning into a "What's in it for me?" scenario.

There had been articles in the press predicting that Brian Bodek and I were about to be asked to leave the board, and each time I met up with Brian he would complain, saying, "They need us, as we understand the club better." I could see his point, but I told him that the club needed investment, and if this deal was approved by the board I was quite relaxed about stepping down, comfortable in the knowledge of the contribution I had made in often difficult financial circumstances. I had a gut feeling that my time was nearly up, and I had already spoken to Joan and the boys to warn them what was about to happen. But I never expected it to happen the way it did.

The bid process slowed down as Shinawatra's assets were frozen in Thailand and he had to renegotiate with our two bond holders, AXA and Banco Spirito Santos, but he officially took over Manchester City on June 21, 2007, with an £81.6 million bid. My involvement at City had already come to the most abrupt of endings the day before.

I was in the production studio with a conference client going through his visuals when my secretary rang me. She said I had a few emails, and that one of them was my resignation letter from Manchester City.

I was stunned. I'd known things were moving behind the scenes with the takeover, of course, and I'd felt the grey suits wheeling and dealing, but I'd never thought it could come to this. Not so suddenly, so abruptly; with no warning, no consultation. It didn't quite seem real, hearing the news like that.

I thought back to the last game I'd seen at the stadium – a derby match against United. A 1–0 defeat confirmed them as champions, but before that disappointment there had been a real moment to remember. We'd issued 44,000 blue-and-white scarves to fans, and before kick-off they'd all been on their feet, spinning them above their heads and singing *Blue Moon*. There was a real sense of their passion and commitment and, even though we'd only just avoided relegation, I'd been reminded of the mood before the first game at the stadium back in 2003 when we'd played Barcelona. That was only a friendly, but when I'd looked around the banks of blue-and-white shirts that day I'd had a real insight into and a confirmation of what I knew was possible for the club. After all the difficulties we'd been through, this had given me that same feeling, that same sense of a club about to explode. The manoeuvring of the grey suits made me uneasy, but I could understand why investors would be interested. This was my club, Manchester City.

But here I was, a month later, contemplating the end. I got my secretary to forward the email to me. I was still in shock but, sure enough, there it was in black and white – my resignation letter, just requiring my signature. Maybe if I hadn't been with a client I'd have reacted differently, but I couldn't take it in. In a daze I kept working until finally I was able to sit down and read the document properly. It was just a stark, standard letter. There was no mention of the work I'd done for the club, no sense of appreciation, just an offer of three months severance pay, which amounted to £7,500. Plain and simple: goodbye.

What really hurt was that nobody had had the decency or courage to speak to me. Alistair Mackintosh had promised me that I would have the chance to present my case, to explain what I'd been doing and what I could do in the future, but I never got that opportunity. I was out.

In preparation for the presentation that I been promised would happen, I'd had two two-hour brainstorming sessions with Jim Cassell, the director of the Academy, during a youth tournament in Javea, Spain, earlier that month. We had gone to the heads of each Academy department and asked them what they needed to take their section forward. We put together a wish-list, a chart detailing exactly what we felt was necessary to keep the Academy progressing, including succession planning, but I never got the chance to show it to anybody. It's still sitting in a drawer in my desk.

David and John Wardle had been instrumental in getting me onto the board, but the elevation of Alistair had driven a wedge between them and had also prompted the resignation of another board member, Chris Bird, who'd been kept in the dark throughout the process and had effectively been shunted sideways.

At the time I said to Alistair, "Chris was the best man at your wedding a few months earlier. Did you not think he should have been told about your proposed elevation and him being moved sideways?"

"It was not my position to say anything," he replied bluntly.

I said I disagreed and then told him, "You have some good skills, mainly financial, and I won't have any trouble working with you." But deep down I knew I wouldn't be comfortable with him.

I was really troubled by the way Bird had been treated after his tremendous contribution as a board member. Four years later, I was being treated just the same. I had recognised a few months earlier that I was quietly being excluded from football discussions, as most of these seemed now to be taking place in the press office of Paul Tyrrell. I'd been chosen to be sacrificed.

I rang Alistair and told him I'd got his email. He was hesitant, embarrassed.

"What could I do?" he asked me.

"I'd have thought, after we'd worked together for five years, after I'd sat next to you in the directors' box talking football, after we'd drawn-up contracts together, that you'd at least have had the courtesy to tell me face to face," I told him.

I was disappointed and saddened, but most of all I was hurt. Hurt at being booted out and hurt by the undignified and unprofessional way in which it was done.

I went back to work, but at 4.30pm I had to dial in for a conference call to approve some documents with the board. Brian Bodek was on the line from London, John Wardle in Manchester, Alistair Mackintosh and Bernard Halford at the ground, and Mark Boler at Ascot races. I sat there, realising with a sick feeling in my stomach that this was it, after almost ten years in the boardroom at City my time was coming to an end, and realising that none of these people, none of my so-called colleagues on the board, had had the courage to tell me about it. And all the time in the background I could hear the racecourse announcer over the tannoy at Ascot.

I knew that nobody on that call had anywhere near my under-standing of football or my love of the game. I had thought City would be different to other clubs. I felt I was representing the real football people who had a passion for Manchester City. I believed that together we could develop a club spirit. I had thought we were putting something special together there. I was wrong.

I was told that the lawyers would be couriering round some documents to my house to sign that night, which I'd decided to do without protest. If this was how the club was going to be run, then I didn't want any part of it.

I was sitting at home waiting when the phone rang. Mark, my son, answered: it was Alistair Mackintosh again. I knew he'd have his usual business head on. As Mark passed me the receiver, it was like the phone turned to ice in my hand. I knew what the conver-sation would be like.

"What did he say," asked Joan, when I put the phone down.

"Nothing," I replied.

There'd been no chat about what was happening. Nothing. Just a series of instructions telling me what to sign.

Joan was absolutely disgusted. She knew more than anyone how many hours I had spent away from home and my business in the cause of Manchester City. I was only ever a non-executive director, but many people thought I was a full-time executive.

Mark asked me, "Is all business like this?"

I was thinking of people like Graeme Whittaker, who ran the northern division of Grant Thornton accountancy firm, and with whom I'd been working in the production of his corporate confer-ences for many years. Graeme was a real maverick, but a successful one and had a great belief in creating a team ethic among his staff. When he heard about the way I received my resignation letter, he rang me and in his usual charismatic style said, "Fuck them. What goes around, comes around." Sadly, Graeme passed away late in 2009 due to cancer at the age of 51.

Soon after, the taxi arrived with the lawyer carrying the papers. She was, of course, wearing a grey suit.

A few days later, I bumped into John Wardle when I was going to collect my tickets for a Rod Stewart concert. I laid into him for not contacting me personally, and said that I felt very let down. He became very humble, apologised to me and then invited Joan and I to join him in his executive box any time we wanted. Bryan Bodek called me after a week of silence and I said to him "Hello, stranger". He had retained a position at the club.

When John, David Bernstein and I had agreed that Francis Lee would leave back in 1998, we decided to let him go with dignity – not because of his record as a chairman but, justifiably, for what he had achieved as a player. I wasn't even allowed to do that.

The grey suits had won.

EPILOGUE

In the days that followed my departure from City, I tried to take stock of what had happened to me. I admit I was shell-shocked by the speed that everything had happened, but I acted as quickly as possible to try and ensure that the Academy and the fund-raising committee remained protected. Unfortunately, the emphasis is definitely on the word "try."

I visited Alistair Mackintosh in his office at the ground and I asked him to ensure that both areas would remain unscathed and untouched as they had been two of the most successful parts of the organisation. Yet shortly afterwards, the committee, which had done so much to raise money for the Academy, was unceremoniously dumped. Steve Bottomley actually went to see Alistair and afterwards was expecting a letter of thanks for the committee's efforts after raising almost half a million pounds in nine years. The committee are still waiting for that letter. Jim Cassell, who in my opinion was the best developer of young football talent in the country, was moved sideways onto other projects. That confused and saddened me hugely.

At the start of the following season, I decided to try and draw a line under the issue and move on, as I have always done in my life. I suggested to Joan that we request a couple of directors' box tickets for the friendly against Valencia. It had always been an unwritten rule at the club that former directors, on request, are offered two complimentary tickets in the directors' box, plus a car parking pass. Ashley Lewis, a former director and boardroom colleague of mine, had also requested two tickets for the game and received them. I submitted my request and was prepared to call in to the club to collect them, but I got a call from Alistair Mackintosh's secretary saying I could pick them up at the Carrington training ground. When I did so I realised that they were two standard tickets at the front of the main stand and no car park pass, so I decided not to go to the game in the end.

After the match a couple of stories appeared in the papers, suggesting I hadn't turned up because I didn't want to sit with the ordinary supporters. Of course, that was not the case at all. After my letter of resignation I'd written a letter to the *Manchester Evening News* thanking the fans for their support over my years as a City player and director and I'm pretty sure someone at the club was behind these stories to try and undermine my credibility with the supporters. I had a little chuckle to myself at the fact that the club executives thought that they were being clever and decided not to respond as I was not going to let people like that, who had no real affection for the club, damage my reputation with the City fans. I have kept those two unused tickets as a reminder of the way I was treated. I did feel lousy for a while, but soon I was able to move on and give my family and my businesses more of my time, which pleased me no end.

Despite the way things ended up at City, I still wouldn't change a thing about my career as a player and a director. I immensely enjoy being in the conference production business as it encourages me to be creative, motivated, and focused, the three things I loved most about my football career. Football gave me everything, and it enabled me to meet people from every walk of life. I met all kinds, and saw the very best and the very worst of people. The camaraderie, the friendship, the loyalty and the dedication that football can inspire is second to none. But football also attracts more than its fair share of piranhas. I met many agents throughout my time as director at City, and was never convinced that enough of them had the players' best interests at heart. With youngsters at the Academy, we were determined that they remain focused and get off to the best possible start in their careers. When a player turned professional, either at aged 17 or 18, Jim Cassell and I would draw up "development" contracts for them. This contract was designed to ensure the youngsters retained a sense of hunger as they were still developing their own character. We specified that we'd draw up the contract with the player and the parents, but very rarely involve an agent. We'd always suggest to the player and his parents that at that age it was always preferable for the player to have an advisor or the PFA rather than an agent whose primary motivation is not the welfare or development of the player but finance.

This guidance was based on my own experience of having an advisor, and what I had begun to observe at City as a director. My advisor, Reuben Kay, stayed with me during and after my playing career, whereas agents often disappear the minute the player's last contract in football ends. A good advisor can guide a player on finances, diet, and lifestyle, and enable the player to build a sound springboard for their life after football. Agents are there for as long as it suits them. The most extreme example I saw of this was with Joey Barton. When he was a young player, Joey's advisor was Struan Marshall, also Steven Gerrard's agent, who was shocked by the way Joey was failing to look after himself off the pitch. He advised Joey on everything – what he needed to have in his life, both on and off the pitch – showing him good habits and how to take care of himself. But then Joey left Struan. And although he may have done well in terms of his contracts after that, Joey needed more than that in his life, and he began to drift and get into some well-documented scrapes on and off the pitch. While Joey will be a very wealthy man when he finished in football, I think even he will agree that he hasn't achieved as much as he should have done as a player.

There is no reason why the vast majority of players can't take more responsibility for their financial negotiations, with an advisor present of course. Many players, and their parents, aren't worldly and simply defer to an agent the whole time. By their very nature agents do not solely have the players' interests at heart. That isn't good for a player's development in the long term, because when footballers retire at 35 or 36 many are suddenly left to deal with looking after mortgages, pensions, car loans and such themselves, and don't know how to do it. It's no wonder that so many footballers, many of whom are extremely well paid, still end up with money problems and virtually no real life experience when they retire because of the bad advice they have received. Young players often place too much faith in their agents, as there is no one else to advise them whether or not the deals they are striking are beneficial to them.

When I was a player, I always wanted to have a proper handle on what was going on with my contracts, and I do believe that the football authorities should monitor the actions of agents far more closely. Until the regulations are changed, agents can only be accused of being greedy by taking advantage of highly talented but naive young players. Too many players have their heads turned between 18 and 21, and they are more concerned about where the next Rolex or Bentley is coming from than whether they are playing well and contributing to the team. My advice to young players is that they should prepare themselves professionally, aim to play well, and then the financial rewards would follow. If all you want is bling in the short-term, then it is very easy to slip into a comfort zone, and the second that happens, your performance on the pitch slips.

In New York, I saw that wealthy football icons such as Franz Beckenbaur, Carlos Alberto and Johan Neeskens never lost their hunger and desire to be successful. That self-discipline is paramount, because if you are set for life when you retire at 36, you still have to have a reason to get out of bed in the morning. You have to have something in your life after football and a good advisor can help you to reset your goals. An increasing number of our football millionaires sink into real difficulties when they retire. Paul Gascoigne is the most infamous example of this, but countless others also sink into gambling and drinking to fill the void after they retire. Paul Merson is one who has really turned his life around after much publicity about his drugs and drinking. He did a couple of personal appearances recently in my conferences and was highly professional. I asked him how he managed this change and he said, "Dennis, because now I have to".

My impression of other directors was also varied. I maintain that just because you have been successful in another business area, it doesn't automatically mean that you will be similarly effective in the football world. The key areas of a club — scouting (both first team and academy), supporter liaison, club finances, legal advice and recruitment – all need experts in charge if they are to prosper. Too few directors have the critical eye required for the job.

In my experience some financial directors are promoted to CEOs because they are good at managing the finances of the business, dealing with facts and figures, but many are not qualified to manage people. The danger with football is that it is becoming attractive to stereotypical, corporate, mercenary career-builders who are desperate to get their nose in the big football money trough, but have no real understanding of the world of football.

It's very easy just to blame the players for the astronomical wages which are paid out these days. On the day of the 9/11 terrorist attacks, we played Notts County in a League Cup game in Nottingham. Prior to the game we were entertained at dinner by the Notts County directors. One of them started to say to me that I must be disgusted with the amount of money players were earning in the current era. I cut him short, saying, "Players are quite entitled to ask for whatever they want in an open and free market. The challenge is for directors like you and I to manage the business efficiently." I don't think it was the answer he was looking for.

Too many directors believe themselves to be the heroes of the show. It's as if they're fantasising that it's they who are on the pitch, they who are scoring the goals and they who are the idols of the fans. But it will always be about the players, and directors should always remember that. I remember that the day before Ian Porterfield died from cancer in September 2007, I spoke to him on the phone. I'd been due to go down to Surrey, where he lived with his wife Glenda, but he was too ill for us to travel to see him. So I rang him, and even though he sounded very weak, we were able to reminisce about Sunderland and 1973. I was in floods of tears. Our hero in the final, who was so strong and calm in the face of pressure from Leeds, and scored that goal, was now being cruelly struck down by such a terrible disease. I kept saying to him, "You'll always be a hero, you'll always be a hero." And he always will be, to me, the rest of the team, and to the Sunderland fans. It's players like Ian who make football the great game it is, not directors.

I'm lucky enough to have come from Newcastle where, as a kid, I was able to see for myself the kind of passion which football can evoke. I am fortunate to have played for Sunderland and Manchester

City, two clubs with monstrous fan bases, and as a player I quickly realised that the core of any club is its fans, and its grassroots links to the local community. I'm a traditionalist in that I firmly believe that any footballer worth their salt can't help but be inspired by the sight of swathes of their own fans cheering them on. It should be what motivates them to perform each week. Of course Sunderland, Newcastle and Manchester City have had rollercoaster rides for many years. Ultimately, I'd like to see all three challenging for honours, because they are genuine football hotbeds and their patient, passionate and loyal fans deserve any success which comes their way.

I'm delighted for Manchester City supporters that finally the club appears to be building a team and a structure which looks set to gain them further success in the next few years. It would have been fantastic, especially in those final years at City, to have had the almost unlimited funds which City's owners have now made available, and I believe that I'd have flourished in the new set-up because the basic core principles of being a director still apply. Running a successful business/football club is not "rocket science" but the appliance of that science is. I've always been successful at managing change, and coping with new demands in my family, my football involvement and my business.

One of the most pleasing elements of the way the new owners are running the club is that they seem to have a long-term strategy, and aren't all about short-term profit. This became clear to me when they signed a 10-year deal with the local council to buy 80 acres of land around the stadium to develop their first-team training and Academy centre to be known as the Etihad campus. Despite my initial misgivings after my meeting with Alistair Mackintosh, I'm delighted to see that much of what we developed; the association with supporters branches, community schemes, and the Academy profile, is still flourishing.

I firmly believe that Roberto Mancini can take City forward. He played the game for 18 years, captained both his club and his country, and as a coach at Inter Milan, one of the most politically sensitive clubs in the world, delivered seven trophies in four years. With that CV, if I'd been a director, he'd have been one of the names at the top of my managerial hit-list. As I would say to my fellow directors, there is no exact template for a successful football manager, but as a board we have to support and help him make more right decisions than wrong. It was interesting on one occasion when Steve McClaren was sitting next to me at a City game during his tenure as England manager, and told me that Sir Alex Ferguson targeted 70 per cent correct decisions.

I'd have loved to play in the current City side. The team Mancini has put together is exactly the system and style of team I played in at Sunderland, City and Cosmos. They have a top-quality goalkeeper, solid defensive base, with flexible and mobile, attacking players who are a nightmare for defenders with their interchangeable movement. Much as I loved the wide open spaces of Maine Road, I'd have thoroughly enjoyed playing at the Etihad Stadium, and I firmly believe that City's supporters, many of whom remember the dark days of playing away at York, Lincoln and Macclesfield, deserve their opportunity to watch such an exciting outfit.

Family, friends and football are what have made me the person I am, and have provided me with the most memorable moments in my life. Joan has been my rock for the last 40 years. She speaks common sense to me, she's unbelievably understanding, extremely supportive and always willing to explain to me that there's more than one side to every story or viewpoint. My three sons Mark, Leigh and John, staunch City supporters, are a source of immense pride to Joan and me every day, and have gone on to prosper in their chosen fields. Mark is a director of Lift Sports, which has Kevin Davies of Bolton Wanderers as a shareholder, and offers financial planning to footballers and other sportsmen all over the country. My middle son, Leigh, a qualified football coach, lives in Vienna and has several coaching contracts with schools and soccer camps. One of the benefits of me not being a City director anymore is that Joan and I now have free weekends so we can pop out to Austria and visit him. My youngest son, John, is currently taking his final Law exams, and I am now able to devote some of my time to supporting him.

Sunderland's FA Cup win in '73 and Manchester City's League Cup win in '76 were unforgettable and fantastic events which I know still burn brightly in the memories of both the players and the fans. My experience in New York was something extra special both in terms of winning the 1978 NASL championship, playing with world stars and experiencing how sport and business work together. Being involved with soccer tours around the world when the Cosmos had the "Hollywood" profile and seeing Maradonna at the age of 17 win a game virtually on his own were the kind of occasions which you dream of as a footballer. As a City director, the double promotion, and particularly the play-off win against Gillingham in 1999, are still a source of immense pride to me along with the style of play that Kevin Keegan brought to the club in his Premier League promotion season and that famous win at Blackburn when the City supporters came out in their thousands to witness Joe Royle's team achieving that first Premier League promotion. There's no doubt that throughout the Nineties, the club was on its knees, and I know that along with David Bernstein, Chris Bird, Ashley Lewis, other directors, and thanks to John Wardle and David Makin's investment and Jim Cassell's fantastic academy production line, I helped lay the foundations on which the new owners have built the modern City.

There is no question that the support of those fans was instrumental in contributing to that resurrection, and at heart I have always been and will always be a passionate football fan. I genuinely believe in "the beautiful game", as Pele so succinctly described it, and I like to think that in my own way I've given football as much as it has given me.

THE TEENAGE AND YOUNG ADULT CANCER CENTRE AT THE CHRISTIE

Cancer has unfortunately played a major part in my life. First, I lost my aunt, Charmaine, at the age of 39 to leukemia – the youngest of my dad's five sisters, she was only three years older than me. I lost another aunt on my mother's side, Rita, to breast cancer in her forties. My father, Norman, died of cancer at the age of 54 after several years of suffering, and his brother, Lawrence (Uncle Lol) died of the disease at the age of 49. My dad's eldest sister, Auntie Doreeen, also succumbed to the disease and her daughter, my younger cousin, Jill, is currently fighting breast cancer. Last December we lost my loving sister-in-law, Pauline, aged 58, to lymphoma after two years of fighting the disease. My brother, Kevin, was diagnosed with a cancerous tumour at the age of 24, but thankfully is still with us today.

When I retired from football, I took up running to keep fit and in 1984 ran the Bolton marathon in its famous "plodder" lane. I decided to make a donation to the children's cancer unit at The Christie NHS hospital in Manchester and raised in excess of £800. The consultant invited me to look around the unit to show me where the money would go. The reality of seeing all these sick children, from babies to teenagers, shocked me immensely. My sons have since run a few half-marathons and all the money raised has gone to The Christie. For my 50th birthday I invited all my guests to make donations and raised £3,015.

When I decided to write my autobiography, I discussed with my wife, Joan, and our three boys about donating all my royalties to the teenage and young adult cancer centre at The Christie. They were in full agreement with my suggestion.

I have since become a patron of The Christie, and their teenage and young adult cancer centre is one of several around the country focusing on helping young cancer patients aged between 16 and 24. The money raised is used to upgrade the facilities and make it more "fit for purpose". Recent research shows that on average teenagers have to make at least four visits to their GP before cancer is diagnosed. More research and development into teenage cancer is essential for early diagnosis and to give our teenagers a greater chance of a full and active life.

As well as enabling The Christie to develop into the UK's premier unit, donations will help fund vital research into new treatments and provide equipment, counselling and activities for patients, support for families suffering financial hardship and overnight accommodation for parents.

We need to raise several millions of pounds to achieve that vision and sustain the centre for future teenagers and young adults. I hope my royalties from the sale of this book will in some small way help our cause.

If you would like to make a donation to The Christie, please visit www.christies.org/donate

The Christie

Charitable Fund

The Christie is Europe's largest cancer centre and an international leader in cancer research.

The Christie treats more than 40,000 cancer patients every year and has sites in Manchester, Oldham and Salford. As a national specialist, around 25 per cent of patients are referred from across the UK.

For more than 100 years The Christie has played a significant role in the development of new cancer treatments. It is home to the world's largest early phase clinical trials unit and has led many break-throughs over the decades. It was the first centre in the world to trial the breast cancer drug Tamoxifen in the 1970s, the first to use cultured bone marrow for leukaemia treatment in the 1980s, and invented photo-dynamic therapy for skin cancer in the mid-1990s.

The Christie charity raises money every year to support extra patient services and life-saving research. Dennis Tueart has supported The Christie charity since 1984, when he ran the Bolton marathon and donated the money raised to charity. In 1999 he even asked for donations, in lieu of gifts, for his 50th birthday. He donated the money to The Christie's teenage and young adult cancer centre, motivated by his own brother's successful treatment for a tumour when he just 24.

Since then, Dennis has continued to raise money for this centre, which has enabled The Christie to make advances in the treatment and care of young cancer patients.

His support always has, and always will be, greatly appreciated.